FLAME ON

The Stackpole Military History Series

THE AMERICAN CIVIL WAR
Cavalry Raids of the Civil War
In the Lion's Mouth
Witness to Gettysburg

WORLD WAR I
Doughboy War

WORLD WAR II
After D-Day
Airborne Combat
Armor Battles of the Waffen-SS,
    1943–45
Armoured Guardsmen
Arnhem 1944
The B-24 in China
The Battalion
The Battle of France
The Battle of Sicily
Battle of the Bulge, Vol. 1
Battle of the Bulge, Vol. 2
Battle of the Bulge, Vol. 3
Beyond the Beachhead
Beyond Stalingrad
The Black Bull
Blitzkrieg Unleashed
Blossoming Silk Against the Rising Sun
Bodenplatte
The Breaking Point
The Brigade
The Canadian Army and the Normandy
    Campaign
Clay Pigeons of St Lô, The
Critical Convoy Battles of WWII
A Dangerous Assignment
D-Day Bombers
D-Day Deception
D-Day to Berlin
Decision in the Ukraine
The Defense of Moscow 1941
Deliverance at Diepholz
Destination Normandy
Dive Bomber!
Eager Eagles
Eagles of the Third Reich
The Early Battles of Eighth Army
Eastern Front Combat
Europe in Flames
Exit Rommel
The Face of Courage
Fatal Decisions
Fist from the Sky
Flame On
Flying American Combat Aircraft of
    World War II, Vol. 1
For Europe
Forging the Thunderbolt
For the Homeland
Fortress France
The German Defeat in the East,
    1944–45
German Order of Battle, Vol. 1
German Order of Battle, Vol. 2
German Order of Battle, Vol. 3

The Germans in Normandy
Germany's Panzer Arm in World War II
GI Ingenuity
Goodbye, Transylvania
The Great Ships
Grenadiers
Guns Against the Reich
Hitler's Final Fortress
Hitler's Nemesis
Hitler's Spanish Legion
Hold the Westwall
Infantry Aces
In the Fire of the Eastern Front
Iron Arm
Iron Knights
Japanese Army Fighter Aces
Japanese Naval Fighter Aces
JG 26 Luftwaffe Fighter Wing War Diary,
    Vol. 1
JG 26 Luftwaffe Fighter Wing War Diary,
    Vol. 2
Kampfgruppe Peiper at the Battle of
    the Bulge
The Key to the Bulge
Kursk
Luftwaffe Aces
Luftwaffe Fighter Ace
Luftwaffe Fighter-Bombers over Britain
Luftwaffe Fighters & Bombers
Luftwaffe KG 200
Marshal of Victory, Vol. 1
Marshal of Victory, Vol. 2
Massacre at Tobruk
Mechanized Juggernaut or Military
    Anachronism?
Messerschmitts over Sicily
Michael Wittmann, Vol. 1
Michael Wittmann, Vol. 2
Mission 85
Mission 376
The Nazi Rocketeers
Night Flyer / Mosquito Pathfinder
No Holding Back
Operation Mercury
Panzer Aces
Panzer Aces II
Panzer Commanders of the
    Western Front
Panzergrenadier Aces
Panzer Gunner
The Panzer Legions
Panzers in Normandy
Panzers in Winter
Panzer Wedge, Vol. 1
Panzer Wedge, Vol. 2
The Path to Blitzkrieg
Penalty Strike
Poland Betrayed
Red Road from Stalingrad
Red Star Under the Baltic
Retreat to the Reich
Rommel Reconsidered
Rommel's Desert Commanders
Rommel's Desert War

Rommel's Lieutenants
The Savage Sky
The Seeds of Disaster
Ship-Busters
The Siege of Brest 1941
The Siege of Küstrin
The Siegfried Line
A Soldier in the Cockpit
Soviet Blitzkrieg
Spitfires & Yellow Tail Mustangs
Stalin's Keys to Victory
Surviving Bataan and Beyond
T-34 in Action
Tank Tactics
Tigers in the Mud
Triumphant Fox
The 12th SS, Vol. 1
The 12th SS, Vol. 2
Twilight of the Gods
Typhoon Attack
The War Against Rommel's Supply
War in the Aegean
War of the White Death
Warsaw 1944
Winter Storm
The Winter War
Wolfpack Warriors
Zhukov at the Oder

THE COLD WAR / VIETNAM
Cyclops in the Jungle
Expendable Warriors
Fighting in Vietnam
Flying American Combat Aircraft:
    The Cold War
Here There Are Tigers
Jack of All Trades
Land with No Sun
Phantom Reflections
Street without Joy
Through the Valley
Tours of Duty
Two One Pony

WARS OF AFRICA AND THE MIDDLE EAST
The Rhodesian War

GENERAL MILITARY HISTORY
Battle of Paoli
Cavalry from Hoof to Track
Desert Battles
Guerrilla Warfare
The Philadelphia Campaign, Vol. 1
Ranger Dawn
Sieges
The Spartan Army

FLAME ON

U.S. Incendiary Weapons, 1918–1945

John W. Mountcastle

STACKPOLE
BOOKS

Published in paperback in 2016 by

STACKPOLE BOOKS
5067 Ritter Road
Mechanicsburg, PA 17055
www.stackpolebooks.com

Printed in the United States of America

10 9 8 7 6 5 4 3 2 1

Stackpole First Edition

Cover design by Wendy A. Reynolds

Library of Congress Cataloging-in-Publication Data

Names: Mountcastle, John Wyndham, 1942- author.
Title: Flame on : U.S. incendiary weapons, 1918-1945 / John W. Mountcastle.
Other titles: US incendiary weapons, 1918-1945 | U.S. incendiary weapons, 1918-1945
Description: Stackpole first edition. | Mechanicsburg, PA : Stackpole Books, [2016] | Series: Stackpole military history series | Originally published: Shippensburg, PA : White Mane Books, 1999.
Identifiers: LCCN 2015039162 | ISBN 9780811716895
Subjects: LCSH: Incendiary weapons—History—20th century. | World War, 1914-1918—Aerial operations. | World War, 1939-1945—Aerial operations.
Classification: LCC UG447.65 .M68 2016 | DDC 623.4/516097309041—dc23 LC record available at http://lccn.loc.gov/2015039162

Contents

Foreword

Incendiary weapons in World War II came in many different packages. Some played critical roles; others were used sparingly, and many others were never accepted for operational use. Other than the official story contained in the series *United States Army in World War II*, little space has been devoted to the development and employment of flame weapons. John Mountcastle's concise, well-documented volume helps correct this neglect.

He provides a proper introduction with a recapitulation of the use of flame in warfare throughout history. The pace quickens during the First World War when the prototypes of most all forms of incendiary warfare were introduced. The interwar period, characterized by disillusionment, disarmament, and depression, boded ill for all things military and especially for the Chemical Warfare Service, which was formally activated in 1920 but whose officers, men, and money soon reached ridiculously low levels. And it must be remembered that gas warfare provided the heart of the Chemical Warfare mission, not the weapons of incendiary warfare. Obviously these weapons had low priority during the interwar years.

Incendiary weapons were diverse. There were both portable and mechanized flame throwers. These weapons were used effectively in the war against Japan because of the dictates of terrain and the enemy. While Great Britain and Germany found the mechanized flame thrower useful in Europe, the United States Army gave it and its portable cousins short shrift. Flame weapons often were unreliable, and General Patton's scorn for the mechanized flame thrower added to that weapon's unpopularity.

The use of incendiary bombs for tactical support, improvised at first, was greatly overshadowed by extensive strategic incendiary bombing against Germany and Japan. The attacks on Japanese cities beginning in spring 1945 were particularly effective. The destruction of Japanese cities and the scattered cottage industries were part of this success. In March 1945 General Curtis LeMay completely altered the Army Air Forces' bombing technique so that one B-29 mission over Tokyo killed 83,793 people and burned out almost sixteen square miles. The entire payload consisted of incendiary bombs.

There is a grim realism in the book's overall conclusion in contrast with some historians who believe that the enormity of modern warfare eventually must lead to its abolition. John Mountcastle, who once commanded the largest armored brigade in Europe, makes no such claim. In fact, the description of incendiaries in World War II provides lessons for the effective development of weapon systems in general. That's what makes this treatise so timely, as well as providing an exciting history.

Brooks E. Kleber

Acknowledgments

This book would not have been completed without the support of a number of people who went out of their way to assist and encourage me. It evolved from research completed during my graduate studies. Colonel Thomas E. Griess, head of the History Department at the U.S. Military Academy, provided me with the opportunity to attend graduate school. At Duke University, Professor I. B. Holley shared his keen insights regarding the development of doctrine and taught me research techniques; Professor Ted Ropp gave unstinting support and interest while asking questions that made me *think*. I wish to thank the dedicated archivists at the National Archives, and also those at the Air University at Maxwell Air Force Base, Alabama. The staff of the Military History Institute at Carlisle Barracks, Pennsylvania, was most helpful. I owe thanks to the Historian's Office at Edgewood Arsenal, Maryland, and to Hannah Zeidlik and Carol Robbins at the U.S. Army Center of Military History. I must thank Dr. Jay Luvaas and Dr. Earl Tilford of the Army War College for their guidance during the preparation of this book; Dr. Dan Spector; Lt. Col. Conrad Crane at West Point; and Professor Alex Roland at Duke were all good enough to read and provide comments on the manuscript. I am deeply indebted to my very talented editors—Beverly Kuhn and Vicki Stouffer at White Mane Books, and Dave Reisch and Brittany Stoner at Stackpole Books—and to my wife, Susan, for her constant support and encouragement. Finally, I wish to acknowledge my mentor and friend, historian Dr. Brooks Kleber, for the great inspiration he provided. The facts presented in this study belong to history. The interpretations of these facts and the conclusions drawn are mine alone.

Introduction

The sun was cutting through the morning haze when the weary troops of the 1st Battalion, 25th Marine Regiment climbed from their foxholes and moved forward to seize an outcropping of volcanic rock known as Turkey Knob. Their attack, which began at 6:30 on 2 March 1945, was preceded by no artillery bombardment, no aircraft strikes. The regimental commander, hoping to achieve surprise, had foregone the usual pre-assault fires, ordering his troops to "Close with and destroy the enemy" by fire assault team. The 1st Battalion had been promised tank support, but most of the Marines knew that, for the attack to succeed, it would be necessary for the tired infantry to root the Japanese defenders from their burrows. After eleven days of fighting on Iwo Jima, the predominance of close quarters combat had reinforced the basic dictum of the Marine Corps: in the last analysis, it is the infantryman who must fight the battle.[1]

The Marines advanced to within twenty yards of the enemy positions along the base of Turkey Knob before a torrent of fire engulfed the lead elements. Hugging each fold in the ground, the troops began the day's business of killing Japanese. Spurred by the shouted orders of their leaders, assault teams inched closer to the firing ports of dug-in positions. Supported now by eight tanks which had begun to pump High Explosive (H.E.) shells in the direction of the enemy positions, the Marine infantry struggled to bring their most effective weapons to bear. Protected by the rifles of each squad were sweating Marines who toiled under the cumbersome fuel tanks and hose assemblies of portable flame throwers. The Japanese would not retreat, nor would they surrender. Determined to die fighting for their emperor, the Japanese continued to shoot even as the flame thrower operators steadied themselves and then pulled the triggers of their weapons.

The distinctive *Whomp! Whoose!* sounds made by the sudden expulsion of pressurized, jellied gasoline were almost immediately replaced by the crackle and roar of flame. The tumult increased as numerous fireballs

engulfed the defenders of Turkey Knob, Okinawa. The roar of flaming gasoline nearly succeeded in drowning the shrieks coming from within the
Japanese bunkers. The ferocity of combat enveloped the young-men-grown-
old on Iwo Jima and their grisly work did not seem to trouble them. Years
later, one said:

> As the Japanese died, the platoon could smell their roasting flesh.
> Some of our men later said that the circumstances made the odor
> seem the sweetest that they had ever smelled.[2]

As the oily billows of black smoke drifted away in the slight morning
breeze, the flame thrower operators exchanged their empty contraptions
for full ones, adjusted carrying harnesses, checked pressure gauges, and fid-
dled with the nozzles of the recently developed, still temperamental
weapons. On signal, the Americans began to move forward and upward
along the slope of Turkey Knob. It would be a long day for the men of the
25th Marine Regiment.[3]

On the same day that Marine flame thrower operators attacked the
Japanese defenders of Iwo Jima and destroyed them in close combat, American bombardiers hunched over the bombsights of B-17 and B-24 bombers
as they guided 406 U.S. aircraft to a target in eastern Germany. Their objective for 2 March was the rail terminal and switchyards of Dresden, a Saxon
city more famous for its delicate chinaware than for any military
significance. But the fortunes of war had placed Dresden in the path of
advancing Russian armies as the victorious Soviet forces pushed into Germany during the early spring of 1945. The Soviets asked for British and
American assistance in destroying the German military forces in Dresden:
forces which, the Russians claimed, menaced a successful offensive. The
Allied airmen complied. A series of devastating air raids by planes of the
British Royal Air Force (RAF) and the U.S. Eighth Air Force would add a
new chapter to the history of the ancient city. As the crews of more than 400
U.S. heavy bombers flew toward Dresden, they were en route to a city
already heavily damaged during raids on 14–15 February.[4]

Once again, on 2 March, the airmen would make use of one of man's
oldest weapons, fire, to inflict untold suffering upon their enemies. The dif-
ference between the application of two types of U.S. incendiary weapons is
immediately obvious. For the Marine infantryman with a flame thrower, fire
warfare was a face-to-face confrontation with an armed enemy soldier. The
results of his duty lingered in his nostrils for days. For the airman bombing a
German city, however, the death and destruction below, while so much
greater than that inflicted by the soldier, was far removed from his immediate

consciousness. For the victims, the results were much the same: stark terror, unbelievable agony, and death.

Many of the crews bombing on 2 March recalled the largest Dresden raid, some two weeks before. They remembered that the target area had been clearly visible to the lead elements of the large bomber formations. German antiaircraft fire, formerly so damaging over targets struck earlier in the Allied Bomber Offensive, was weak and ineffectual that day. The heavy bombers droned on until the bombardiers released their loads and signaled "bombs away!" The clouds of bombs falling earthward were composed of high explosive and incendiary bombs. Most were provided with fuses which would delay detonation until the bomb had penetrated the roof and upper stories of the typical German structure. Some were specially equipped with extended delays which provided for an explosion hours after the bomb had dropped. In this way, rescue and firefighting operations would be seriously hampered.[5]

Tail gunners in the leading flight had reported seeing a great deal of fire and smoke on and near the target as the heavy bombers wheeled in a tight turn after releasing their bombs. The great billowing clouds of rising smoke demonstrated the incendiary effect of the thousands of thermite-filled bombs that had been dropped, but also obscured the target for the succeeding waves of bombers. Lacking any clearly defined aiming point, the trailing aircraft jettisoned their bomb loads into, and around, the great mass of flames below.[6]

The bombs of the follow-on aircraft proved most devastating to the masses of civilians huddled in air raid shelters near the Dresden rail terminal. As more bombs fell and the incidence of fire increased, the temperature at ground level rose to unbearable levels and the lack of oxygen caused large numbers of those in underground shelters to faint. The cowering refugees had but two choices: remain in their shelters and face almost certain asphyxiation or flee into the burning city, hoping to escape the flames all around them. Many chose to attempt an escape and died in the *Feuersturm* that had engulfed large sections of the city. The raids of 14–15 February were devastating. By the time the fires and explosions finally ceased, an estimated 135,000 people had perished. The Russians had little difficulty occupying what was left of the smoking ruins of Dresden soon after the six massive raids of February and March were completed.[7]

The question of "area" bombing versus "precision" bombing was much discussed during World War II, with most American air commanders contending, at least until late 1944, that pinpoint bombing was possible. The bombing of Dresden was clearly an example of area bombing. The great loss of civilian lives in Dresden prompted a prominent British airman, Air Marshal Sir Richard Saundby, to later comment:

That the bombing of Dresden was a great tragedy none can deny.
That it was really a military necessity few... will believe. It was one of
those terrible things that sometimes happen in wartime, brought
about by an unfortunate combination of circumstances.[8]

The foregoing accounts of combat in the Pacific and over Europe
demonstrate two types of incendiary weapons employed by the U.S. armed
forces during World War II. The U.S. flame weapons of the period 1942–
1945 were numerous and possessed varying degrees of lethality. Some were
designed to be used as tactical weapons in close combat, like the portable
flame thrower. Others, like armored flame throwers mounted in tanks and
bombs filled with jellied gasoline (dropped by fighter aircraft in support of
front-line troops), were destined to be employed in the island campaigns of
the Pacific and in the European Theater of Operations. The most widespread use of incendiary munitions was by the U.S. Army Air Forces in the
strategic bombing campaigns waged against Germany and Japan.
        American flame weapons not only were designed with different roles in
mind, but these devices varied considerably in their effectiveness. In every
case, the first experimental models required a great deal of improvement
before the combat forces charged with the employment of the flame
weapons in combat accepted them. The identical type of flame weapon or
munition might function satisfactorily in one theater of operations while
being regarded as nearly worthless in another. Terrain, climate, the enemy,
and the tactical or strategic environment in which they were employed all
affected the record of the U.S. flame weapons of World War II.[9]
        As diverse as the many American flame weapons of World War II were,
they all had one thing in common. *None* of the incendiary munitions that
were used by U.S. forces in the defeat of the Axis had been a part of the U.S.
arsenal prior to the outbreak of the war. Each weapon had been developed
by the United States only after World War II was being waged in Europe.
        In 1940, while German combat engineers demonstrated the frightful
effectiveness of portable flame throwers when employed against French and
Belgian fortifications, and German bombers showered several British cities
with incendiary bombs, the U.S. Army belatedly recognized the potential for
destruction embodied in modern flame weapons. But the United States had
not a single flame thrower, or a solitary incendiary bomb. As General
George C. Marshall stated in his biennial report to the Secretary of War in
1945: "We have tried since the birth of our nation to promote our love of
peace by a display of weakness. This course has failed us utterly...."[10]
        It would be 1943 before U.S. soldiers and airmen were equipped with
dependable incendiary weapons. Why, in a modern industrial state richly

blessed with technological and industrial might, had flame weapons been largely ignored since they were introduced to modern warfare during World War I?

We must answer this question before the principal area of inquiry in this study may be addressed. Key to our understanding of the role played by U.S. incendiary weapons during World War II is the answer (or answers) to this question: Why did it take the armed forces of the United States until the last two years of World War II to exploit the capabilities of modern incendiary weapons?

In searching for answers, this book will investigate not only technological matters of design, manufacture, and experimentation, but will also explore the less well-defined aspects of man's moral aversion to flame weapons and the institutional and organizational problems that frequently cut across branch or service boundaries and often served to retard both development and employment of incendiaries.

This is a study of the problems inherent to the development and employment of new and specialized weaponry. The questions posed and the conclusions drawn should speak not only to flame weapons of World War II, but should suggest broader questions about the procedures by which defense establishments select and utilize the weapons that make up their arsenals. For despite the diverse and far-reaching effects of modern technological processes that have characterized the fifty years since the end of World War II, today's defense planners still face many of the vexing financial, moral, and doctrinal problems that loomed so large before, during, and after that colossal struggle.

CHAPTER 1

An Ancient Fear in Modern Form: The Introduction of Flame Weapons During World War I

Flame throwers and incendiary bombs, like so many of the weapons employed during World War II, were improved versions of devices introduced during World War I. The machine gun, tanks, submarines, and aircraft were, like incendiary weapons, tested during that great first conflict. The experience gained by armies between 1914 and 1918 would, in many cases, influence the decisions made by politicians and military men during the two decades following the armistice of 1918. The decision makers were products of their past as they sought to prepare for the next war by applying the lessons of the last in the uneasy truce that passed for peace.

Before examining the reaction of the U.S. Army to the use of incendiary weapons during World War I, before appraising the actions of the peacetime planners, one must first understand what sort of devices these flame weapons were. In the most basic terms, the flame projectors and incendiary bombs of World War I represented a marriage of twentieth-century technology and man's basic and ancient fear of fire. And to comprehend fully the psychological impact of the less-than-perfect fire weapons of 1914–1918, it is necessary to remember that fire warfare has been practiced since biblical times.

The idea that fire might be useful as a weapon must have occurred soon after the first careless caveman burned his finger in his cooking flame. The fact that humans learned to fear fire because of the pain it could cause was probably sufficient to warrant its use as a psychological, as well as a casualty-producing, weapon. The Old Testament is full of references to instances in which fire was credited with destroying the houses of wicked sinners, serving as a vehicle for sacred pronouncements, or consuming unbelievers.[1] The inherent fear of flame was incorporated into the Judeo-Christian religious tradition and capitalized upon by religious leaders. Not until the seventeenth century was the practice of burning the ungodly at the stake given up.

The use of fire against one's enemies was illustrated in the Old Testament Book of Judges. Samson, angered by his Philistine neighbors, is said to have caught three hundred foxes. Tying them tail-to-tail, he sent them running through the Philistine wheatfields, dragging lighted firebrands behind them. The fields of his enemies were soon consumed by flames. This example of incendiary warfare, which took place around 1140 B.C., is certainly one of the earlier military uses of flame on a grand scale.[2]

Although knowledge of the use of flame weapons in times past is quite sketchy, some clues may be found which indicate a certain refinement in the practice of incendiary warfare. Not content to rely on foxes running into wheatfields, warriors began to experiment with flaming arrows, pots of boiling oil, and naptha as means of burning enemy structures, inflicting casualties upon enemy troops, and creating panic in the ranks of their foes. The bas-reliefs of the ancient Assyrians, for instance, depict warriors using a type of liquid fire, although nothing is known of its composition. Only much later in history did written accounts of flame warfare survive.[3]

The early Greeks understood the value of fire as a weapon. The forerunner of what was later to be known as "Greek Fire" was described by Thucydides in *The History of the Peloponnesian War*. The Boeotians, in their attempt to capture the walled fortifications at Delium in 424 B.C., had been unsuccessful until they used fire:

> Various methods of attack were employed, and in the end they took the place by means of an engine constructed in the following manner. They took a great beam, sawed it in two parts, both of which they completely hollowed out, and then fitted these two parts closely together again, as in the joints of a pipe. A cauldron was then attached with chains to one end of the beam, and an iron tube, curving down into the cauldron, was inserted through the hollow parts of the beam. Much of the surface of the beam itself was plated with iron. They brought up this machine from some distance on carts to the parts of the wall that had been principally constructed of vines and other wood. When it was close to the wall, they inserted into their end of the beam large bellows and blew through them. The blast, confined inside the tube, went straight into the cauldron which was filled with lighted coals, sulphur, and pitch. A great flame was produced which set fire to the wall, and made it impossible for the defenders to stay at their posts. They abandoned their positions and fled; and so the fortification was captured.[4]

Augustin M. Prentiss, in his book *Chemicals in War*, has said, "The greatest impetus to the use of incendiaries in war came with the introduction of 'Greek Fire.'"[5] This sticky, highly inflammable mixture was never reduced to a set, published formula. The Syrian Kallinokos, about the year 660 A.D., found that by adding niter and oil to the mixture of sulphur, coals, and pitch already in use, he could produce a viscous substance that burned with an intense heat and could be propelled over considerable distances. The emperor Constantine IV (Pogonatus) utilized this Greek Fire during the siege of Constantinople being carried out by the Saracens in 673 A.D. By mounting tubes on his warships, he was able to propel this flaming liquid onto enemy vessels where it burned fiercely. Because of its composition, it was not easily extinguished by water. The psychological effect that this burning, unquenchable substance had on the crews of the wooden ships was considerable.[6]

Much later, in 1190, the Moslems used this same weapon against the Frankish crusaders besieging Acre. At Mansura, too, the Saracens flung great vessels of burning liquid into the Christian camp by means of large arbalests. After the Crusades, however, the use of Greek Fire diminished. We may surmise that this was due in large part to the general lack of scientific information available to many Europeans, especially until after the Renaissance.[7]

Naval commanders of the seventeenth and eighteenth centuries recognized the value of solid shot heated red-hot and fired at wooden sailing ships, and burning "fire ships" were utilized to set enemy fleets at anchor ablaze; nevertheless, there was little success in producing a modern version of the ancient Greek Fire projectors. An attempt in 1702 by the Prussian artillery to develop a "serpentine fire sprayer" (*Schlangenbrandespritze*) was abandoned after repeated failures. The flammable mixture being tested, which was designed for propulsion by a bellows through a wheeled tube, was too viscous and consistently burned the projector. If flame was to be placed effectively upon enemy positions, some means of propulsion other than a "serpentine fire sprayer" would have to be found.[8]

Man's continuing fascination with flame found expression from time to time in the schemes of those who searched for a novel means of destroying enemy forces while minimizing friendly casualties. One such plan, advanced repeatedly by the Englishman Lord Cochrane, the earl of Dundonald, called for the creation of toxic sulfuric fumes by vaporizing sulphur with burning coke. This proposed use of fire to produce a lethal attack on military (and civilian) enemies was rejected by several boards appointed by British prime ministers between 1812 and 1854 on the grounds that Dundonald's idea was technically unfeasible. Opposition to this scheme on ethical grounds was also cited and came mainly from within the British military establishment.

Dundonald's only encouragement came from Lord Palmerston in 1854. Palmerston, then the prime minister, suggested that the War Office permit Dundonald to conduct his experiment in the Crimea. War Office concurrence would be contingent upon Dundonald's agreement to personally supervise the creation of his toxic gas cloud. Should it fail, Palmerston reasoned, Dundonald would shoulder the blame, not the British government. It would appear that the use of "dirty tricks" was acceptable to some—as long as they were not called to account for their actions.[9]

Advances in the design of artillery shells during the nineteenth century provided those interested in ordnance development with a vehicle that could feasibly be used to deliver incendiary material over some distance. Hollow shells, fused to burst after a specific time in flight or upon impact, might be filled with a substance with which to burn a target. The outbreak of the American Civil War added impetus to the work already begun by several inventors in the United States. Notable among those men working with incendiary munitions in the North were Levi Short and Alfred Berney. They took their place in the jostling throng of gadgeteers and inventors who besieged the War Department and the Navy during the opening days of the conflict. Some, though not all, were persistent enough to receive an audience from the harassed Ordnance Department officers and were allowed to demonstrate their devices. In January 1862 Levi Short exploded several artillery shells of his own design which impressed the Army officers attending his demonstration being held in honor of President Lincoln.[10]

Levi Short sold more than a hundred of these shells to the U.S. Army for use by General Benjamin Butler in his campaign to capture New Orleans in 1862. That same year, Short went into partnership with Alfred Berney. Like Short, Berney had put on a display for President Abraham Lincoln in early 1862, showing off his pump-operated flame projector and several types of incendiary shells.

Although his flame thrower failed to operate successfully, the shells were quite effective. Impressed, Lincoln ordered his Chief of Ordnance, General James W. Ripley, to purchase several thousand of the devices for use against fortified cities. Melding their talents, Short and Berney were able to produce enough shells during the first six months of 1863 that Union forces besieging Vicksburg, Mississippi, were able to burn a large part of the city before the Confederate surrender in July.[11]

The team of Berney and Short also produced the large incendiary shells that were fired into Charleston, South Carolina, in August 1863 by Union artillerymen. Although short-lived and only marginally effective, this means of delivering flame to the noncombatant inhabitants of a city was to presage by eighty years the large-scale fire bombing of European and Japanese cities during World War II. Damage to morale was considered as important as material destruction. The psychological reaction of the civilian inhabitants of the target cities was quite similar and proceeded in stages from curiosity to defiance and, finally, to terror.[12]

Given the ability of these incendiary shells to destroy enemy cities and to terrorize their populace, it may seem strange that the inventions of Berney and Short were not enthusiastically accepted by the officer corps of the Union forces. However, even in a war that knew no parallel in the American experience for sheer destructiveness, the "terror" weapons were considered by most to be abominations. More effort was expended to restrict the use of such hellish devices than was directed toward improving them.[13]

A growing fear of unbridled destructiveness and the wanton carnage committed by Union forces had spurred the Union Secretary of War, Edwin M. Stanton, to attempt to find a means of holding destruction in check. After only a year of conflict, he approached a noted German-American jurist, Francis Lieber, and asked him to formulate a code that would govern the actions of the Union armies in the field. When the document was completed in February 1863, it stated, in part:

> Men who take up arms against one another in public war, do not cease on this account to be moral beings, responsible to one another and to God. Military necessity does not admit cruelty—that is, the infliction of suffering or for revenge....[14]

That neither the Union nor Confederate armies conducted themselves in accordance with these principles does little to diminish the significance of this early attempt to ameliorate the often unwelcome results of "progress."

It would be several years before an international body attempted to grapple with the legalistic and moral questions about weapons that surfaced in Europe, especially after the Franco-Prussian War. In spite of the lack of any sanction against weapons judged to be inhumane, the flammable munitions used during the Civil War were rejected by the professional officer corps of the miniscule armed forces of the United States in the years that followed Appomattox. Professor Alex Roland, in his study of underwater weapons (mines, submersibles, torpedoes) during the age of sail, concludes that line officers frequently felt a strong antipathy toward inventors and their newfangled devices:

> Inventors who proposed these weapons were often tactless in dealing with military professionals. They claimed over-much for their weapons ... and generally treated officers with condescension

and impatience. Worst of all, they undertook to instruct a professional in how to conduct his profession—a chancy business in any
realm, but a particularly hazardous one in military circles.[15]

During wartime, with the Army and Navy swollen to many times their
normal size and peopled by volunteers and draftees, the Regulars often
relaxed their vigil on their self-ascribed codes. When faced with moral dilem-
mas, these old-line keepers of the flame gave way to the gadgeteers if and
when it appeared that the inventions could aid in restoring peace, which
would mean a return to the old ways of doing things so cherished by the Regular officer corps. Professor Roland says of this, "When faced with the reality
of the 'usages of war,' officers overcame their prejudices, but never without
pain and reluctance."[16] With the return of peace, the military returned to its
jobs of fighting Indians and showing the flag at foreign ports of call.

While no more was heard about incendiaries on this side of the Atlantic,
readers of European newspapers may have noted several references to the
use of flame weapons in 1871. Correspondents covering the social upheaval
that gripped Paris during the first half of 1871 mentioned the employment
of petro-filled bottles and balls of incendiary gum or Greek Fire by female
supporters of the Paris Communard. These female firebombers, or
Petroleuses, allegedly hurled their flammable devices at homes, stores, and
factories owned by adherents of the Versailles government that came to
power following the defeat of Napoleon III by Prussia. Hailed as heroines by
members of the Paris Commune, cursed as arsonists by the Versailles forces,
the *Petroleuses* were less effective and certainly less numerous than either side
believed. Their effectiveness, such as it was, lay not in any distinct capacity
for material destruction, but with their ability to arouse the public's age-old
fear of, and fascination with, flame.[17]

During the years preceding the outbreak of World War I, there were
those who viewed with alarm the increasing lethality of modern weaponry.
In an attempt to regulate the ways and means of waging war, international
conferences were convened at the pleasure of the crowned heads of European states. At St. Petersburg in 1868 and 1907, and the Hague in 1899 and
1907, delegates negotiated in search of common ground on which some
consensus could be reached concerning the conduct of war during this, the
new Age of Reason.

Representatives of European governments grappled with the multitude
of questions raised by the portentous employment of the imperfectly understood weapons of modern warfare. In the course of these discussions, incendiary devices were barely mentioned. Only in the Declaration of St.
Petersburg, 1868, did the signatories prohibit the use of any projectile

coated with fulminating or inflammable materials. In this attempt at sparing combatants from "needless suffering," the conferees specified that the prohibition concerned those missiles weighing 400 grams or less. While the Hague Congress of 1907 prohibited the use of phosphorus weapons, nothing was said about incendiaries as such.[18]

The motives of the delegates were, at the same time, humanitarian and self-serving; their pronouncements at once too general and too specific. But incendiaries were as yet little understood. As one historian has observed:

> One does not, in international law, outlaw a specific weapon until its actual design shows what, exactly, is to be legally controlled. One simply puts it in a basket labelled 'dangerous' until further development shows the need for control. So the Hague delegates spent more time on dumdum bullets, both dangerous and in the arsenals, than on submarines, which were, at this stage, just where they were both clearly dangerous and useful, though it was hard for the delegates to visualize just how dangerous to international law or how useful militarily.[19]

Given this insight, the student of the period can better understand why the agreed-upon rules proved inadequate to the great test of 1914–1918. There existed, then, no effective restraint upon a country with an advanced chemical industry, a country that would develop, within a short time, both poison gas and a modern version of Greek Fire.

The growing militancy of the Kaiser's Germany and the various properties of refined petroleum were to provide the fetus and a hospitable climate for the development of a new fire weapon: a weapon not for use against cities, but for use on the battlefield against enemy soldiers. In 1900, a Berlin chemical engineer, Richard Fiedler, was conducting tests on nozzle designs for the propulsion of petroleum under pressure. In the midst of his experiments, he was struck by the possible military application of streams of gasoline, shot from a pressurized tank, and then set ablaze among enemy troops. He halted his initial experiment and began to work full-time on his new idea. In 1901, Fiedler first presented his concept to the German High Command and received funds for continued testing of his prototype apparatus. By 1908, work had progressed sufficiently for field testing by a special Engineer Test Company (*Pioneer-Versuchskompagnie*) to begin.

The Fiedler device consisted of a welded metal vessel containing a mixture of gasoline and oil which was pressurized by means of nitrogen stored in another metal cylinder. The cylinders were strapped to an operator's back by means of a knapsack-type harness. When the soldier opened a needle valve, the pressurized fuel was expelled from a hand-held nozzle connected to the fuel tank by a rubber hose. At the mouth of the nozzle, an ignition device, not unlike that of a cigarette lighter, lit the fuel as it shot out of the nozzle. The operator could direct a stream of burning fuel for nearly thirty meters toward a target. The test model of this early flame thrower (*Flammenwerfer*) weighed approximately fifty pounds when fully loaded and could spray a continuous stream of fire for one minute.

The Germans recognized the limitations imposed on mobility by the weight and bulk of the device and, during the period 1908–1914, continued to test and improve the basic model as well as experiment with a larger model which would not be portable, but would be emplaced in defensive positions and used to combat attacking troops. In addition to the work that was done on the apparatus itself, numerous tests were conducted to devise suitable assault tactics for engineer troops armed with flame throwers while supporting infantry attacks. The test results showed that troops specially trained with the flame thrower would be necessary for its effective employment. With its delicate valve mechanism and ungainly characteristics, it was not a weapon easily mastered.[20]

To ensure that the flame thrower troops possessed the required degree of expertise, the German High Command directed in late 1914 that those engineer troops that had been trained in the use of flame throwers be consolidated in one unit. This first battalion, consisting of forty-eight officers and men and commanded by Captain Hermann Redemann, conducted the first large-scale flame attack to take place on the Western Front.[21]

On 26 February 1915, the battalion attacked trenches held by French troops in the forest of Malancourt, north of Verdun. A German account of the attack describes it thus:

> The fiery serpents which, as if rising out of the earth, fell roaring and hissing on the enemy's trenches and drove him to precipitate flight, leaving behind their weapons and equipment. Even in the rear positions and in the adjacent positions to the right and left the enemy fled from the trenches and left important war material in our hands.
>
> The first flame attack showed that the use of flame projectors could be very successful, if the apparatus was correctly used as regards tactics and technique and if the flame projectors were properly fitted into the general plan of attack and into the duties and formation of the assault infantry.[22]

Heartened by this success, the German High Command authorized an increase in the size of the flame unit. The energetic Captain Redemann was promoted to major and the unit, now officially known as the Third Guard Pioneer Battalion, was enlarged to 800 men in April 1915. Equipped with a shipment of improved weapons from the Fiedler Flame Thrower Works in Berlin, the pioneers trained hard during the spring months in preparation for an attack against British troops when the opportunity presented itself.[23]

Major Redemann and his pioneers first had to prove themselves during the Battle of Ypres in July 1915. The objective was a line of trenches which British troops had seized after bitter and costly fighting. The British positions created a salient near the ruined village of Hooge, Belgium, and presented a threat to German units on either side of the penetration. The mission of the German assault troops was to straighten the line by recapturing the works held by the enemy.

During the night of 29–30 July, the troops of the British Eighth Rifle Brigade became uneasy because of the unnatural quiet which pervaded their portion of the front. No sound had been heard since sundown from the Germans, even though their trenches lay only fifteen feet away in some places. A Canadian historian, citing official British accounts of the action, describes what occurred during the early morning hours of 30 July 1915 in this way:

> Then at 0325, with dramatic suddenness, came the carefully planned German attack. The site of the stables of the chateau was blown up, while a sudden hissing sound was heard by the two rifle companies on either side of the crater. A bright crimson glare over the crater turned the whole scene red. Jets of flame, as if from a line of powerful fire hoses spraying flame instead of water, shot across the front trenches of the Rifle Brigade and a thick black cloud formed. It was the first attack on the British with liquid fire. At the same time, fire of every other kind was opened....[24]

Those soldiers still alive after the first searing wall of flame inundated the position may well have marveled at the strange, humpbacked figures moving steadily toward them through the rolling clouds of oily black smoke. The loads they bore bent them over as they negotiated the tortured terrain with an oddly crab-like gait. The realization that these strange creatures were human, after all, did nothing to lessen their terror as they saw the Germans open valves on their machines and begin to hose streams of flame into the trenches filled with wounded and stunned British soldiers. The few survivors of the explosions and flame visited upon them by the German assault engineers abandoned their positions to the assault force.

When, several days later, the British were able to recapture the positions lost in the flame attack, two German flame throwers fell into their hands.

These were found to consist of a cylindrical steel vessel about 2 feet high, and 15 inches in diameter, fitted with straps for carrying, and divided internally into a compression chamber and oil reservoir. The propellant was nitrogen at 23 atmospheres contained in the upper chamber. A short length of flexible hose ended in a nozzle in which was fitted the ignition device. As the oil emerged under pressure, it forced up the plunger of a friction lighter and ignited a core of fuze mixture surrounding the nozzle which remained alight long enough to enable a number of shots to be fired.[25]

While Redemann and his flame thrower troops continued attacks along the trench lines of the Western Front and sent detachments of engineers to conduct flame operations against the Russians, scientists working with the German Air Service were busy developing an aerial incendiary bomb. The result of their experimentation was a simple device designed to start fires in enemy cities when dropped from an airplane or zeppelin. Dubbed the "bucket bomb" by the British, the first German effort weighed twenty pounds and consisted of a thermite core tightly wrapped with balls of compressed cotton that had been saturated with naptha and tar. A simple detonator was provided to ignite the tin-cased bomb when it hit the ground or a structure. The Germans dropped over two hundred of these bombs in air raids against Channel ports during the last two months of 1915. While the accuracy and overall results were something of an embarrassment to the Germans, the public outcry over this latest "Hunnish" action was considerable. The demand for retribution grew during the early days of 1916.[26]

As so often was the case in this fledgling air war, the action-reaction syndrome soon took over and the French and British began to develop their own incendiary bombs. After examining several German bombs that had failed to ignite, British engineers concluded that the greatest shortcoming of the German munition was its inability to generate a heat of sufficient intensity to ignite any but the most inflammable structures. Accordingly, the British began tests on two different bomb designs, each filled with a variety of inflammable materials. The two bombs being tested were the "Carcass" bomb (50 lbs), and the Mark IV or "Baby Incendiary" (6½ oz) which would be dropped in clusters of three hundred.[27]

During a period of extensive testing of the two bombs in 1916, the British selected a highly flammable mixture of sodium nitrate, sulphur, rosin, and powdered aluminum as the filler for their Carcass bomb. The Baby Incendiary, really a tin-cased dart with a weighted nose containing an igniter, was filled with "Thermalloy," a combustible blend of powdered aluminum and thermite.[28]

Working in concert with their British allies, the French also produced large and small incendiary bombs during 1916. The *Davidsen* bomb, containing a mixture of thermite, sulphur, and gasoline thickened with paraffin, and the *Chanard* incendiary dart were the products of French research. By early 1917, French airmen were employing the *Chanard* against German installations in France and against industrial and transportation complexes just over the German border.[29]

The early incendiary bombs employed by the belligerents were steadily improved during the war. Scientists on both sides recognized the characteristics that a proper incendiary must possess. By identifying these key properties (which still guide the developers of incendiary munitions), the scientists and engineers laid the groundwork for improved fire bombs, not only during the latter stages of World War I, but during World War II as well. They concluded the ideal filler material for an incendiary bomb should possess the following characteristics:

1. It should burn persistently for an appreciable length of time with a very high temperature.
2. It should burn vigorously and not be easily extinguished.
3. It should be of such character as to distribute itself over a fairly large area.
4. It should be safe to handle, and should not ignite by shock or by being pierced by bullets.
5. It should not deteriorate in storage.
6. It should be provided with a detonator/igniter that assures positive ignition.[30]

By the time aviators began to employ incendiaries in appreciable quantities, ground troops in the trench lines that stretched beneath the bombing aircraft had become accustomed to fire warfare as well, for the British and French had fielded their own versions of the German *Flammenwerfer.*

The British effort in the field of flame thrower development was part of a larger chemical warfare program. Early in 1916, a unit was activated under the command of Colonel C. H. Foulkes. This unit, designated the Special Brigade, had one company, "Z" Company, with a mission of conducting flame warfare. This company was commanded by a chemical engineer, Captain W. H. Livens, who was to design not only various flame throwers, but several poison gas projectors as well.[31]

When the Special Brigade deployed to France in July 1916, Z Company took portable flame throwers designed by engineers working under the direction of the British Ministry of Munitions. Referred to as the Hall

Projector, after its designer, the weapon weighed fifty pounds, carried four gallons of highly flammable oil, and could throw a fire stream about thirty meters. The Hall Projector differed from most other models used in World War I because its fuel tank was not cylindrical in shape, but was a doughnut-shaped "O" ring. This design, much improved over the years, was to be used by the British until the end of the Second World War.[32]

Once in France, the British flame unit experimented with another portable flame projector, the Lawrence model, which was unlike any then in use. Instead of a fuse wick ignition system, it employed a battery-powered electric spark to ignite its flame fuel. The British troops found it more comfortable to carry over rough terrain (it weighed only forty pounds), but discarded it when autumn rains and the dampness of trench conditions often caused the batteries to fail.[33]

The static nature of trench warfare, coupled with the difficulty encountered by flame troops in negotiating the shell-torn landscape while carrying their bulky loads, led the British to invest quite a bit of effort in the development of large flame projectors that could be emplaced semipermanently in fixed positions close enough to the enemy to fire streams of flaming oil into the German works. Captain Livens of Z Company found that, in areas where trench lines were within fifty meters of one another, he could use emplaced flame throwers and accomplish his mission of killing Germans while sparing the lives of some of his own troops. Before receiving any large emplaced projectors from England, he had already devised a workable system of his own. Livens used discarded shell shipping containers from artillery units to make short, large caliber mortar tubes. From these tubes he fired thin-skinned drums of highly flammable flame fuel. The drums split open on impact in the German trenches, soaking into the soil and splashing into underground bunkers. After sending over a few of his homemade shells, he would fire incendiary shells into the same area. If all went well for the British, the German position and its occupants would go up in one loud *whoosh* of flame and black smoke.

Livens' experiments produced a large projector that was manufactured in England and shipped to the Front for use in late 1917. Weighing nearly a ton, it could throw a stream of flame eighty meters. A similar model, the Vincent projector, was also used by Z Company during 1917. The time and effort required to emplace these machines outweighed the benefits they provided and only fourteen Livens and ten Vincent projectors were actually used in combat. The war of movement that followed the Germans' spring offensive of 1918 put an end to the British use of emplaced flame throwers. Portable flame throwers continued to be used by the British until the armistice was signed in November 1918.[34]

The French army formed seven units which were equipped with flame throwers. Designated *Campagnies Schilt,* after Captain Schilt who had designed the French portable flame thrower, these units, of about 200 men each, fought until the end of the war. Schilt had designed the French machine while on duty with the *Sapeurs-Pompiers* engaged in the defense of Paris. Using many aspects of the German design, he produced several different models. His Model No. 3 passed French field trials in late 1915, and by June 1916, the first French Schilt companies were in action. The Model No. 3 was much like other portables with the notable exception of its fuel. Instead of heavy oil, it burned a thinner mixture made up of gasoline and naptha.[35]

The French also developed large emplaced flame projectors. Unlike the British, the French never put them into actual combat use, primarily because of the excessive amount of fuel that the machines consumed.[36]

The massive battles along the Somme, at Verdun, and during the abortive Nivelle Offensive of 1917 saw an increased use of flame throwers by all sides, especially during trench raids and limited attacks. While the German army had lost its monopoly on the flame thrower, it continued to rely more upon this weapon than did either the French or the British.

Redemann's original unit had doubled in size in March 1916 and, by April 1917, had been redesignated the Guard Reserve Pioneer Regiment. Made up of over 3,000 officers and men, the unit provided highly trained assault teams to each German corps fighting on the Western Front and sent other groups to train Austrian *Flammenwerfer* teams fighting in Italy. The assault teams were composed of one officer, nine NCOs, and thirty-four enlisted men. In addition to their flame throwers, the German soldiers carried new light machine guns and explosive charges designed to neutralize enemy strongpoints.[37]

Although the Germans continued to improve the tactics by which flame throwers were employed, the overall effectiveness of the German program began to suffer as a result of the ever-tightening British blockade of German home industries. Plagued by shortages in petroleum, brass (for valve fittings), and rubber, the Fiedler company was hard-pressed to supply the steadily expanding needs of the enlarged flame outfit after mid-1917. In an attempt to overcome the problems of lessened support by industry, the engineers set up field shops where they not only repaired many of their flame throwers, but actually manufactured rather crude copies of the Fiedler projector.

Prior to the entry of the United States into World War I, all the major participants of the fighting in France had become accustomed to flame attacks. As was the case with certain other weapons that depend largely upon fear for much of their impact, the flame thrower was beginning to lose some of its effectiveness as troops realized how vulnerable the flame thrower operators were, particularly once their flame fuel was exhausted. By mid-1917, the flame projector had been accepted as a valuable weapon which was most effective in the hands of specially trained and highly motivated operators.[38]

General John J. Pershing's arrival in France with the first contingent of what was to become the American Expeditionary Force (AEF) in June 1917 marked the beginning of the end for German war hopes. The American contribution of men and materiel was enough to swing the balance in the favor of the British and French. Important as the American infusion of strength may have been, it was largely expressed in terms of raw resources. The will to fight was perhaps the greatest asset the Americans possessed. However, the AEF lacked combat experience and equipment. These short-comings were particularly noticeable in the field of chemical warfare. When the AEF headquarters group landed in France, it had no experience in planning chemical warfare operations, no authorization to conduct chemical operations, and no troops trained in the use of poison gas or flame.

Moving with the drive that was to typify his command of the AEF, Pershing soon requested that the War Department grant him the authority to establish a special service in his forces that would be charged with the planning and prosecution of chemical operations. At the urging of British advisors, and even before he received a reply from the War Department, he ordered his chief of staff to provide funds, troops, and the authority required by an officer chosen to "create and handle" an organization devoted to the conduct of chemical warfare.[39]

The AEF Gas Service, established on 15 July 1917, was expanded in mid-August when the War Department granted permission for a Gas and Flame Regiment. Lieutenant Colonel Amos A. Fries, of the Corps of Engineers, was appointed commander of the new regiment on 15 August 1917. Fries immediately established a close relationship with Colonel C. H. Foulkes of the British Special Brigade that was to last throughout the war.[40]

From the beginning, Fries' main concern was the use of poison gas and the equipping and training of American troops to contend with gas, what came to be known as "gas countermeasures." One company of the regiment, initially designated the 30th Engineers (Gas and Flame), was charged with the conduct of flame operations. This unit, never filled to its allotted size, busied itself learning about the various types of flame projectors in use during the early months of 1918. Like gas masks, flame throwers were not part of the equipment brought to France by the Americans. The American flame engineers trained with borrowed weapons and waited for a call to action that never came. They shared the frustration felt by many members of the regiment at large. American commanders, ignorant of chemical warfare matters, and distrustful of the capabilities of the unit (redesignated as 1st

Gas Regiment in August 1918), simply did without much of the support they might have received had they but asked.[41]

While U.S. chemical troops in France tried to learn about chemical warfare as quickly as possible, and the tiny U.S. Army Air Service tested French *Chanard* incendiaries, the War Department established an agency in Washington, D.C., to coordinate the divergent efforts of five different agencies charged in some way with the support of the American chemical warfare effort.[42] Two of these agencies, the Bureau of Mines and the Army's Corps of Engineers, were responsible, respectively, for research into chemical agents (including flame fuels) and the development of flame projectors. The Bureau of Mines let a contract with American University for experiments with flame fuels in early 1918.[43] The Corps of Engineers experimented with various portable flame throwers and, in mid-1918, approved a copy of the British Lawrence projector as the standard American model. Known as the Boyd No. 3, it could expel flaming oil for nearly forty meters, but weighed eighty pounds. The few Boyds that were shipped to France for service tests were quickly rejected as being too heavy for a combat-equipped soldier to manage.[44]

In September 1918, a large steam-driven flame projector on caterpillar treads was shipped to the AEF headquarters for tests. Invented in the United States by a Major Harold Adams of the Corps of Engineers, it was demonstrated for General Pershing at Chaumont, France, in early October. Firing flame over eighty meters, it impressed the gathered officers until Colonel Fries, the AEF Chemical Officer, demonstrated how easily it could be destroyed as he moved to a position in front and a little to one side of the powerful fire stream. Dropping to his hands and knees, Fries crawled under the jet of fire to within six feet of the device. The firing crew, blinded by glare and the shimmering heat waves, had not seen him approach. The Adams flame thrower tank was discarded.[45]

During the last year of the war, the British and French continued to improve their aerial incendiaries. They experimented with new bomb casing designs and began to employ, on a limited scale, spontaneously inflammable liquid fillers. In October 1918, the U.S. Army Air Service dropped several copies of an American-made incendiary bomb in a test at Edgewood Arsenal, Maryland. Designated the U.S. Mark III, this bomb weighed forty-six pounds and measured 6" x 36". Within a steel casing weighing ten pounds, it carried ten pounds of thermite and sixteen pounds of an oil emulsion. The Ordnance, Air, and Chemical Service officers who witnessed the demonstration were so impressed by the results that they persuaded the Chief of Ordnance to order the production of 25,000 bombs. More than 2,000 had been produced by November 1918, but none were shipped to France. The Allied victory canceled any further testing of incendiary weapons in the United States. The bombs already delivered to Edgewood Arsenal were moved to a temporary storage area to await disposition. Halted too by the armistice was the German employment of their recently developed *Elektron* bomb. Weighing just over two pounds (1 kilo), this magnesium bomb had demonstrated its capability to generate intense heat when, in clusters of 228, it had been dropped on Paris during raids in September 1918. The production of this very efficient munition highlighted the disparity between the German and American incendiary programs.[46]

The end of hostilities on 11 November 1918 closed a chapter in the history of flame warfare. The impact of flame throwers and fire bombs had been felt throughout the period 1915–1918, but was most pronounced during 1915 when the shock effect of fire was greatest. With regard to the flame thrower, usually identified with the German army, Allied journalists had been quick to point to its shortcomings. The *London Times*, in its yearly illustrated history of the conflict, advised its readers that the effect of the burning liquid was to saturate and set on fire the clothing of the men it hit, and that the results gained by this brutal weapon were of no special military value. The history contained the following report of a British officer:

> Its effect may be very easily exaggerated. When you see it for the first time it rather gives you the jumps. It looks like a big gas jet coming towards you, and your natural instinct is to jump back and get out of the way. A man who thinks nothing of a shell or a bullet may not like the prospect of being scorched or roasted by fire. But in my experience, the effective range of the flammenwerfer is very limited, and the man who manipulates it as often as not is shot or bombed by our fellows. They call it devil's fire, but when they recover from their first fright they care for it as little as for the devil himself. The actual cases of burning by devil's fire have been very few! There was, however, evidence to show that at first the flammenwerfer did produce considerable effects, and it is certain that these were obtained at the cost of great torture to the men hit.[47]

While experienced troops might suffer flame attacks with equanimity or even become somewhat blasé after repeated exposure to flame warfare, the effects of flame upon troops unacquainted with it were much the same in 1918 as they had been in 1915. Thus, the reaction of American troops subjected to a flame attack was fear, followed by outrage. On 6 October 1918, a battered group of U.S. 77th Division troops was attacked by flame thrower units in the Argonne Forest. This body of soldiery, which would win fame as the "Lost Battalion," came very close to surrendering when assaulted by German Death's Head Pioneers attached to the 254th Reserve Infantry Regiment.[48]

After running out of fuel, the Germans withdrew. Had the Germans been able to press the attack, the story of the Lost Battalion would probably have had a different conclusion. When the beleaguered force was relieved the following day, they were nearly out of ammunition, famished, and clearly on the verge of collapse. As the authors of the Lost Battalion's history have said, the survivors of the action tended to confuse many specific points of historical detail when relating their experience in the Argonne, but they all remembered the flame throwers.[49]

Flame warfare during World War I capitalized more on humanity's inherent fear of flame than upon the efficiency of the incendiary weapons themselves. The practitioners of fire warfare in the air and on the ground found that the limitations of their flame weapons revolved around the improvised nature of the equipment, the lack of any clearly thought-through tactical doctrine, and the insufficient training of those soldiers charged with the actual employment of the weapons. When the natural hazards associated with unproven weapons are magnified by the knowledge that the operator could, as the result of an accident, become a human torch, it is little wonder that those troops handling incendiary weapons of all kinds were often less than enthusiastic about their jobs.

Successful flame attacks, as practiced during the First World War, were all conducted by Europeans. As the war ended, only Europeans possessed any sizable body of technical information on flame warfare. The Americans had little if any practical knowledge that could be gained from experience with flame weapons in combat. Intimate knowledge of the strengths and weaknesses of various flame devices, flame training methods, and organizational concepts of flame thrower and aviation support units belonged to the French, British, and Germans—not to the Americans. With the rapid dismemberment of the wartime U.S. Army soon after the armistice, the little information garnered by wartime soldiers was largely lost as they returned to their peacetime pursuits and tried to forget the war.

Some American officers, particularly those in the soon-to-be-disbanded 1st Gas Regiment, may have wondered about the fact that there had been no talk among the Europeans of scrapping their flame weapons or that the French and British would continue to train young officers in the techniques of flame combat. Many Americans seemed to regard the flame thrower, especially, as a highly overrated weapon. That the U.S. Army had failed utterly to equal the Europeans in developing flame weapons may have caused some patriotic Americans discomfort. This failure was easy to forget if one could rationalize it by disclaiming the incendiary weapons altogether.

In spite of all the shortcomings of the early flame weapons, those on both sides who were enthusiastically committed to the concept of flame warfare had produced weapons that shocked those unlucky enough to encounter them on the battlefield. Through innovation and determination these champions of fire warfare had provided a modern form for one of mankind's ancient fears. In the process, they sparked an argument that would smolder for the next twenty years in the U.S. Army; a question that would only be resolved with the dissolution of peace and a return to war.

CHAPTER 2

The Doldrums: 1920–1939

Upon their return to the United States, the officers of the AEF Chemical Warfare Service faced a new battle, for serious questions were being raised about the continued need for a separate chemical service in the rapidly shrinking peacetime army. The Army Chief of Staff, General Peyton C. March, and even General Pershing, the driving force behind the creation of a Chemical Warfare Service (CWS) overseas, now felt that the Corps of Engineers could carry out the gas and flame mission.

However, Amos A. Fries was unwilling to give up the fledgling organization that he had led for one and a half years in France. After returning from overseas, he had reverted to his regular grade of lieutenant colonel. As the Chief of the AEF CWS, he was in a delicate position, for a major general in Washington also presumed to speak for, and about, the Chemical Warfare Service. Since June 1918, Major General William L. Sibert had functioned as Chief of the CWS, National Army. In command of all chemical troops and installations in the United States, General Sibert was somewhat discomforted by the arrival of Fries and his staff from the battle area. In spite of this strained relationship, Fries began his campaign to save the Chemical Service.[1]

The determined colonel first persuaded the Secretary of War, Newton Baker, to extend the life of the CWS for one year to hear arguments on both sides of the question regarding the CWS. Then, taking his fight to Congress, Fries won the support of two very influential politicians: Representative Julius Kahn, chairman of the House Military Affairs Committee, and Senator George Chamberlain, chairman of the Senate Military Affairs Committee. Because of his determination and aggressive recruitment of supporters, Fries overcame the antipathy of General March, and neutralized Pershing's opposition.[2]

Fries' efforts were repaid when, on 4 June 1920, Congress amended the National Defense Act of 1916, and in so doing provided for the creation of a new Chemical Warfare Service as a permanent branch of the Regular Army. The lawmakers charged the CWS with the development, procurement, and supply of gas, smoke, and incendiary materials. In addition to training, equipping, and organizing Chemical Service troops, the new branch would become responsible for educating the rest of the army in the offensive and defensive techniques of chemical warfare.[3]

Amos A. Fries was appointed as Chief of the new branch and regained his wartime rank of brigadier general. Initially he had 108 officers and 1,544 enlisted men in his command. Within a year, though, the CWS would shrink to less than one hundred officers and fewer than five hundred enlisted troops.[4]

Undaunted, Fries established his headquarters in the hastily constructed buildings at Edgewood Arsenal, which had sprung to life as a chemical munitions site in 1918. As soon as housekeeping details were ironed out, Fries set about convincing the Army and the nation at large of the importance of a strong toxic gas defense for the protection of the United States. The task would not be easy. The nation had turned its attention to peaceful pursuits and was little inclined to maintain a high level of defense spending. Horrified by the employment of poison gas in World War I, a number of different groups were already working to have toxic chemicals banned by international treaty. Lacking money, and thoroughly alarmed by the antigas sentiments of pressure groups, Fries directed his staff to begin publishing a monthly newsletter to be mailed to former CWS officers now returned to civil life, to maintain and cultivate contacts with the civilian chemical industry, and to take a hard look at current CWS programs to see what expenses might be cut, thereby streamlining the Edgewood operation. His fears were well founded, for the CWS received only $1,350,000 for its entire operation in Fiscal Year 1922. In the following year's budget, this already meager sum was cut to a mere $600,000![5]

One of the first cuts made by the CWS staff was in the research and development program for incendiary weapons. General Fries had not been favorably impressed by flame throwers or incendiary bombs during World War I and saw no need to expend his meager funds on continued development of weapons he deemed distinctly subordinate to toxic gas. Contributing to the problems of continued experimentation with incendiary bombs was the fact that the Ordnance Corps (not the CWS) had been charged with the design and manufacture of all aerial bomb casings used by the new Army Air Service.[6]

As early as June 1920, Fries had made his feelings concerning flame throwers known in a reply to a farmer asking about the possibilities of buying war-surplus flame throwers.

...I have to advise you that they [flame throwers] are entirely too inefficient to be useful for burning weeds.

Notwithstanding the wide advertising they have received they were the most inefficient weapons introduced in the war.[7]

The CWS Chief did not confine his adverse remarks about flame throwers to official correspondence. Within two years after returning to the United States from France, Fries had completed a book (coauthored by Clarence J. West) which was to serve as an unofficial history of the AEF Chemical Warfare Service during World War I. The book, entitled *Chemical Warfare*, was designed to project Fries' concepts and to argue in favor of gas warfare. Widely read by military men in England and the United States, it was also translated into French and German and began to draw notice on the Continent as well. In its discussion of the activities of the American chemical troops during the war, the book dealt almost exclusively with their major function, the use of poison gas. Fries argued forcefully for continued development of the various toxic gasses, which he felt might be primary weapons in any future conflict. In the book, he brushed aside the objections of those who called for an end to the development of toxins, insisting that if everyone had powerful weapons, no country would be tempted to attack its neighbor. As far as Fries was concerned, "Every development of science that makes war more universal and scientific makes for permanent peace by making war intolerable."[8]

Fries' comments on the desirability of increased universality in weapons did not, it seems, apply to incendiary weapons. The reader is able to sense a rejection of incendiary weapons not solely on technical grounds, but upon a personal repugnance as well. The general made his case against flame throwers by saying:

Of the incendiary materials used [in World War I] the least valuable is the flame thrower. In the Chemical Warfare Service it has been the habit for a long time not to mention the flame thrower at all, unless questions were asked about it.... Even the German, who invented it and who, during the two years of trench warfare, had full opportunity for developing its use, finally came to using it largely as a means of executing people that he did not want to shoot himself. Men falling in that class were equipped with flame throwers and sent over the top. The German knew, as did the Allies, that every man with a flame thrower became a target for every rifle and machine gun nearby.[9]

While the Chief of the CWS was not always able to convince the general public of the necessity for maintaining a strong antigas defense posture, his personal influence over the tiny chemical branch of the Army was surely pervasive. And, as a West Point graduate with a successful career as an Engineer officer in the years before World War I, Fries was equipped to deal with the intense intramural rivalries that afflicted the U.S. Army. In the peacetime Army of the 1920s, the general holding the chair of "chief" of each branch not only was the final arbiter for disputes within his service, but was regarded as the legitimate official spokesman for his branch by the other service chiefs. His control over his subordinates was enhanced by the fact that he had approval authority over all promotions, transfers, and job assignments within his service. Until his retirement in 1929, General Fries could be assured of seeing his orders promptly obeyed and his priorities served. He was, within his sphere of influence, a very powerful person.[10]

While developmental work continued during the 1920s on toxic gasses and various defense measures designed to reduce gas casualties, little effort was made to keep abreast of British and French advances in flame weaponry.

Having scrapped the few Boyd flame throwers produced during World War I, the CWS rid itself of the last vestige of its wartime association with incendiaries in September 1921. During July and August, Army Air Service planes under the command of General Billy Mitchell had conducted test bombings of several old German battleships in Chesapeake Bay. He had requested that the CWS provide him with bombs that could be dropped to create a smoke screen. At the direction of General Fries, the last Mark III incendiary bombs left in the Army arsenal were emptied of their thermite filler and refilled with white phosphorus. The *Chemical Warfare* journal carried an article several months later in which the daring tactics of the airmen were extolled as the bombing technique of the future. One had only to approach the target at 200 feet, drop the smoke bomb on the battleship deck, and fly away. Unfortunately, the process by which this bombing technique was perfected had required all the incendiary bombs manufactured during 1918.[11]

Twenty years later, when the U.S. Army Air Forces requested incendiary bombs and air staff officers began to look for a plausible explanation for the lack of these items, some must have blamed General Fries for the failure to develop new incendiary bombs after World War I. Certainly Fries must share part of the onus for American unpreparedness in the field of incendiary weapons, but his personal antipathy toward flame was only a part of the pervasive problem of unpreparedness that afflicted the U.S. Army prior to World War II. The bases for U.S. unpreparedness lay in national policy after World War I and in the failure of the Army General Staff to identify requirements for new weapons and doctrine. The conservative attitudes prevalent among Army leaders combined with an imperfect system for testing new concepts to seriously degrade the ability of the U.S. Army to prepare for war. These factors were as important as the lack of monies so often cited by official histories as the culprit.

Alex Roland, in studying military opposition to new types of weapons, has stated that conservatism, morality, and pragmatism all seem to be involved in the problem of weapons development. Aside from General Fries' personal feelings regarding the importance or desirability of fire warfare, his objection to flame weapons on the grounds that they had not worked well in World War I seems to fit Roland's analysis.

> The pragmatic objection stemmed from the simple fact that the weapons did not work.... However, their [officers'] pragmatic objection was also a self-fulfilling prophecy. The [U.S.] military refused to adopt these weapons because they had failed in combat —[and the weapons failed] largely because the military had failed to adopt them.[12]

In spite of Fries' assertions that flame throwers did not function well, there was still some lingering interest in the weapon. During the 1920s and early 1930s, requests for information about flame throwers continued to arrive at Edgewood Arsenal. The correspondents were as varied as their reasons for wanting a flame thrower. The fire warden of a forest preserve in New Jersey, a farmer in Florida who thought that a good dose of flame might cure his cabbage plants of two-spot mites, and the military attaché at the Polish Embassy in Washington all wanted to obtain flame throwers. The civilians were told that the CWS had no old flame throwers for sale. The Polish officer was advised that:

> Flame projectors are not a part of the equipment of the troops pertaining to the Chemical Warfare Service, nor are such devices kept in store by this service for any probable use.[13]

By 1926, the translated version of Fries' book had been circulated throughout Europe. Predictably, it had prompted a strong reaction from German proponents of flame warfare. As evidenced by its wartime enlargement and reputation, the German flame regiment had been highly regarded by many German army officers.

Despite German officers' positive opinions of the *Flammenwerfer*, the German army had just been forced to scrap all of its "offensive" weapons by the terms of the Treaty of Versailles. The Guard Reserve Pioneer Regiment was demobilized and its officers transferred or retired. To retired Colonel

Redemann, Fries' remarks about German flame throwers and the assignment of German troops to the flame regiment as punishment for previous
offenses constituted gratuitous and unfounded abuse.[14]

Redemann's rejoinder to Fries was sent in a long letter forwarded with a
translation by the U.S. military attaché in Berlin. Redemann refuted all of
Fries' assertions about flame weapons and backed up his argument with a
number of enclosures in the form of statements from high-ranking German
war leaders who had seen the flame unit at work during the war. The statements of Generals Schmidt von Knobelsdorf, von Loszberg, and the former
Crown Prince display a strong, even emotional, bias in favor of the German
weapons and tactics employed. Despite their obvious attempts to skew their
recital of past actions in favor of the German side, the meticulous manner in
which the generals attested to the lethality of flame throwers employed by
well-trained assault teams lent credence to Redemann's assertion that Fries
and West were guilty of rather shoddy research or, worse yet, simply had
relied upon the accounts of dubious sources of information. In his letter,
Redemann said:

> Apparently their knowledge of this means of combat is not
> personal, but, on the contrary, they have accepted newspaper
> accounts and the verbal statements of others, which as so often was
> the case in the World War—are absolutely false.[15]

General Fries replied to Colonel Redemann, acknowledging that "Here
and there in the book will be found rather unimportant statements which in
the light of present knowledge, the facts do not bear out." Continuing his
reply, Fries maintained that, to the best of his knowledge, none of the
former Allies were still interested in flame thrower development, that American troops had never been attacked by flame throwers, and that, "The use
of any such equipment in any army today has been discarded as not being of
sufficient worth."[16]

It may seem incomprehensible that the Chief of the CWS was truly
unaware of the continued experimentation being carried out on flame
weapons by the British and French, for during the 1920s the faculties of the
British and French chemical schools regularly corresponded with the faculty
at the CWS school at Edgewood Arsenal. A careful review of the records of
the CWS leader reveals no evidence of any request by Fries for information
on foreign flame developments. One might expect a graduate of the
Military Academy to pursue a more scientific approach to weapons analysis.

The failure of Amos Fries to encourage the members of his small headquarters to seek information on foreign developments or to allocate scarce

resources to flame research may well have stemmed from the common tendency to reinforce success rather than attempting to reverse an earlier failure. In the CWS of the 1920s, toxic gas was regarded as a weapon of almost unlimited potential for future wars. The successful employment of gas by U.S. forces during the Meuse-Argonne Offensive of October 1918 had done much to convince CWS officers that poison gas was effective. The fact that many officers in other branches did not share the CWS optimism only increased Fries' determination to continue improving the offensive and defensive gas warfare material in the CWS inventory. As Fries frequently noted in articles as well as in his book, toxic gas was able to produce enemy casualties while at the same time reducing U.S. casualties among protected troops. In this matter, the official reports of the Army Surgeon General seem to support Fries, for the death rate among AEF troops admitted to hospitals during World War I was far less for those who had been gassed than those who had suffered some type of gunshot or shrapnel wound.[17]

In contrast to the often touted advantages of toxic gas, the problems attendant to the early flame projectors were considerable. The World War I flame thrower had frequently appeared to present as great a threat to the hapless operator as to his intended victims. The failings of the early flame throwers were sufficient to disqualify them from any remedial effort on the part of the U.S. Army. This decision, made by the CWS Chief, deprived the Army of a weapon that Great Britain and France were continuing to improve. To reject flame weapons on the basis of only limited information regarding their past use, to deny that any potential existed without a fair testing of the weapon, would seem to indicate a serious lack of vision on the part of the CWS Chief and his staff. This failure was exacerbated by an inadequate assessment of foreign developments in weaponry.

The Chemical Warfare Service was not the only branch of the U.S. Army that was attempting to develop modern weapons without the very real benefit of pertinent information about foreign developments in its field. The Ordnance Department also suffered. In an official history of the Ordnance Department, the authors comment upon the reasons for this dearth of information from overseas.

> Americans had long realized that information about the types of equipment in use or under development by foreign armies was an aid, if not actually a starting point, for ordnance research and development work for the U.S. Army. But during the 1930's technical intelligence, that is, data on details of foreign design and manufacturing methods, was so intertwined with military intelligence that what filtered through to the Department was casual and tended to leave

research to proceed in a near vacuum. The U.S. Army's disregard of developments in foreign munitions before 1940 is a perpetual source of astonishment to the European.[18]

In mid-1930, though, there was evidence of increased interest of some members of the CWS staff with regard to flame weapons. The Redemann correspondence had floated through the staff sections at CWS headquarters for several weeks during 1928. Perhaps coincidentally, the year after General Fries retired, the American attaché received a request for information that had been forwarded by the War Department G-2 Staff. The new chief of the CWS, Major General Harry L. Gilchrist, had asked that the attaché secure two lecture outlines from the French Army Chemical School. The two lectures, normally presented to French staff officers, were the only lectures that the CWS was interested in having, although many such outlines had been offered under the information exchange program that year. The original letter from the Headquarters, CWS, to G-2 Intelligence had stated:

> ...the Chemical Warfare Service is interested in two of the documents offered [*sic*] in paragraph (b) of the basic communication, viz. "Flame Throwers: Portable Light Flame Thrower," and "Flame Throwers: Heavy Type Flame Thrower."[19]

Possessing only the limited information on foreign developments that filtered down to the branches from the War Department G-2 Staff, and hamstrung by personnel and money shortages, the CWS was also restricted by the role it played within the Army as a whole. As a technical service the CWS, in large measure, depended on the combat arms for impetus in weapons or tactical equipment development.

Charged by the Defense Act of 1920 that created the CWS with the development, procurement, and supply of gas, smoke, and incendiary materials, an important part of the CWS mission was the support of the combat branches: Infantry, Cavalry, Air Service, Artillery, and Engineers. Upon examining the structure of the CWS during the 1920s, one is struck by the fact that the small service was better organized to facilitate response to initiatives advanced by the combat arms than to conceptualize and develop weapons that might or might not have some future utility. Prior to his retirement, General Fries had organized a board of CWS officers charged with coordinating the technical developments of the CWS with the tactical doctrines and methods of using combat arms. In addition to CWS officers, the board meetings were attended by representatives of the combat arms. Known as the Chemical Warfare Committee, this organization attempted to analyze all important developments in combat tactical doctrine vis-a-vis the chemical munitions or equipment required to support the new developments.[20]

In the fifteen years following World War I, the combat branches of the Army did not request CWS assistance in developing incendiary weapons of any kind. A CWS index published in 1934 which listed all official U.S. Army publications dealing with chemical warfare did not include any mention of incendiary weapons. Clearly, the Infantry, Air Corps, and Engineers had envisioned no future role for flame throwers or fire bombs. Lacking any demand for flame weapons from outside the CWS, the staff at Edgewood filed away the information it had received in 1931 about French flame throwers and fire warfare tactics and continued its self-defined primary mission of experimentation with toxic gas and gas defense.[21]

While the U.S. Army struggled along on its small budgetary allowances during the Depression era, the British, French, and Italians (also hard-hit by a depression) managed to continue improving World War I flame weapons. After ensuring that the Germans and their former allies were stripped of incendiary weapons, the victorious European powers proceeded in the development of flame weapons, secure in the knowledge that there was no legal prohibition to constrain them.[22]

Although there had been some attempts to outlaw incendiaries during the framing of the Geneva Protocol of 1925 and at a disarmament conference sponsored by the League of Nations in 1933, these attempts had failed to win support. One student of the period states:

> ...several attempts have been made to restrict or prohibit incendiary weapons by international agreement; indeed the disarmament conference of the League of Nations seemed close in 1933. But...the awesome use of poison gas during World War I overshadowed incendiary weapons in the post-war legal discussions....[23]

The absence of American interest in incendiaries may have reflected some concern about the morality of this type of weapon, which was viewed by critics as causing needless suffering to its victims. Mainly, however, the lack of progress between the two world wars with regard to flame weapons can be ascribed to a failure of the U.S. Army to anticipate the need for this type of weapon in the future.

History shows that the introduction of new weapons has often mandated a change in the tactical doctrines of the force employing the weapon. In the peacetime U.S. Army, the mechanism for evaluating the relationship between weapons and doctrine was ungainly and often ineffective. Branch loyalties and the pervasive influence of branch chiefs cannot be discounted, but the lack of interest in flame weapons seemed to speak to an even greater problem afflicting the U.S. Army of the period. In a study of the development of new weapons and doctrine, one historian has said:

> ... the greatest stumbling block to the revision of doctrine was probably not so much vested interests as the absence of a system for analyzing new weapons and their relation to prevailing concepts of utilizing weapons.[24]

The problem of devising a system for evaluating new weapons and the probable effect that these innovations would have on established procedures was exacerbated by the parochialism of the separate branches. An official history of the U.S. Army explains the system extant during the 1930s:

> ... the Chief of Staff of the U.S. Army had the final voice in decreeing American doctrine of the tactical use of weapons ... each of the using arms worked out its concept of the best means of accomplishing its own mission, [and] the Chief of Staff had to approve them or resolve conflicts of doctrine arising between one arm and another. The Ordnance Department [or the CWS] was then responsible for designing the fighting equipment with which to execute the maneuvers planned. If evolution of doctrine were tardy, then design would also be delayed, for design of weapons for any army is necessarily shaped by the purpose for which the weapons are to be used.[25]

In a land where political leaders eschewed any military intervention in foreign affairs, where the public felt that the World War had been the "war to end all wars," where the only serious prospect for war lay in the far reaches of the Pacific, the chiefs of the combat branches of the U.S. Army were hard put to know just which weapons would be most needed in the future. Those military planners charged with identifying probable requirements for weapons may well have rankled under the admonition of Giulio Douhet, who had warned:

> Victory smiles upon those who anticipate changes in the character of war, not upon those who wait to adapt themselves after the changes occur.[26]

Although there continued to exist only limited interest in incendiary weapons within the active Army, a professor of chemistry at Columbia University, Enrique Zanetti, sounded a prophetic warning about incendiaries in

1934. Professor Zanetti, a CWS Reserve officer who had served in the AEF CWS in 1918 as a liaison officer to the French chemical branch, cautioned of the potential destructiveness of incendiary bombs. Speaking to a group of chemists in Chicago, he stated:

> Each of these small [incendiary] bombs holds within itself the devastating possibilities of Mrs. O'Leary's cow.

Most of the U.S. Army Air Corps officers attending the Chicago meeting were committed to high explosive and toxic gas bombing, as advocated by the noted Italian theorist Giulio Douhet. Zanetti took pains to emphasize the fact that "Explosives dissipate, fire propagates."[27]

Reserve Colonel Zanetti would have been considerably cheered had he attended a meeting of CWS and Air Corps officers held in April 1934 to discuss Air Corps proposals for the development of new toxic gas and smoke bombs. Apparently, Zanetti was not the only person thinking about incendiaries. Voicing a minority opinion at the conclusion of the meeting, Army Air Corps Captain George C. Kenney requested:

> That a priority be given to the development of an incendiary bomb which is capable of igniting materials that are resistant to fire.... [And] is more satisfactory than either the existing H.E. bomb or any W.P. [White Phosphorus] bomb developed to date in this country.[28]

Captain Kenney, from the Air Corps Tactical School at Langley Field, Virginia, was not expressing the opinion of the faculty of the school, but his own. A graduate of the Army Command and General Staff School and the Army War College, Kenney had already established a reputation as an innovator. He would continue to conceptualize new approaches to problem solving throughout an illustrious career that saw him rise from a brigadier general in 1941 to a full general in 1945.[29]

This request for incendiaries, the first since 1918, resulted in the approval for a limited investigation of various types of incendiary bomb fillers that might produce a more suitable incendiary effect when dropped *en masse* upon an enemy city. The Technical Division of the CWS began actual experimentation in 1936 at Edgewood, using bombs supplied by the Ordnance Department, and filler materials identical to those developed during the last year of World War I. It was a case of going back to square one with regard to U.S. incendiary bombs.[30]

The lack of CWS interest in incendiary bombs that characterized most of the interwar years was highlighted in a book authored by a CWS officer.

Published in 1937, *Chemicals in War*, by Lieutenant Colonel A. M. Prentiss, contained only a short chapter on incendiary bombs (and almost nothing on flame throwers). Prentiss urged his readers to prepare for the possibility of large-scale attacks upon civilian populations in any future war. While he saw poison gas as the greatest potential danger to unprotected populations, he also warned that incendiary bombs might also be extensively employed. Given Prentiss' concern, it would appear that some active duty CWS officers were aware, at least, of the potential destructiveness of fire bombs.[31]

During the period 1935–1937, the Chief of the CWS, Major General C. E. Brigham, called upon Reservist Zanetti on several occasions with regard to incendiary bombs. In 1935, Colonel Zanetti had received, from the science editor of the *New York Times*, the remnants of an Italian incendiary bomb that had been discovered by a *Times* correspondent covering the Italian invasion of Ethiopia and mailed back to New York. Zanetti mailed the bomb to the Chief of the CWS for analysis. Engineers at Edgewood found that this bomb, with a magnesium alloy casing and thermite filler, was far superior in igniting capacities to anything the U.S. Army had developed during World War I and turned the sample over to the small group of men who were scheduled to begin testing incendiary bombs in the near future.[32]

When the obvious disparity between U.S. fillers and the Italian sample was reported to General Brigham, he asked Colonel Zanetti to come on active duty for a time during the summer of 1936. Zanetti agreed, and at the request of General Brigham, traveled to England, France, Italy, and Germany in search of more information about European advances in incendiary bomb technology. Upon returning, Zanetti provided the CWS Chief with considerable information about European developments in aerial incendiaries. He had discovered that the Germans, having thrown off the restrictions of the Versailles Treaty, had resurrected their 1-kilo *Elektron* bomb and were selling a number of these munitions to Italy, Russia, and several South American countries. While taking a guided tour of the Chemische Fabrik H. Stoltzenberg in Hamburg, Zanetti was given very limited access to production areas. Nevertheless, he was able to see that the Germans were also developing a bomb filled with thickened gasoline and seemed to be ready to begin mass production.[33]

Having received the fruits of Zanetti's labor, the CWS might have been able to step up its own test program had the increased funding so necessary been made available. Unfortunately, the Air Corps was not in a position to provide more money, the Ordnance Department was totally committed to the development of newer HE bombs, and the CWS was ploughing all of its "extra" money into the improvement of the 4.2-inch chemical mortar. The experiments with incendiary bombs continued, but in a desultory fashion for want of personnel, money, support, and command enthusiasm.[34]

Life continued at a rather leisurely pace at Edgewood Arsenal in 1937 and 1938. In Europe, however, political and military events began to occur with dramatic frequency. The Mediterranean, too, was in the news. Mussolini's Italian conquest of Ethiopia and the Spanish Civil War made headlines in American newspapers. After seeing a newsreel depicting Italian flame throwers mounted on armored cars and light tanks, the new Chief of the CWS, Major General Walter C. Baker, asked on 16 March 1937 that he be provided with more information about the Italian flame vehicles. In his letter to the War Department G-2 Division, the general asked:

> ... that the appropriate military attache obtain such information on this subject as may be available without disclosing the interest of the Chemical Warfare Service in this equipment. This information should include, if possible, description of the flame thrower, composition of the flame producing material, types of motor vehicles in which used, effectiveness, and contemplated use.[35]

It took more than a year for Colonel G. H. Paine, the attaché in Rome, to gather sufficient information to be of real value. The data requested was eventually received in the form of a well-written comprehensive report which outlined the mechanical functioning of the Italian weapon, plans for its tactical use, photographs, and additional comments regarding the Italian portable flame throwers. Concerning the flame thrower mounted on a light tank [*carro d'assalto*] Paine said, in part:

> The Italian flamethrower ... consists of the flame-throwing apparatus on the tank, and a small two-wheeled light armored trailer which carries the liquid, which may be crude oil, kerosene, gasoline, or a mixture of any or all of these. ...
>
> The jet of flame is only about 25–30 meters when the tank is stationary, but the range is increased to 65–70 meters when the tank is moving and the pump gets added power from the tank's transmission.
>
> It is understood that the portable flame thrower will no longer be used in offensive operations, as it has been found that the casualties to flame thrower personnel have been excessive.[36]

Colonel Paine's report was read carefully, then filed. In spite of proof that the Italians had used their mechanized flame throwers in Ethiopia and that German tanks with mounted flame throwers had been combat-tested by

Franco's forces during the Spanish Civil War, the CWS made no attempt to develop experimental prototypes of flame throwers. The CWS was not prepared to initiate any work on flame thrower design until a request was received from the War Department in behalf of one of the combat arms of the Army. The Second World War would be almost nine months old before such a request was made.[37]

CHAPTER 3

Europe Aflame: The American Reaction, 1940–1942

For West Europeans, World War II really began during May 1940. The six-week campaign that followed, leading to the fall of France, will be remembered as a period of total chaos. As German armies surged through most of western Europe, many people far removed from the battlefields anxiously devoured every scrap of information available on the German victories. The tactics, weapons, and organizations which had been so successfully melded to carry out the *Blitzkrieg* came under intense scrutiny, especially in Moscow and Washington.

Among the Americans carefully analyzing the German advances were a group of officers in the Army Corps of Engineers. They marveled at the methods used by the *Wehrmacht*'s engineer troops for neutralizing French and Belgian fortresses. The speedy German capture of the heavily defended Belgian fort of Eben Emael on 10–11 May 1940 fired the imagination of the U.S. officers. Airborne and amphibious engineers using demolitions and flame throwers had cracked the morale of the Belgian defenders while battering the defenses of the "impregnable" fortress. For several months after the fall of France, U.S. military journals were filled with articles on the German success. Several, written by an American military attaché, Captain Paul W. Thompson, concentrated on the role played by the German engineer troops during the Blitz. An engineer officer himself, Thompson praised the élan and technical expertise of the Germans. Of the attack on Eben Emael, Thompson wrote:

> The works were still strong, still intact, still angry. And now began the action to which all that had gone before was simple preparation. Those throwbacks to medieval war, the flamethrowers, opened up against the embrasures. The engineers moved forward, yelling, into their final assault.[1]

This stirring account of battlefield action was a far cry from the mundane peacetime activity of the U.S. Army Corps of Engineers. As was quite evident from official and personal reports, the Germans had worked hard during the late 1930s, training their engineer troops for combat. New explosives and flame throwers had been used not only in France and Belgium, but in Poland as well. The Germans had developed a new portable flame thrower, the Model 1935, and had used it, along with a tank-mounted flame thrower, the *Sd. Kfz. 122*, which had been tested during the Spanish Civil War.[2]

One of the Americans closely following events in Europe was Major General Julian E. Schley, Chief of the Army Engineers. After studying suggestions from his staff and before the battle of France was finally decided, Schley directed his assistants to prepare several letters for submission to the War Department. These contained requests for funds and equipment which would, if received, assist the Engineers in ridding themselves of their peacetime "civil-works" image. Soon afterwards, new tables of organization were drafted for combat engineer units, bringing them more into line with German standards, and increased emphasis on weapons training for engineer recruits was proposed.[3]

General Schley must have realized that his requests for additional funds had at least a fair chance of approval, for after 1939, five Engineer Corps officers were assigned to key positions on the War Department General Staff. If the hopes of Schley and his staff were realized, the Engineers could adopt a new identity. By mid-1940, members of the General Staff began to use the term "combat engineers" with increased frequency. Many members of the Corps of Engineers began to think of themselves as members of a combat arm like the Infantry or Artillery. Study groups at the Engineer School, Fort Belvoir, Virginia, concluded that the Engineers should begin preparing themselves for a combat mission in the not-too-distant future.[4]

One of the weapons the Chief of Engineers wanted for his troops was the portable flame thrower. Having been informed that the CWS had no flame throwers in its inventory, Schley submitted his formal request to the Adjutant General, War Department. The original request for flame throwers dispatched on 24 July 1940 said this:

1. I request that the Chief of the Chemical Warfare Service be directed to develop as soon as practicable a suitable flame thrower for individual use.
2. Intelligence reports indicate that such flame throwers have been used with considerable success in attacks upon mechanized vehicles

and permanent and semi-permanent fortifications. The use of such
a flame thrower should be given serious consideration in the development of equipment for engineer troops.[5]

This request, growing as it did from an increased sense of urgency on
the part of the Corps of Engineers, was sufficient to launch a research and
development program that would provide the U.S. Army with its first
portable flame thrower in over twenty years. Events in Europe that had led
to the request had been closely monitored by the CWS staff in Washington
and at Edgewood Arsenal. The obvious superiority of the German position
in the field of flame warfare must have impressed the Chief of the Chemical
Warfare Service. He lost no time in replying to a query from the Adjutant
General's Office concerning the Engineer request. On 30 July 1940, the
Chief of the CWS wrote:

1. It is recommended that... the Chief of the Chemical Warfare Service be directed to initiate the development of flame throwers....
2. Sufficient funds are available to the Chief of the Chemical Warfare Service to initiate this development.
3. ...It is expected that working models can be produced within
   three months time.[6]

The Army General Staff considered the Engineer request in light of
which branch of the service should be tasked with testing the new flame
throwers. Generally, the Ordnance Department was in charge of weapons
development. Because of the nature of the flame thrower's "ammunition"
(petroleum), the War Department G-4, acting for the Army Chief of Staff,
directed that, "based on precedent" the Chemical Warfare Service would be
given the overall control of flame thrower design and development.[7]

Unknown to the Chief of Engineers, another branch of the Army was
interested in developing flame weapons. Even as the Chief of Engineers was
considering the possibilities afforded by flame throwers, the commander of
the First Armored Corps, General Adna R. Chaffee, had requested in May
1940 that the War Department G-4 provide funds for experimentation by
the Armored Force in the field of "Flame projectors mounted on light tanks
or combat cars."[8] The War Department G-4 replied that while there was no
opposition expressed by the Army Chief of Staff to experimentation by the
Armored Force in this field, no funds would be available until the next fiscal
year began in July. The tankers at Fort Knox, Kentucky, were authorized to
contact the Chemical Warfare Service and, in conjunction with the CWS,
begin tests as soon as was practicable.[9]

With War Department approval granted to the Engineers and to the Armored Force, the Chief of the CWS instructed the Technical Division of the CWS to establish separate committees to work with the two branches. In doing this, the CWS Chief, Major General Walter C. Baker, set a precedent that was to hamper communications between the two testing groups throughout World War II. Immersed in their own problems, the two groups operated almost independently.

PORTABLE FLAME THROWER DEVELOPMENT, 1940–1942

The initial request for flame throwers sent by the Chief of Engineers was based in large part upon the assumption that, should the United States become involved in the World War, the engineer units assigned to each army division would be the troops called upon to reduce enemy fortifications, strongpoints, or roadblocks. The Engineer planners were correct in theory, for the flame thrower, though utilized in a variety of roles during World War II, was first and foremost a device used for capturing stubbornly held, strongly built enemy positions. The only discrepancy in their initial concept was the supposition that the employment of flame throwers would fall strictly under the province of the Corps of Engineers. As it turned out, the flame thrower was to be used not only by engineers, but by tankers, and to the greatest degree of all, by Army and Marine infantrymen. In its initial developmental stages, however, the portable flame thrower was almost solely an Engineer-CWS project.

The War Department General Staff, upon approving the Engineers' request for flame throwers, instructed the Chief of the CWS to work closely with the Engineers in the initial stages of designing and testing the weapon prototype. According to the War Department directive, the portable flame thrower should meet certain basic criteria. It had to be of such size, shape, and weight that a soldier could carry it on his back and capable of projecting a stream of flame at least ten yards, and the flame fuel should not be easily extinguishable with water. Other than these broad guidelines, the CWS was given nearly a free hand in the design of the test weapon. A research and development program for Fiscal Year 1941 was somewhat cautiously funded: the sum was $10,000.[10]

Early in August 1940, the Technical Division of the CWS began work on the portable flame thrower project. Since the Army had scrapped all of the old Boyd model flame throwers developed during 1918, the CWS technicians had to start from scratch. Because of the short period that the CWS had in which to produce a prototype (three months), the Americans did not attempt to secure British flame throwers, all of which were still rather intricate doughnut-shaped projectors based on the World War I models. Collecting whatever information there was in the files at Edgewood Arsenal, the committee began seeking ideas and assistance from industry.

Lacking any demand for flame projectors in industry or business, the civilian community was unable to provide a flame thrower "off the shelf" as it so often did when the military needed a bulldozer, crane, or truck. The CWS technicians contacted a number of producers of insecticide sprayers, in hopes of gleaning some information on recent innovations in pressurized containers. By late August the CWS had located a New York firm that manufactured fire extinguishers. The Kincaid Company was willing to produce several models based on CWS specifications. CWS officers must have reasoned that if Kincaid could produce fire extinguishers, it could surely fabricate fire projectors.

The CWS purchase order and diagrams of the device required were sent to the Kincaid firm in early September. Concept drawings provided only general guidance concerning the performance characteristics and physical dimensions desired in the working model. A packet of photographs of the U.S. Model 3 (Boyd) flame projector were attached to the drawings. An actual copy of the flame weapon developed in 1918 would have been better, of course, but the CWS had not saved a single Boyd flame thrower after 1919! By failing to provide the Kincaid Co. with precise requirements, the CWS Technical Division abdicated its role in the design process in favor of the manufacturer.[11]

The finished product from Kincaid was returned to the CWS at Edgewood Arsenal in October 1940. The first model is described by an official CWS historian in this way:

> This ... model consisted of four main components: a storage system for fuel, a storage system for compressed gas, a flame gun and an igniter. ... The first fuel tank was a vertical cylinder having two components, the upper holding nitrogen under pressure and the lower containing five gallons of fuel—at that time diesel oil, fuel oil, or a blend of gasoline and oil. The filled weapon weighed seventy pounds. The fuel oil flowed through a flexible tube into the flame gun. The gun was a metal barrel to which was fastened an igniter consisting of a battery and two triggers, one to release the fuel and the other for ignition as it issued from the nozzle. When the weapon was fired, compressed nitrogen blew the oil through the hose and gun at the rate of one half-gallon per second. At the nozzle an electric spark from the battery lit a small jet of hydrogen, which in turn set aflame the oil. The stream of burning oil had a range of fourteen to twenty-one yards.[12]

The technicians from Edgewood Arsenal studied the finished product from the Kincaid Co. During laboratory tests conducted by the CWS the model seemed to work. In retrospect, one wonders why the technical officers at Edgewood accepted the device from Kincaid. Labeled the Model E1, it was akin to a large oil drum in size and weight. No normal man could have carried the device for long. The fact that the big drum wobbled from side to side on its poorly devised carrying harness made it nearly impossible for the operator to move at anything other than a sedate walk while balancing this ungainly load between his shoulder blades. Perhaps the E1 seemed acceptable in the Technical Division office, if only as a starting point for further development. In any case, the project officers at Edgewood Arsenal decided to send the E1 to the Engineers for field testing.[13]

The Engineer Test Board received three flame throwers for testing. Field tests were conducted during the winter months of 1940–1941 at Fort Belvoir, Virginia. The board was not favorably impressed with the E1 for several reasons. A number of serious shortcomings were found with the basic design of the prototype. Overall, this device was cumbersome, heavy, and most uncomfortable for the soldiers who had conducted the tests. The Engineer Test Board found it unsuitable for employment in combat. Obviously, the Model E1 represented the efforts of a group of well-meaning amateurs trying to play catch-up in a game that had started two decades before.[14]

Upon receiving the dismal report on their first effort, the CWS personnel working on the portable flame thrower redesigned the apparatus. Once again, the Kincaid Company produced a sufficient number of the improved model for testing purposes and had them back to the CWS at Edgewood by late March 1941. The new model, labeled the E1R1, was still heavy (fifty-seven pounds when loaded), but appeared to be an improvement over the E1. When the new weapons were ready for testing, they were delivered to the Infantry Test Board at Fort Benning, Georgia, as well as to the Engineer Test Board at Fort Belvoir.

The decision to have both the foot soldiers and the engineers test the E1R1 was made even before the testing of the first model was completed. The G-3 Operations and Training Division of the War Department had recommended that, for future testing, the facilities of the sprawling infantry center at Fort Benning, Georgia, be used as well as the somewhat more limited test ranges available at Fort Belvoir. Because the Engineer Test Board needed personnel and time to conduct the many tests of new engineer equipment being introduced in 1941, the G-3 Division designated the Infantry as the primary testing agency for the improved version of the portable flame thrower.[15]

The Chief of Infantry told the President of the Infantry Test Board on 11 May 1941 that his agency would be conducting the primary evaluation of the improved flame thrower. While the minimum requirements for the weapon were those originally set by the War Department, the Chief of Infantry outlined the specific goals of the test:

1. To determine the suitability, powers and limitations and probable use by the Infantry.
2. To determine the maximum effective range and the fuel consumption per second of operation.
3. To determine the number of men required for this operation and the distribution of the loads of the operating crew.[16]

Given the mission of conducting a test of an engineer weapon, the Infantry Chief was also interested in determining whether the flame thrower could be of value to his troops. This seemingly peripheral point signaled the opening round in a controversy that was to last throughout World War II: namely, *who* was to carry, maintain, and operate the portable flame thrower, the infantry or the engineers?

When the Infantry Test Board received its test weapons in late May, a small test section had already been formed. This group consisted of officers and noncommissioned officers of the Infantry and Chemical branches. The Test Section decided to employ average troops detailed from an infantry unit in all phases of the flame weapon's test. This would ensure that the findings of the test section would reflect not only data on the mechanical aspects of the weapon, but on the "human engineering" factors of the flame thrower. In other words, the testers wanted to find out if a typical infantryman could operate the flame thrower. While this may seem a rather obvious step, there are countless examples of weapons systems developed by armies the world over which appear to function perfectly when in the hands of a twenty-year veteran on a test range. These same weapons, when adopted and issued to ordinary troops, do little more than confound and frustrate their users.[17] Combat conditions, of course, only make matters worse.

Field trials of the E1R1 began immediately after the test board staff members were fully acquainted with the weapon. The flame project was provided with a training area to conduct the tests under simulated combat conditions. Several different scenarios were used. In all sorts of weather conditions, the flame throwers were tested in the assault of fortified positions, in the defense of fixed positions, in attacking tanks, and in supporting infantry assaults over open ground. To observe the effects of the bulky equipment on the operators, the infantrymen using the equipment were often marched to their training sites with the E1R1s strapped to their backs. They were then required to rush forward from one position to another, seeking cover and concealment as they approached their objectives.

Several important observations were made by the test control personnel. They found that the flame thrower was quite uncomfortable for the soldiers to wear and thus the operator would not, or could not, move as quickly as he should in a combat situation. Although the E1R1 was consistently able to exceed the flame-throwing distance of ten yards (average distance was twenty-five yards), no more than 10 to 15 percent of the flaming gasoline or fuel oil actually reached the target. Most of the flaming stream of fuel had consumed itself in its flight to the target. The soldiers then mixed diesel oil with the gasoline to reduce the speed with which the fuel burned. More fuel then reached the target. These targets were generally cloth dummies in fox-holes, pillboxes, or tanks. The greatest drawback from thickening the flame fuel, and one which could not be solved at Fort Benning, was that the pressure required to throw this heavier mixture blew out the valve connections and ruptured the fuel lines on the E1R1.

The stream of burning fuel made a loud rushing noise and generated a great deal of black smoke which concealed the operator after the first few bursts were fired. Unfortunately, this smoke also tended to obscure the target and the fire stream was subject to the vagaries of the wind. Several test group soldiers were badly singed when they neglected to consider the wind direction before firing their weapons. The flame thrower developed mechanical breakdowns with increasing frequency as the tests continued. In spite of the mechanical problems, which were caused primarily by fittings, handles, and valves which were not rugged enough to withstand sustained use, all of the initially scheduled tests were conducted.

The report of the Infantry Test Board, submitted on 20 June 1941, provided the CWS with information on specific problems which needed to be corrected. The back pack, hose, igniter, and valves all had to be strengthened to withstand the rigors of combat operations. In its summation, the report as submitted to the Chief of Infantry stated:

24. The Test Section concludes:
   a. That the subject Flame Thrower, if modified as indicated ... will be suitable as a Special Infantry Weapon.
   b. That the maximum range is 25 yards.
   c. That due to its bulk and weight it should be confined to the following uses:
      (1) Defense of special installations when close contact with the enemy is probable or imminent.

     (2) Attack of enemy positions where due to cover (artificial or natural), the flame thrower may close to within 20 yards or less of the objective.

     (3) As an incendiary in destroying material.

  d. That the fuel consumption is about one quart per second of operation.

  e. That it requires one man to operate the subject weapon and an additional man per extra charge to be carried.

  f. That the carrying pads should be improved along the lines suggested. . . .[18]

This test report, with its generally favorable tone, provided the encouragement needed by the CWS personnel working with the flame thrower project. As they worked on the improvements recommended by the Infantry Test Board, the E1R1 was being shown to a group of Marine Corps officers at Quantico, Virginia. The Marines had expressed an interest in the flame thrower even before the initial tests of the E1 were conducted at Fort Belvoir during the previous winter.

On 25 July 1941, a representative of the Kincaid Company demonstrated the Model E1R1 for the Marine Corps Equipment Board at Quantico. After witnessing the demonstration, the President of the Equipment Board recommended that the Marine Corps not purchase any of the Kincaid products at that time. The Marines, habitually short of funds, simply could not afford the prices quoted by the factory representative. Kincaid wanted $680 per weapon. If the Marines purchased more than a thousand E1R1s, the price would drop, but only to $375. As it had often done, the Marine Corps postponed buying the new weapon until it was improved at Army expense.[19]

During the fall of 1941, nearly all of the CWS personnel working on flame throwers bent their efforts toward refining the improvements already made on the E1R1. The work already accomplished had resulted in its adoption as a standard weapon in early August. Labeled the M1, it had been improved in several ways. The M1 had a longer range, was sturdier, and possessed a more dependable ignition system. One of the greatest improvements had been made in the design of a new, more effective nozzle on the flame gun. This new design had come, not from the CWS, but from a group of civilian chemists and engineers working for an organization known as the National Defense Research Committee.[20]

The NDRC, which was destined to assist the CWS in so many ways during World War II, had been established on 27 July 1940 by order of the Council of National Defense. This organization of scientists from industry and the universities was to assist in solving problems faced by the Army and Navy. The president of the Carnegie Institute, Dr. Vannevar Bush, served as the chairman of the NDRC throughout the war. A special branch of the loosely knit organization had been established in October 1940 to deal with problems related to incendiary weapons. The Chief of the CWS Technical Division asked this group, designated Division 11, in February 1941 to assist the CWS in studying ways of improving the nozzle design of flame throwers and to discover, if possible, a truly effective method of thickening flame fuel.[21]

The immediate problem of improved nozzle design was attacked by groups of NDRC scientists who, in 1941, studied the projection of jets of liquid at the Massachusetts Institute of Technology. Various nozzle designs were then tested at the fire prevention laboratory of the Associated Factory Mutual Fire Insurance Companies (an organization devoted to reducing industrial fires). The two groups came up with a much-improved nozzle design that was to last for three years before being replaced.[22]

Upon approving the portable flame thrower for standardization as the M1, the War Department General Staff had planned to purchase 1,000 of the weapons. The new flame throwers would be issued, according to the initial plan, only to engineer units. Under the provisions of the first staff study, each engineer battalion assigned to support combat units would be given two M1 flame throwers and sufficient repair parts to maintain them. A reserve of flame throwers and spare parts would be kept in field depots. The infantry was not allocated any flame throwers. This brought on a new round in the debate between the Engineer and Infantry branches over who was to operate flame throwers in combat.[23]

The Chief of Infantry made his feelings known to the Chief of the Operations Division of the General Staff. During the late summer and fall of 1941, a debate continued over how many flame throwers should be procured and which branches should receive them. In a memorandum to the Army Chief of Staff, General Marshall, the G-3 (Operations) and the G-4 (Supply) sections urged that a much larger number of flame throwers be bought. They felt that the initial number authorized (1,000) should be produced at once and that the chiefs of the two branches (Infantry and Engineers) should be required to reassess their need for flame throwers. This memorandum, dated 22 August 1941, suggested that to equip an army of 1,750,000 men, a production run of 5,000 flame throwers would be much more appropriate than 1,000. The Chief of Staff agreed with his two staff members, and the two branch chiefs were directed to review their needs and reply not later than 15 October 1941.[24]

In the fall of 1941, it became apparent that the portable flame thrower would present problems for troops untrained in its use. After being briefed on new weapons development, the Secretary of War directed the Chief of Staff to order the Chief of Engineers and the Infantry Chief to prepare a study which would produce a usable doctrinal statement for all troops armed with the flame thrower. This study, when approved, would be printed in pamphlet form and distributed as a training circular. It must explain the Army's concepts involved in the tactical employment, limitations, and maintenance of the M1.[25]

The two branches produced the document on the concepts of the tactical employment of the flame thrower. Couched in plain language, it attempted to explain the flame thrower to the soldier who found himself carrying one without having any knowledge of how it was to be used, or in many cases, even how to turn it on. In its final form, this pamphlet was issued as Chemical Warfare Training Circular No. 72. By the time it reached the troops, the United States was no longer a spectator in the wide world conflict. The Japanese attack on Pearl Harbor had taken place and Americans were fighting Japanese in the Philippines. The Kincaid Company went on double, then triple, shifts to supply the Army with the M1 as the country began its all-out war effort.[26]

EARLY EXPERIMENTS WITH TANK-MOUNTED FLAME PROJECTORS: 1940–1942

While some CWS engineers worked to design a portable flame thrower, another group of officers in the Technical Division of the CWS attempted to devise a flame thrower that could be mounted in a tank or armored car. The development of mechanized flame projectors began in June 1940, as a result of General Chaffee's request for funds to equip his armored forces with a suitable flame thrower. Although the War Department, in its 1940 decision, had given the Armored Force the responsibility for developing this type of weapon, the CWS was the branch of the U.S. Army most able to accomplish this task. The General Staff had also provided minimum standards for mechanized flame throwers. The War Department continued to circulate the original staff study, adding comments and suggestions from nearly all sections of the General Staff. Within two months, the study began to resemble a book. Out of the stack of comments, indorsements, and appendices came these requirements: The weapon must have a range of at least fifty yards, utilize a slow-burning, hard-to-extinguish fuel, and be small enough to be mounted in a tank or combat car. Additionally, the fuel supply, which could be carried inside the vehicle or in a trailer pulled by the vehicle (as were the British and Italian models), had to be in a fuel tank armored heavily enough to deflect a 30-caliber bullet.[27]

The CWS technicians at Edgewood designed a large prototype flame projector powered by compressed air in June 1940. This flame gun was mounted on a frame referred to as a "Cunningham mount" that would, theoretically, replace the main gun on a tank. After demonstrating this first device at Edgewood Arsenal in September 1940 for representatives of the Armored Force Test Board, the CWS technicians began work during the winter of 1940–1941 at Fort Knox, designing a system that might be mounted inside an actual tank for test purposes. While they worked, the Armored Force continued to gather information and ideas about mechanized flame throwers from a variety of sources.[28]

Army observers and attachés in Europe had sent an increasing number of reports that dealt with flame thrower tanks being used by the German army. One report stated that British troops interviewed had felt that "Flame throwers, in conjunction with roadblocks . . . form the best defense against the German flamethrowing tanks."[29] The Armored Force commander wrote to the War Department G-2, asking for more information on this report. If the German flame tanks, loaded with flame fuel, were vulnerable to other flame throwers, would it be wise to develop such a death trap for a tank crew? General Chaffee had envisioned the tank-mounted flame thrower as a weapon for use against enemy infantry. What would happen if the Americans had to fight other tanks armed with flame throwers? Would the yet-to-be developed U.S. tank have a greater range than the current German models?[30]

As more and more private citizens became interested in news reports from Europe, suggestions from individuals and business firms began to arrive at military headquarters all over the United States. One such letter, which came to Washington in 1940, suggested that, instead of trying to propel ignited gasoline at an enemy, the flame tanks should shoot jellied fuel at an enemy position, then ignite the fuel with tracer bullets. The tankers testing flame throwers at Fort Knox had no way of knowing that, within the next five years, this procedure would become a common practice for American mechanized flame thrower crews in combat. Their biggest worry in 1941 was devising a device that would propel fuel at all.[31]

The CWS technicians working at Fort Knox had a weapon system mounted on an old light tank that was ready for a test in June 1941. On the day of the test, everything that could go wrong did. Gasoline leaked from the fuel reservoir and started a fire inside the tank turret. The fire extinguished, the technicians tried again to fire the tank. The compressed hydrogen being used to expel the fuel had leaked and the flame fuel drizzled out of the flame gun, setting fire to the rubber treads of the tank tracks.[32]

After this first failure, the Armored Force and the CWS project manager designed a different system which was mounted in an obsolete M2 medium tank. This model also replaced the tank's main gun, leaving only the machine guns for protection of the crew if the flame gun failed. This "main armament" flame projector differed from earlier models in that its fuel was propelled by compressed nitrogen. The apparatus was supplied with fuel from two 60-gallon reservoirs mounted inside the tank turret. Three commercial metal gas bottles contained the nitrogen. An electrical spark at the mouth of the flame gun was provided to ignite the flame fuel as it shot out of the nozzle. The M2 flame tank could generally fire a stream of flame for about fifty yards.

A critical test of the flame projector came in September 1941 when the Armored Force Test Board conducted a series of Armored performance trials to determine if the flame weapon was worthy of standardization and acceptance. The rigorous field testing proved too much for the delicate seals and fuel lines which broke down with distressing frequency. The Armored Force test report recommended rejection of the CWS device because of its unsolved mechanical problems. Citing the unreliable nature of the flame projector, the Board concluded that "Because no requirement currently exsits [sic] for the continued testing of this weapon, further expenditure of funds and man hours is not recommended." Thus the development of mechanized flame throwers in the United States was all but abandoned on the eve of the Pearl Harbor attack.[33]

This report, combined with the great difficulty experienced by the CWS in securing tanks on which to evaluate experimental flame thrower models, often reduced the CWS to using trucks as simulated tanks. That the British were developing several different models of flame tanks did not impress the American tankers of 1941. The Americans were more interested in spending money on the development of an American tank that could challenge the Germans in tank-to-tank battles fought with armor-piercing shot. As it turned out, the Americans were not wrong in anticipating a mechanized war against Germany. But if more progress had been made on a flame thrower tank in 1941, fewer Americans would have died on Pacific battlegrounds in 1943. The near-abandonment of the mechanized flame project by the Armored Force caused the CWS to shift its emphasis in flame thrower development to the portable flame thrower in late 1941.[34]

INCENDIARY BOMB DEVELOPMENT: 1940–1942

Along with flame throwers, the first year of war in Europe had brought about the employment of incendiary bombs by the German air force.

The *Luftwaffe* had spent the summer engaged in an attempt to destroy the Royal Air Force, then switched its main effort to British cities. As large cities like London, Liverpool, and Bristol were bombed, Fiorello LaGuardia, the mayor of New York City, determined to send a team of trained observers to London to learn what they could about civil defense against aerial incendiaries. LaGuardia, who had served as an Army pilot during World War I, was more aware than most of his mayoral counterparts of the potential destructiveness of incendiaries.

The report compiled by a team of two battalion fire chiefs and a senior fire inspector was published in 1941 by the U.S. Conference of Mayors. Entitled "Wartime Fire Defense in London," the report described German incendiary bombs, explained bombing techniques, and provided detailed discussion of the procedures used by London's fire department and Civil Defense teams to combat the German air attacks.[35]

The small-scale testing of incendiary bombs and fillers that had been conducted at Edgewood since 1937 was stepped up in response to an Army Air Corps request on 10 May 1941 which asked the CWS to produce (in conjunction with the Ordnance Department) a small incendiary bomb similar to the German 1-kilo *Elektron* bomb.[36]

While London and other British cities continued to feel the impact of German air raids during the summer of 1941, the Chief of the CWS began a schedule of biweekly meetings with a small team of technicians from the Technical Division of the CWS. The topic was the production of magnesium/ thermite and oil-filled bombs to meet Air Corps requests. In August 1941, General Baker revealed to this group that Colonel Enrique Zanetti had been recalled to active duty several months earlier and had been in London as a special observer since June. On his return to Edgewood Arsenal, Colonel Zanetti would head a special incendiaries branch of the Technical Division. The CWS was beginning to respond to the increasingly frequent queries from Army aviators about the progress being made with incendiaries, demonstrating once again the need for external pressure to activate CWS activity in fields other than toxic gas.[37]

During September 1941 a number of important events electrified Colonel Zanetti's group. Work begun in May had resulted in the acceptance and standardization in September of an incendiary bomb produced by the Ordnance Department with technical assistance from the CWS. This bomb, designated the AN-M50, was a copy of a British 4-pound incendiary that combined a thermite filler with a magnesium alloy casing which would also burn. It would be modified and improved throughout the war and would become the mainstay of the Allied incendiary attacks against German cities in 1943–1945.

Not all of the developmental tests produced munitions as useful as the M50. CWS tests were conducted with various types of incendiary "leaves" which could be dropped over enemy forests and grain fields, both of which could be considered strategic resources. Carried to the target in a liquid solution, the leaves would theoretically burst into flame when they dried in the sunlight after fluttering down all over the target area. In 1942, various types of cellulose leaves were dropped on Federal forest lands in the western United States. The experiments failed because an estimated ninety percent of the leaves never ignited. Those that did proved to be incapable of starting a major fire. [Although the incendiary leaf idea was scrapped after two years of work, the concept of burning an enemy's raw materials retained its attractiveness and would be revisited by the U.S. Air Force during the Vietnam War.]

No more successful than incendiary leaves was an idea that germinated in the Technical Division of the CWS during 1941. In a rush to catch up with the European nations in the incendiary warfare field, the CWS Technical Division chief approved the expenditure of research funds on a project to design a large flame projector for an Army aircraft. The aircraft, probably a medium bomber, would fly over enemy positions, then burn enemy troops with a large flame thrower mounted in its belly. Although a far better means of delivering napalm on enemy troops was evolved in the napalm belly bomb, it was 1945 before the CWS technicians working on the "aeroflame" project were finally told to cancel any further experiments.[38]

Much better news was received in September. Progress was being made in the search for a means of thickening fuel for bomb fillings. Dr. Louis F. Fieser, of Harvard and the NDRC, was working diligently with chemists and engineers from major firms in his search for an effective thickening agent that could be used with the only incendiary bomb then available to the rapidly expanding and recently renamed U.S. Army Air Forces.

A development of great significance to the incendiary specialists was the War Department decision to transfer the total responsibility for the design, testing, and procurement of incendiary bombs to the CWS. The Ordnance Department, still devoted to high explosive bombs, agreed without argument and quickly passed to the CWS a War Department order for the production of 125 million M50 bombs! The War Department order threw the CWS into a quandary regarding the ways and means to procure such a large order on short notice, but it was a welcome step in that the responsibility and authority in the incendiary field now rested solely with the CWS, thereby eliminating much of the jurisdictional wrangling that had marked Ordnance–CWS relations from 1937 on.[39]

These events in the early fall of 1941 were to provide the impetus for the incendiary bomb program that would, by the end of the war, be the single greatest CWS contribution to the Allied war effort. Although Zanetti and his associates were gratified and masked their concern with a "better late than never" attitude, time was running out for the United States.

After December 1941, the United States faced three enemies, all of whom had working flame throwers, both portable and tank-mounted. In contrast, the U.S. Army possessed only one standardized flame thrower, the M1 portable, which was just beginning to reach engineer units still untrained in its use. While the Marines had bought 180 M1s in November 1941, they were no more ready than the Army to employ these weapons in combat. Although experimentation with incendiary bombs was now proceeding more rapidly than before, the CWS had yet to develop a truly effective means for thickening gasoline for fire bombs. In the German *Luftwaffe*, the U.S. had an adversary fully knowledgeable regarding the effective employment of incendiary bombs.

Clearly, the United States was incapable of employing incendiary weapons of any type at the beginning of its active involvement in World War II. Several years, vast effort, and previously undreamed-of sums of money would be spent before U.S. incendiary weapons came of age during World War II.

AFTER PEARL HARBOR

Americans had little to cheer about in 1942. Old-time regulars, called-up reservists, and overworked civilians struggled to train and equip the burgeoning U.S. forces while outnumbered Americans in the far Pacific fought desperately to hold back the Japanese advance. At Edgewood Arsenal, the CWS was fully aware of the threat posed by the possibility of gas warfare. President Roosevelt had promised to retaliate if the Germans or Japanese initiated poison gas attacks. During the months following the Japanese attack on Pearl Harbor, the CWS applied most of its resources to training and equipping not only service personnel, but civilian defense groups in the proper procedures to be followed in the event of a poison gas attack against the United States.[40]

Although the possibility of gas warfare was the primary concern of the CWS, the Technical Division felt obliged to carry on with subsidiary programs in the fields of battlefield screening (smoke), the refinement of the 4.2-inch chemical mortar, and incendiaries. The work being done on the flame thrower, which centered around the procurement and issue of the M1 portable, received added impetus in February 1942 when word reached Edgewood that the Japanese had used flame throwers against American and Filipino troops on Bataan Peninsula and that a number of CWS troops in General MacArthur's command had lost their lives.[41]

The prewar CWS had been a small, tightly knit organization. Stories of Japanese atrocities on Bataan that were circulated through Army posts in the United States spurred the soldiers at Edgewood in their development of the flame thrower and incendiary bombs. For many of the CWS officers, essentially technicians, the war took on a highly personal importance. Any lingering questions surrounding the use of flame weapons tended to fade at Edgewood by mid-1942. The important questions about the incendiary weapons became much more utilitarian. Who should use them? How can they be employed to the best advantage? How can the weapons already developed be improved?[42]

For the remainder of 1942, a year of delaying actions by the Allies in the Pacific, in Russia, and North Africa, the CWS worked to answer these basic questions about the flame weapons. Most of the effort went toward the portable flame thrower and incendiary bomb projects. The Armored Force, fully aware that its primary role would be to challenge German armor, expressed very little interest in continued development of mechanized flame throwers. Once fears of a German or Japanese invasion of the United States subsided, the development of large emplaced flame projectors was halted. In the case of the portable flame throwers, the CWS suffered from the lack of a combat-tested doctrine of flame thrower use and from conflicting ideas concerning the type of troop units which could best employ the weapon.[43]

Attempting to resolve the question about the proper place for the flame thrower in the Army, the Chief of the CWS turned to the General Staff for guidance. Citing the 1941 report of the Infantry Test Board in which the Board had recommended that the flame thrower be adopted as a "special infantry weapon," the CWS Chief asked if he should increase his procurement schedules of the M1s. In June 1942, only the engineer troops attached to various type of combat units were authorized flame throwers. The table below outlines the number of flame throwers authorized:

Number of M1s authorized	Type of unit equipped
2	Per Combat Regiment, Squadron, Armored Battalion & Combat Engineer Battalion
12	Per Infantry Parachute Regiment, to be held in depot for special operations
6	Per Infantry Parachute Regiment, for training purposes

A year had passed since the tests of the E1R1 had been conducted at Fort Benning. Did the Infantry want flame throwers for themselves? The CWS needed to find out.[44]

The reply sent to Major General William N. Porter, the wartime Chief of the CWS, displayed the "wait and see" tone that was prevalent throughout the Army in 1942. In their letter, the staff planners at HQ, Army Ground Forces said that while "The Infantry feels that the flame thrower has a very definite place as an offensive and defensive weapon..." it had no definite idea of how it might be best utilized or by whom. The Infantry suggested that the weapon should be regarded as a special purpose weapon (like assault boats) or that whole units equipped with flame throwers be established. The staff letter concluded that if improvements were made in the current flame thrower, "the future of the flame thrower may be greatly changed, and it may become a weapon that the Infantry can use successfully for normal missions, but this cannot be foreseen positively at this time, and no change in basic policy is warranted.... "[45]

For tactical doctrine concerning flame thrower employment, the CWS would rely primarily on its first effort, Training Circular No. 72. Only one addition was made to previously published tactical doctrine during 1942. In a new field manual published in July 1942, entitled *Tactics of Chemical Warfare*, the CWS cited permanent or semipermanent field fortifications as the primary targets for flame thrower assaults. Another year would pass before the Corps of Engineers and the CWS would produce manuals that dealt more specifically with flame tactics.[46]

The problems of the M1 were numerous. As pointed out in a letter from the commander of the 4th Motorized Engineer Battalion, the M1 was subject to broken fuel lines, leaky valves, and frequent loss of pressure. On some occasions, the delicate, battery-powered ignition system failed to produce a spark and unlit fuel shot toward the target. Or, the hydrogen cylinder which provided the pressure to expel the flame fuel would malfunction and the stream of burning gasoline would dribble out, surrounding the operator with a puddle of burning fuel. Worst of all, the M1 might eject nothing but unsettling gurgling noises which left the hapless operator wondering just what was going to happen. The average soldier's lack of confidence in the weapon boded ill for units slated for overseas movement.[47]

Amid all the different ideas advanced by the "flame crowd" at Edgewood for ways to improve the M1, two proposals were generally agreed upon. First, only combat operations would uncover *all* of its deficiencies, and second, the most pressing need was for an improved flame fuel. The gas and diesel oil mixtures were unsatisfactory. The flame stream burned itself up on its flight from the flame gun to the target. A more viscous fuel was needed—one that would burn more slowly and could deliver more fire *on* the target. Early experiments with fuel thickeners composed of soap, raw rubber, or crankcase oil, some of which dated back to World War I, had all proved disappointing.[48]

Division 11 of the NDRC had been working on the flame fuel problem since February 1941. Several groups of scientists were engaged in this research. One of these teams was located at the laboratories of the Standard Oil Development Company, where research chemists had been working diligently to discover a method of lowering the flash point of gasoline. They experimented with various compounds built around aluminum hydro-chloride which, when combined with gasoline, formed a jellylike substance. The Standard Oil team also found a rubber-based thickener called "IM" (isobutyl methacrylate). It formed a substance which had the consistency of applesauce when added to gasoline. Unfortunately for Standard Oil and the CWS, the Japanese advance into Malaya cut off most of the rubber supplies upon which wholesale use of IM would depend. In tests conducted by the CWS and the Army Air Forces (AAF), both mixtures functioned well as a filler for incendiary bombs. Both, however, had a serious shortcoming. These mixtures would not remain in the desired gelled state over an extended time and tended to break down into their original components, especially when being handled during shipment. Thus, incendiary bombs could not be filled in the United States and then shipped overseas. These compounds would also be unsatisfactory as a flame thrower fuel because rigid control had to be maintained during the mixing process lest tempera-ture or humidity variations caused unwanted chemical reactions in the gel. The average soldier, working under less-than-ideal conditions in the battle area, might blend the fuel incorrectly.[49]

During the second half of 1941 another group of scientists, under the direction of Dr. Louis Fieser of the NDRC, had been working on the flame fuel problem. Their efforts would provide the CWS with the substance it needed to produce a much more efficient filler for bombs and flame throw-ers. After a great number of unsuccessful experiments, Fieser's group tried blending the fatty soaps extracted from aluminum napthanate and alu-minum palmitate. Having produced a gooey substance, the scientists bor-rowed a meat grinder from the dining hall at Harvard and ground the compound into what looked like plump worms. The worms were then added to gasoline. The chemical reaction that resulted transformed the whole mixture into a compound that, like IM, had the look and consistency of applesauce. When dried, this material could be separated into marble-sized balls and packed in tightly sealed containers. On being mixed with gasoline, the chemicals in the compound would cause a thickening of the gasoline, thus lowering its burning flash point.

In a series of Army Air Force tests conducted at Edgewood Arsenal in the summer of 1942, the Fieser compound showed no ill effects from being mixed under simulated field conditions the day before bombs filled with the mixture were dropped. The bombs produced impressive fires when dropped and the CWS was convinced that it had found a workable substitute for IM, which was also in high demand for its use in producing aircraft canopies and turrets. Pressed for a name for his discovery, Dr. Fieser elected to name it by using let-ters from the first syllables of the two main elements: it was called napalm.[50]

Although this substance provided the Army with the badly needed fuel thickener for incendiary bombs, it also presented a new problem. The M1 flame thrower was simply not powerful enough to handle the thicker, more viscous fuel. Faced with the requirement of redesigning the M1, the CWS once again turned to the NDRC for help. The CWS Technical Division Chief, Brigadier General Kabrich, established an *ad hoc* committee at Edgewood Arsenal which was charged with the design of a new flame thrower.

Meeting on 23 August 1942, the flame thrower committee agreed that the best and quickest course of action would be to modify the existing M1 flame thrower so that it might use thickened napalm fuel. By 1 October, the committee had prepared a report for the Chief of the CWS which outlined three major changes: replacement of the fuel valve, adjustment of the pressure regulator, and the use of thickened fuel. The Chief of the CWS accepted the report, and by November 1942, the three firms manufacturing the M1 had retooled and were turning out the improved version called the M1A1.[51]

The new flame thrower still had problems. To save time, the CWS had not attempted to change the old model ignition system. It continued to present problems, particularly in tropical climates. The M1A1, however, did serve its primary mission. It gave the Americans a portable flame thrower that could throw a stream of thickened fuel for fifty yards, nearly twice as far as the older M1. The fuel stuck to whatever it hit and burned with a very hot flame. Perhaps most important was that troops already trained with the M1 did not have to learn a completely different type of weapon. The CWS pressed on with the production of the M1A1 and continued to work closely with the Engineer School at Fort Belvoir in the development of tactics for flame gunners.[52]

To many of the soldiers and civilians who found themselves busily engaged at the CWS facilities which had sprung up so rapidly during 1942, the sheer size of the wartime chemical branch must have seemed overwhelming. The swirl of activity that engulfed formerly sleepy Edgewood Arsenal was at once confusing and exhilarating. Immersed as they were in their own projects, most probably failed to appreciate the full magnitude of what was being accomplished. In effect, a new and different Chemical Warfare Service had been created and was continuing to expand as CWS personnel departed the United States for service in overseas commands.[53]

The official histories of the CWS point with obvious pride to the astounding accomplishments of the Service during the first full year of war after Pearl Harbor. The dedication of the hastily formed staffs and units is justly praised. What seems to be overlooked is that the CWS was largely incapable of meeting the challenge of war without the help of a great deal of "imported" talent from civil life and the Army Reserve. The prewar research and development program, limited mainly to the development of defensive measures for use against toxic gas, was the province of the small staff sections created by Amos Fries in the 1920s. The organization, although enlarged during the period since 1939, still failed to provide truly adequate means for testing new concepts in weaponry not directly related to poison gas.[54]

What was absent, it seems, was a clear understanding of the *process* by which organizations may respond to unusual requirements. Lacking even a skeleton staff for incendiary weapons development in prewar years, the CWS was forced into a situation where new staffs and officers proliferated to fill this void in the organization. Slipshod management of vital programs was sometimes the unfortunate result. The ability to make a smooth transition from peace to war is a part of a nation's arsenal that is too often overlooked.[55]

As 1942 drew to a close, the CWS in the United States continued to wrestle with new problems, and created *ad hoc* committees to deal with them. At camps and test facilities, CWS technicians waited for word from the fighting forces overseas who would depend on their support as they began the long and perilous journey to Berlin and Tokyo.

CHAPTER 4

An Uphill Battle: Flame Throwers in Europe, 1942–1945

The year that followed Pearl Harbor sped by as the U.S. Army prepared for the first strike against that Axis enemy deemed most dangerous by Allied policymakers. Different strategic concepts, national egocentricism, and interservice rivalries clouded the issues surrounding the lack of transport ships, troop availability, weather, and geography as the leaders of the Grand Alliance wrestled with the questions of "when" and "where" to strike first at the German war machine.

The spirit of compromise that was to characterize (albeit imperfectly) the Allied campaigns against Hitler led to the decision to attack before the end of 1942 and to begin the assault on Germany on the faraway beaches of northwest Africa. As U.S. troops in England and the United States boarded transports bound for invasion beaches near Algiers, Oran, and Casablanca, they carried with them a great deal of equipment previously untested by American troops in combat. One such item was the portable flame thrower, Model M1.

Engineer combat battalions that were assigned to each U.S. division participating in Operation TORCH had been hastily equipped with twenty-four M1 flame throwers after these units were selected for TORCH. The amount of training with the M1s varied from unit to unit, but as a general rule, those battalions staging in the United States had received the flame throwers before units already overseas in camps scattered throughout the British Isles. In no case were a sufficient number of spare parts issued and in many units the flame throwers had not even been uncrated for an inspection before being loaded for shipment to North Africa.[1]

Once ashore, U.S. engineers found that there was no need for flame throwers. The cease-fire negotiated between the Americans and the Vichy French obviated the requirement to assault coastal fortifications or enemy strongpoints with fire. With the dawn of 1943 and the race for control of Tunisia that occupied U.S. troop formations, engineer units quickly became caught up in the war of movement that characterized combat in the Western Desert. Only supply sergeants took note in late May and June 1943 when shipments of the new napalm-firing M1A1 flame throwers arrived to replace the M1s. The first great Allied offensive ended without a single use of a U.S. flame thrower.[2]

Although flame throwers were again available to engineer units participating in the next stage of the Mediterranean offensive, the conquest of Sicily (Operation HUSKY), there was only one recorded instance of their use. American troops used portable flame throwers to burn a large grain field suspected of harboring German snipers. Army engineers in Sicily were hard-pressed to accomplish their primary jobs of minesweeping, road construction, and bridge building. If occasional opportunities for flame weapons presented themselves, the flame throwers were not on hand, but far to the rear of the American spearheads. Before this equipment could be filled with gasoline and napalm gel, charged, and brought to the front lines, the infantry or armored troops would reduce the obstacle by some other means. With hard-charging General George S. Patton in command of the U.S. forces on Sicily, no serious thought was given to delaying the advance to introduce flame throwers into the battle. The German strongpoints in Sicily were destroyed by artillery, tanks, or demolition teams working with the ubiquitous infantrymen. The official report of the Sicilian operation published by General Patton's headquarters indicated that flame throwers had contributed nothing to the American success.[3]

As U.S. planners considered what weapons should be used in the impending invasion of the Italian mainland, Chemical Warfare Service officers reminded them of the possibility of determined resistance in the numerous Italian cities and towns that would have to be conquered. The CWS staff officers felt that the portable flame thrower might play an important role in reducing the German and Italian defense pockets that could be expected in built-up areas. The flame thrower was included in the long equipment lists drawn up for combat engineer battalions.

Following the original doctrine established in 1942, the U.S. Army in Europe was still saddling the overworked engineer troops in each division with the responsibility for maintaining as well as employing the often untrustworthy flame weapons in combat. In many cases, engineer soldiers taught to operate the M1A1 were transferred to other duties or became casualties. The episodic training sessions that took place behind the front lines left much to be desired, as the CWS officers who conducted the classes were sometimes less than knowledgeable about the flame thrower.[4]

As in Sicily, the flame throwers brought ashore at Salerno were often consigned to behind-the-lines storage areas where, for lack of care, seals dried and cracked and steel fittings corroded. Not surprisingly, these neglected weapons usually failed to function properly when employed against German defenses like those in the Gustav Line. The failure of the flame throwers further damaged their reputation with infantrymen and engineers alike.[5]

Reports submitted by units fighting in Italy only occasionally mentioned the use of flame throwers. In most cases where flame throwers were employed, the weapons just happened to be readily available. Although the senior American headquarters in Italy, the Fifth Army, published a training memorandum which directed units to form flame thrower assault teams similar to those that were being employed in the Pacific, no teams of this type were used in Italy. Instead, infantrymen or engineers used the flame throwers when, and if, the weapons were available and were deemed appropriate for the task at hand. In May 1944, for example, infantry lieutenant Robert G. Waugh of the 85th Infantry Division grew disgusted at the slow progress that his rifle platoon was making in its attempt to breach a part of the German Gustav Line. He requested flame thrower support from a nearby engineer unit. The engineer commander agreed to furnish several weapons, but declined to provide engineer troops to operate them. Waugh read the slim operator's manual that accompanied the flame throwers and then led his platoon in a successful assault that opened the way for a major breakthrough. Waugh credited the flame thrower with the victory.[6]

Once the Allied offensive had passed Rome and advanced into the rugged mountains of northern Italy, the flame thrower was largely abandoned by the Fifth Army. The weight, limited range, and requirements for continued maintenance led troops fighting in mountainous country to disregard the potential of the flame thrower. The U.S. units relied upon their abundant artillery support and tank-supported infantry assaults to overcome German defenses.[7]

Unlike the U.S. troops, British and Canadian soldiers fighting in Italy steadfastly maintained their portable and mechanized flame throwers. The high regard with which British troops held the flame thrower can be ascribed to the continued improvement in flame weapons that had gone on in England since 1918. The British army had, by continuing training with flame throwers, inculcated its troops with confidence in flame warfare. The effective employment of flame weapons by British and Canadian soldiers in Italy served as a prelude to an even greater British dependence upon these weapons in northwest Europe. There, Commonwealth and British troops equipped with flame throwers demonstrated the careful planning, research and development, and training that had taken place in preparation for the assault on France.

The British had combined the talents of the Royal Engineers, the Royal Armoured Corps, and the Petroleum Warfare Board to produce an efficient tank-mounted flame thrower. As part of the overall program to provide the invasion forces with a number of special purpose tanks ("Funnies"), the British developers selected the Churchill Mark VII tank for modification with a flame thrower system. When completed, the flame tank was christened the "Crocodile."

The Crocodile system consisted of a flame projector mounted in place of a bow machine gun, the pump apparatus within the tank hull, and an armored trailer carrying 400 imperial gallons of thickened flame fuel which was pulled behind the tank. When fired, the flame projector had a range in excess of 125 yards, and could sometimes reach targets 200 yards away. By retaining the tank's 75-mm gun, designers permitted the tank to fight as a standard tank if need be, although the amount of ammunition carried was reduced to make room for the flame thrower apparatus. The British weapon so impressed U.S. observers at demonstrations held in 1943 that the commanding general of the European Theater of Operations, U.S. Army (ETOUSA) requested that 100 of the flame units be bought for installation on specially modified M4 Sherman tanks.[8]

In addition to the Crocodile and the portable flame throwers that British troops would take on their return to France, there was another mechanized flame thrower in the British arsenal. Called the "Wasp," it consisted of a Canadian "Ronson" flame projector mounted in a lightweight tracked carrier. Designed by British and Canadian engineers, the Wasp could accompany infantry units over rugged terrain and would be available to provide responsive flame support when needed. British and Canadian units had their full complement of flame throwers and carried out rigorous training with their flame weapons in preparation for D-Day.[9]

Like the British, the Germans had continued to improve the flame throwers that had made headlines in 1940. They had also developed several types of heavy emplaced flame throwers for static defense lines and a lightweight (24 lb) flame thrower for use by airborne troops which was called the *Einstoss Flammenwerfer*. Yet for all their inventive genius in the field of flame warfare, the Germans could not prevent the steady erosion of their ability to conduct flame operations. The greatest problem lay in providing fuel for the numerous flame weapons issued to German troop units.[10]

German flame fuel formulae called for gasoline to be thickened with aluminum stearate and creosote by-products. During the early campaigns of World War II, German engineer troops utilized a mixture that was nearly identical to the FRAS (Fuel Research Aluminum Stearate) that the British army used throughout the war. As aluminum and petroleum became increasingly

scarce, the Germans developed ersatz mixtures of low grade fuel oil and pep-
tized creosote as substitute flame fuels. By 1944, however, even the ersatz fuels
became scarce and German units frequently abandoned their empty *Flammenwerfers* as they retreated toward their homeland.[11]

In the sprawling American camps that dotted England, CWS staff officers
worked with engineer and infantry troops to familiarize U.S. troops with the
only flame weapon available, the M1A1. Assuming that the weapon would be
useful against German coastal defenses, U.S. planners had increased the
allotment of flame throwers for each assault and follow-on division. CWS officers worked diligently to prepare the combat troops for flame warfare. Plans
were made for CWS support units to land on D-Plus-1 to service and repair
flame throwers at a number of sites immediately behind the front lines.[12]

As reports from the invasion beaches filtered back on 6 and 7 June, it
became apparent that flame throwers had contributed little to tactical success. The U.S. troops landed at UTAH Beach had moved inland with little difficulty and had often abandoned their flame throwers as excess weight.
Those troops landing on bloody OMAHA Beach had lost many M1A1s in the
surf or abandoned them when it was found that the German pillboxes were
too well defended to approach with a flame thrower. The troops on OMAHA
had to rely on naval gunfire to knock out the German positions. Lacking an
armored flame thrower, the Americans were unable to burn out German
positions as the British had done at GOLD and SWORD Beaches with their
Crocodile and Wasp armored flame weapons. The importance of armored
protection for flame throwers became more evident as Allied troops fought
their way inland from the invasion beaches.[13]

The only important service rendered by U.S. flame throwers following
the Normandy invasion occurred on the Brittany Peninsula near the ancient
and heavily fortified city of Brest. In August and September 1944, American
troops armed with flame throwers did succeed in overcoming some
stubborn German strongholds. On several occasions, flame thrower operators, usually combat engineers, did not actually try to burn the German
defenders, but only shot their flame throwers near the German positions.
The Germans feared and respected the flame throwers and surrendered
rather than face a flame attack. Despite the demonstrated effectiveness of
the flame throwers, U.S. troops did not use them very frequently for some of
the same reasons that had restricted flame thrower employment in Italy.
Unfamiliar with these weapons, and lacking trained operators, infantrymen
assaulting German fortified positions resorted to hand grenades, tank fire,
artillery, or, in most cases, demolition charges.[14]

Elements of the U.S. 29th Infantry Division keenly felt the lack of
armored flame throwers when, on 14 September 1944, they were faced with

the difficult and dangerous mission of overcoming the German SS defenders of Fort Montbarey, near Brest. Artillery fire and infantry assaults proved fruitless. As casualties mounted, the infantrymen tried to use portable flame throwers, but the operators were cut down before they could fire their weapons. In desperation, the commander of the 116th Infantry Regiment requested flame thrower assistance from the British.

Luckily, the British 141st Tank Regiment was in the vicinity of Brest and sent two platoons of Crocodiles to attack Montbarey. Forcing their way through the rubble of the fort, the British tankers spewed flame into bunkers and embrasures. The German defense held for another twenty-four hours, but when subjected to a second flame attack they surrendered, with over sixty troops marching off to P.O.W. compounds.[15]

Reports of the success of the Montbarey operation rekindled some interest in flame-throwing tanks among U.S. commanders in Europe. The CWS, though, could only respond to this interest in a limited way. The research and development effort that had been undertaken in the United States in response to requests for armored flame throwers had limped along on small budgets and a minimal staff for three years. Most of the work that had been accomplished was done by CWS technicians and civilian firms, without any substantial assistance from the Armored Force. The tankers in the U.S. Army remained unenthusiastic about special purpose tanks throughout the war, relenting only after British Funnies demonstrated what could be accomplished by the specially equipped vehicles. Despite the industrial might of the American automotive industry, the demand for standard tanks armed with the 75-mm gun was never satisfied during the war. Supplying not only the U.S. Army and Marine Corps, but the British and Russians with Sherman tanks caused the Armored Force to protest any large-scale program that would involve the production of sizable numbers of special purpose vehicles.[16]

By late 1944, however, several types of flame throwers for tanks were available for shipment to Europe. The model favored by the still-skeptical Armored Board was designed to replace the bow machine gun in the tank hull, but did not preclude the continued use of the main gun. Designated the Model E4-5, this "auxiliary" flame thrower had been demonstrated in England prior to D-Day and had been approved for production on a limited scale. Equipped with two 25-gallon fuel tanks, the E4-5 could place a "rod" of thickened fuel on a target up to fifty yards away. General Bradley's Twelfth Army Group requested more than 300 of the flame units in anticipation of their use during the hard fighting expected once the U.S. forces reached the heavily defended Siegfried Line. Because of a shipping label incorrectly printed, all of the E4-5s sent to Europe prior to November arrived with only one of the two 25-gallon fuel tanks. Although some units in the First Army installed the flame throwers with only one fuel tank, the majority of the weapons were not installed until November 1944. At that time, the First Army received 75, the Third Army got 30, and the Ninth Army, 45.[17]

Like the M1A1 portable, the U.S. tank-mounted auxiliary flame thrower coming into active service late in 1944 was the butt of much criticism. The Model E4-5 was sound in design and should have performed satisfactorily in Europe. On several occasions, it was credited with causing the surrender of German troops who had held out tenaciously against other forms of attack. But the E4-5, later standardized and redesignated the M3-4-3, was never employed on a large scale by the U.S. armored forces in Europe.

A combination of mechanical breakdowns, haphazard maintenance, and very limited training of operators militated against the successful employment of the U.S. weapon. In addition, there was little command interest in tank flame throwers once the flurry of comment after the Brest assault had blown over. General Patton set the tone for many of his subordinates in the Third Army when, after witnessing a less-than-impressive demonstration of an M3-4-3, he compared its flame stream to a "piddle." The resulting publicity in the *Stars and Stripes* troop newspaper prompted the Chemical Officer of the Twelfth Army Group to write to Brigadier General Kabrich of the CWS Technical Division, saying:

> I have hopes that you are doing something to modify this new M3-4-3 so as to give it more volume and range. It is a beautiful unit, but I am sick and tired of hearing about the Wasp and Crockodile [*sic*] being held up as examples.[18]

Although a few CWS officers might chafe under the frequent comparison of U.S. and British flame throwers, the majority of the U.S. troops in Europe were unaware that any problem existed. Especially in those American outfits that fought alongside British and Canadian units, flame thrower support was provided by British Crocodiles or Canadian Wasp flame throwers. The support rendered by the flame thrower troops was almost always sufficient to meet tactical exigencies and was carried out in a professional manner. Having trained with the flame equipment prior to going into combat, the British and Canadian troops understood their weapons, were proud of their accomplishments, and displayed a *panache* that was lacking in many U.S. units.

American commanders who expected heavy combat in the attempt to breach the Siegfried Line were proved correct when their units confronted German troops in the network of bunkers, minefields, and tank traps that made up the string of defensive works along the Franco-German border. Some U.S. units increased training with portable flame throwers for infantry units while selected tank units began to install the E4-5 flame throwers in their vehicles. Other units, notably Patton's Third Army, conducted little or no flame thrower training and simply stored the newly arrived auxiliary flame throwers.[19]

The costly fighting that took place during the campaign to overwhelm the German border defenses saw one of the few instances when German troops employed flame throwers against the U.S. Army. On the night of 16 September 1944 Germans with flame throwers mounted in armored half-tracks [*Sd.Kfz.251*] attacked a company of the 28th Infantry Division. The Germans routed the U.S. troops and sent the few survivors scampering to the rear to spread tales about the fate suffered by their less fortunate comrades. Dramatic and successful, the attack was nevertheless a rarity. A drastic shortage of flame fuel and the concentration of German flame throwers on the Eastern Front were responsible for the limited employment of German flame weapons in the West.[20]

A number of the castoff weapons fell into Allied hands in the fall of 1944. On several occasions, the captured weapons were turned on the retreating Germans. One American commander reported that he especially favored the German Model 1942 portable flame thrower because it could shoot a jet of unlighted fuel at a target. The drenched target could then be lit by firing a stream of fire on the next shot. In this respect the German weapon differed from the U.S. M1A1 because the American weapon was provided with a "hotspot" ignition system designed to ignite the flame fuel as it passed through the nozzle of the flame gun. The German Model '42 had an igniter which consisted of a cartridge magazine loaded with ten blank 9-mm cartridges. The fuel ejection system and igniter worked off separate triggers, thus providing the operator with more flexibility in his mode of target engagement. This flexibility, combined with a lighter weight than the M1A1, made the Model '42 a fairly popular weapon with the few American units that would go to the trouble to fill and charge the tanks of the captured weapons.[21]

U.S. troops *did* employ the M1A1 upon occasion in their advance through the Siegfried Line. An official Army history of the campaign cites several instances when German defenders surrendered rather than fight U.S. troops armed with portable flame throwers. As was the case in 1915, the soldier's fear of fire led him to give up rather than face death by burning. That the flame thrower was as much a psychological weapon as a casualty-producing weapon is demonstrated by these reports from *The Siegfried Line Campaign*:

A prisoner captured earlier went inside the pillbox with word that if the Germans failed to surrender, they must face death from a flame thrower. Nine Germans filed out.

and;

Operating a flame thrower, Pvt. Henry E. Hansen spotted a German standing near the entrance to a bunker. As the German whirled to face him, Pvt. Hansen caught him full in the face with a blast from his flame thrower. A moment later, ten Germans pushed open the [bunker] door and rushed out to surrender.[22]

Still, flame throwers were not popular with U.S. troops despite their occasional success. During World War II, the CWS received numerous requests and suggestions for a lightweight, one-shot disposable flame thrower for use by assault troops. Although developmental work was begun on this type of weapon in 1943, it was never produced in any quantity during the war. Had it been in the hands of troops assaulting the Siegfried Line in 1944 and 1945, the role of the flame thrower could have been much greater.[23]

Another example of the type of support provided to U.S. units by the British can be found in the combat journal of the 84th Infantry Division. During late November 1944, a regiment of the division was delayed for some time in its advance into Germany by a very determined German garrison in the town of Sueggerath. The U.S. regimental commander, dismayed by the casualties suffered in several attempts to storm the German positions, requested Crocodile support. A company commander later told of the effect of the flame tanks on the defenders of Sueggerath:

The Crocodiles pulled into our C.P. at 1500. The British tank leader asked about German positions, then said his men would be ready to go on into the town in half an hour, after they got briefed. We advanced behind the tanks at about 1545. A few squirts from the flame tanks, and the Germans poured out of their holes. The bastards are afraid of those flame throwers and won't be caught inside a pillbox.[24]

Lieutenant General George S. Patton had a number of tanks in Third Army equipped with flame throwers mounted in the bow machine gun aperture. He was delighted with the results. During the final push into Germany that followed the Allied crossing of the Rhine, British, Canadian, and U.S. flame tanks were frequently used as a means of frightening German troops in hopes that they might surrender without a costly battle. While the German soldier might fight tenaciously, he seemed to draw the line at burning to death while defending a position. In many cases during the last three months of the war, a burst or two of flame where German troops could see it would bring them out of their bunkers with their hands in the air.[25]

When German troops could not, or would not, surrender, the Crocodiles destroyed them. One member of a flame tank unit, the 141st Tank Regiment, described the grisly results of an attack on a German position on the Belgian/German border:

> There were [German] bodies which seemed to have been blown back by the force of the flame and lay in blackened heaps. Others were caught in twisted positions as if the flame had frozen them. Their clothes were burned away. Only their helmets and boots remained, ridiculous and horrible.[26]

Despite the demonstrated effectiveness of both portable and mechanized flame throwers in the hands of well-trained and highly motivated soldiers, the U.S. Army in Europe never depended upon flame throwers as did the British. Mechanical shortcomings in the weapons, insufficient training and indoctrination in the techniques of flame warfare, and an abundance of other weapons all conspired to reduce the role of U.S. flame throwers in the ETO. The German soldier associated fire warfare with the British, Canadian, or Russian armies, not the U.S. Army.

Although front-line German soldiers of 1945 had little contact with U.S. flame weapons, their families did—in firebombed German cities. As the civilians knew, aircraft bearing U.S. markings were just as likely to drop incendiary bombs as were aircraft of the British RAF. Although slow to begin, the U.S. incendiary bombing program, once in operation, contributed to the widespread destruction of the German soldiers' homeland and the damage to German morale that took place after 1943.

CHAPTER 5

Aerial Bombardment of Germany: The Role of Incendiary Bombs

Within months after the attack on Pearl Harbor, U.S. ground troops and Army Air Force units began to arrive in the British Isles. The presence of these forces sustained flagging British and Russian morale to some degree and served notice on Hitler that the Third Reich would be the first priority target for the Allies. From mid-1943 until V-E Day, the U.S. Army Air Forces in Europe made a significant contribution to the Allied war effort. Most important to this study are the ways in which aerial incendiaries were used by the American airmen and their British allies as their combined air offensive carried the war to millions of Germans.[1]

By mid-1942, the U.S. Army had established several headquarters in England. One of these headquarters was to serve as the nerve center of that mighty bomber fleet designated Eighth Air Force. A tiny segment of the rapidly enlarging Eighth AF staff was devoted to implementing chemical warfare and chemical defense. Headed by CWS Colonel Crawford M. Kellogg, the Eighth AF Chemical Section assumed air staff responsibility for directing all chemical training and supply within the command. The Chemical Warfare Service personnel working for Colonel Kellogg also had to convince bomber unit commanders to utilize the only offensive aerial weapon produced by the CWS: the incendiary bomb.

For more than a year prior to the Japanese attack on Pearl Harbor, CWS officers had been conducting a series of seminars at Edgewood Arsenal during which their growing interest in the wartime potential of incendiary bombs had been nurtured. As noted in chapter 3, Colonel Enrique Zanetti was the foremost champion of incendiary bombs in the prewar CWS. Shortly before being recalled to active duty, Zanetti had written in the *Chemical Warfare Bulletin*:

> Whether one is prepared to accept the long-foreseen "all-out" type of warfare, in which the destruction of civilian morale plays such an

important part, or whether one condemns it as brutal, inhuman, and uncivilized matters little. All-out warfare is here and must be faced.

It is elementary that the achievement of conflagrations should be the aim of users of incendiary bombs when attacking combustible areas of large cities.[2]

The CWS staff at Edgewood, anticipating a call for incendiaries from the Eighth AF, began shipping small quantities of 100-lb, M47 incendiary bombs to Colonel Kellogg in June 1942. After receiving the first small shipments, Kellogg set out to oversee their use.[3]

As he traveled around England, Kellogg found widespread evidence of the earlier German success with the *Elektron* and 110-kilo oil bombs that had been dropped on British cities during 1940 and 1941. Royal Air Force (RAF) officers explained to Kellogg that the British had been steadily increasing their use of incendiary bombs in the retaliatory raids against German cities that had begun in 1941. The RAF, while recognizing the importance of destroying German war industry, was also committed to destroying the will of the German people. As one study of the Allied air offensive reports:

> In May 1943 Air Marshal Lord Trenchard advocated repeated night and day bombing attacks on military targets in German towns so that bombs which either overshot or undershot the target would fall on the civilian population.... The Chiefs of Staff accepted Trenchard's thesis that civilian morale provided the most vulnerable target in Germany.[4]

In spite of the British enthusiasm for incendiaries, the majority of the newly arrived U.S. air commanders were determined to rely on the high explosive (H.E.) bombs with which they had trained in the United States. Not only had the Americans committed themselves to high-level, daylight precision bombing, but they had an aircraft, the B-17, that promised the in-flight stability necessary to carry out "pin-point" bombing. Coming as they did from a land untouched by enemy bombs, the U.S. airmen may not have been as inclined to bomb civilian population centers as were the British.

During the summer of 1942, Colonel Kellogg took every precaution to ensure that the rapidly growing Eighth AF bases contained sufficient quantities of protective equipment in case of a German toxic gas attack. This part of his mission completed, he turned his attention to the impending U.S. participation in the bombing of German installations on the Continent. Given the stated U.S. position on using toxic gas, it was clear to Kellogg that, if the CWS was to contribute to the air assault on Germany, it would be through the use of incendiary bombs developed by the chemical branch.

In attempting to "sell his product" to the airmen of the 8th Bomber Command, Kellogg devised a two-pronged strategy. He asked the British for help in persuading U.S. commanders to try incendiaries. Of course, if the RAF should succeed in this, many more incendiary bombs of different types would be needed in England. Assured of British help with the first part of his plan, the energetic CWS colonel turned to the second part of his task. Purposely overstating the demand for incendiary bombs in a message to Edgewood, Kellogg hoped to ensure that a sufficient number would be available to the bomber crews. He was gratified when the CWS Supply Division informed him that more bombs would be shipped to him on a top priority basis.[5]

Royal Air Force officers contacted by Kellogg responded enthusiastically to his request for assistance. In addition to RAF personnel, a number of civilian technicians volunteered to assist the American in his campaign for incendiaries. Many of the British incendiary experts were members of an operational research organization known as RE/8 [Research and Experiment Station, Section 8]. In conjunction with British bomber crews, the personnel from RE/8 demonstrated the various types of British incendiary bombs (and U.S.-made M50 magnesium bombs) for groups of U.S. officers. The British also invited Colonel Kellogg and several of his subordinates to join an informal organization known as the Zoroastrian Society. The group was devoted to the scientific study of incendiary weapons and to the improvement of incendiary bombing techniques. A great deal of useful information was provided by the British members of this *ad hoc* group to their American cohorts. In this manner the Eighth AF Chemical Section was able to overcome, to some degree, the lack of information on incendiary bombs that hamstrung their early efforts to promote the use of fire bombs.[6]

Throughout his tour of duty as the Eighth AF Chemical Officer, Colonel Kellogg continued to apply his energies to the accomplishment of the CWS and Army Air Force mission. He personified the innovative and imaginative CWS officers that filled many overseas posts. Cut off from their own branch of the service, functioning as staff officers in combat unit headquarters, many of these CWS officers were painfully aware of the pitfalls that await the man who would serve two masters. That Kellogg was able to finally convince many U.S. airmen of the importance of incendiaries by overcoming their reluctance and ignorance of flame weapons serves as testimony to his persistence.

Colonel Kellogg was not alone in his attempt to overcome the reluctance of U.S. airmen to use what was, to them, still an unproven munition. Also urging the Eighth AF to utilize incendiaries was Horatio Bond, an expert on industrial and urban fires serving as an attaché from the Office of

Civil Defense at the U.S. embassy in London. In a memorandum to the staff
of Lieutenant General Ira C. Eaker, the commander of the Eighth AF, Bond
said, in part:

> We may be overlooking an important weapon if we do not take full
> advantage of damage to the enemy that can be caused by fire. . . . It
> seems to me, therefore, that a very definite policy should be devel-
> oped for looking into the use of fire as a weapon. We need to use
> fire bombs like those being employed by the British with such prom-
> ising results.[7]

Colonel Kellogg would have been gratified to know that staff papers
concerning incendiary bombs had begun to circulate not only around
Eighth AF headquarters in early 1943, but in the Washington, D.C., headquarters of the Army Air Forces. In April 1943, General Henry H. (Hap)
Arnold received a memo which provided a bleak assessment of U.S. incendiary bombs: "We have absolutely no incendiary bombs that will meet the Air
Force requirements and standards for precision bombing of specific continental targets." The Air Force commander ordered his staff to report to him
within two weeks on the comparative effectiveness of various types of incendiaries, and on the availability of incendiaries by mid-1943. Their response
listed four different types of incendiaries and what the comparative effectiveness was believed to be:

RELATIVE EFFECTIVENESS AGAINST TYPICAL EUROPEAN TARGETS

Nomenclature	(max. 10)	
AN-M50,	4 lb magnesium thermite	10
AN-M54,	4 lb thermite steel case	2
AN-M47,	100 lb napalm	8
AN-M69,	6 lb napalm	17*

* Later experience showed this figure to be grossly inaccurate. The M50,
though rejected by the RAF because of a high dud rate in early 1943, was
improved and became the favored U.S. incendiary for use in Europe.[8]

On orders from General Arnold, the Eighth AF began experimenting
with various types of incendiaries in 1943. Because of mechanical failures in

fuses and bomb design, many airmen in the 8th Bomber Command remained unconvinced of the suitability of incendiary bombs. The majority of the airmen felt that H.E. bombs were the only ones capable of destroying sturdy German structures. Many skeptics were to change their minds before the end of the summer of 1943, for in late July the RAF demonstrated what massive incendiary attacks could do to a modern German city. The scene of this vivid spectacle was Hamburg, one of Hitler's major industrial centers and the home of over two million people. The RAF campaign aimed at the destruction of Hamburg by fire was code-named Operation GOMORRAH.

Hamburg was chosen as the target of an all-out, ten-day attack for several reasons. The shipyards of this city in northern Germany were the chief producers of submarines for the *Kriegsmarine*. A major rail center, Hamburg also contained other industrial sites and military installations. Petroleum refineries, truck factories, and armaments works all vied for space within the confines of greater Hamburg. The concept of an attack by fire had been outlined in an earlier RAF study on incendiary bombing, which explained:

> The destruction of a city by fire can only be obtained by creating a large-scale conflagration in the vulnerable built-up area of the city, which generally lies about its centre. In this form of attack, the basic requirement is to drop a sufficient number of potential fire-raisers in the form of incendiary bombs to saturate the fire guard and fire brigade service. In addition, H.E. bombs must be used to harass and lower the efficiency of the fire fighters, to break water mains, and to deny access to the fires by blocking structures, etc.[9]

Operation GOMORRAH was carried out by the RAF Bomber Command under the command of Air Marshal Sir Arthur ("Bomber") Harris during 24 July–3 August 1943. The British bombers conducted 3,095 sorties at night, while 255 B-17s of the U.S. Eighth AF made two daylight follow-up attacks.

Four major night raids were launched during the ten-day operation. The attack of 27–28 July was the most devastating. On that night, the RAF force of 787 heavy bombers was able to bomb without being molested by German night fighters. Denuded of fighter interceptor protection by the British ploy of dropping aluminum chaff (code-named WINDOW) to confuse the German radar operators, Hamburg lay at the mercy of the bombers, protected only by its antiaircraft guns.

The first British pathfinder aircraft began dropping large flares and incendiary markers on the target (the shipyards) shortly before midnight. The fires started by the pathfinders were burning and provided effective markers when the main force arrived over the target area at 1:00 A.M. on 28 July. The loads carried by the Lancaster and Wellington bombers were composed of H.E. and incendiary bombs of various sizes. The fires that sprang from the incendiaries fed on the dry buildings in the city and grew to such an intensity that there developed in Hamburg what came to be called a "Fire Storm."[10]

The *Feuersturm* was caused by the intense heat generated by the burning city. There was little surface wind that night, and the great mass of super-heated air rising from the growing conflagration rushed upward at great speed. A vacuum resulted at the base of the fire. Into this void poured cooler air from the surrounding area. Winds of hurricane force developed as the air rushed through the streets of Hamburg to fuel the fire.

The magnitude of the resulting inferno and the destruction it wrought have been documented by several German authorities at the scene. Horatio Bond, in *Fire and the Air War*, has cited several of these German officials in reporting:

> Police engineers in Hamburg estimated that the temperatures in the burning city blocks went as high as 800 C. (1472 F.). Literally hundreds of people were seen leaving shelters as the heat became intense. They ran across the streets and were seen to collapse very slowly like people who were thoroughly exhausted. They could not get up.
>
> Many thus killed were found to be naked. The heat and flames destroyed all clothing except shoes. Most of these people were not burnt to ashes when recovered but were dry and shrunken, resembling mummies.
>
> In the shelters, bodies assumed various aspects corresponding to the circumstances under which death had set in. Bodies were frequently found lying in a thick, greasy black mass, which was, without a doubt, melted fat tissue.[11]

That the effects of the attack on Hamburg were felt for some time was acknowledged by Albert Speer, Hitler's Minister of Armaments and War Production. Speer said after the war, "Fires made the greatest impression on the general morale of the population, which after the events in Hamburg and elsewhere was extremely afraid of the outbreak of large area conflagrations."[12]

The staff at Eighth AF headquarters was also impressed by the British success at Hamburg, especially when aerial photos showed massive damage to all major industrial sites in the city, including the shipyards. Huge dock-yard cranes and tramways, though still standing in most cases, were rendered unusable because the intense heat of the fire storm had warped their steel girders. With proof of the effectiveness of incendiary bombs against industrial targets, American commanders began using more incendiaries. From July 1943, when only 250 tons of incendiaries of all types were dropped by the Eighth AF, the monthly expenditure rose until the U.S. bombers were regularly dropping over 5,000 tons of incendiaries each month in 1944 and peaked at 7,726 tons in March 1945.[13]

The increased interest in fire bombs at Eighth AF was recorded by the Chief of the CWS, Major General William N. Porter, who later said in a memorandum for record:

> There was a great deal of prejudice at the start against incendiaries, largely because Ordnance officers in England were opposed to their use. They were finally "sold" to AF largely because Jerry Kellogg finally persuaded Curtis LeMay to try them.... at last, when their effectiveness was apparent after GOMORRAH, Eighth AAF began to scream for incendiaries, the situation was reversed, and CWS was hard put to meet the demand.[14]

To meet the increased requirement for improved incendiaries, the CWS would turn to the talented civilian scientists of the NDRC and, with the expenditure of large sums of money, succeed in providing the airmen with effective fire bombs. The research and development effort of 1943–1945 demonstrated the strength and flexibility of American industry and academe.

RESEARCH AND DEVELOPMENT: A CATCH-UP GAME

For more than a year prior to the British fire bombing of Hamburg, the Technical Division of the CWS had been working very closely with Division 11 of the NDRC on a variety of projects aimed at producing better incendiary bombs. Those men working to develop a satisfactory means of thickening gasoline for bomb fillings had been successful with the production of napalm, a mixture that was being used in the 100-lb M74 by early 1943. Other scientists were searching for ways of making the thermite-filled magnesium bomb, the M50, more reliable. The increase in the Army Air Forces interest prompted the CWS Chief to transfer more technicians to the bomb projects in the spring of 1943 and to solicit ideas from his staff and the NDRC on ways to test the incendiary bombs more thoroughly before shipping them overseas. General Porter was very anxious to provide the airmen with dependable incendiary munitions. A "bad press" was damaging to reputations and none of General Porter's CWS staff wanted the Ordnance Department to be able to say, "I told you so."[15]

On 12 May 1943, General Porter announced that funds had been allocated for the construction of several test sites for incendiary bombs. His concept was basically simple. If one wished to evaluate an incendiary bomb's performance against German buildings without having to go to Germany the thing to do would be to construct a "German" town in the United States. Thanks to a greatly increased research and development budget, the CWS was going to do just that. In June 1943 work would begin on model German and Japanese towns at Eglin Field in Florida; at Dugway Proving Ground, Utah; and at Edgewood Arsenal. To ensure that the German structures truly represented the types of building being attacked in Germany, General Porter secured the services of three eminent architects to design the target structures. Eric Mendelsohn, Joseph Heufeld, and Joachim Wachsmann, all Jewish refugees, had each owned architectural firms in Germany before fleeing the Nazi regime.[16]

The effort expended in constructing the mock towns was enormous. At Dugway, for example, buildings designed by the architects covered a five square mile area. Constructed of brick, wood, and tile at an estimated cost of $575,000, the German structures were authentic even in their furnishings. Heavy German furniture, bedspreads, rugs, and draperies were installed. The attics were insulated and all debris was removed that might feed a fire (intelligence reports indicated that this type of house cleaning had recently been ordered in Germany!). An Army Air Force observer said this about the German-style buildings at Dugway Proving Ground:

> To describe the target as a series of "typical" enemy structures would be a gross understatement and an injustice to the talent which was employed in making these buildings as truly authentic as humanly possible down to the last detail. They were "typical" even insofar as the curtains, children's toys, and clothing hanging in closets were concerned. Nothing was overlooked. Those houses represent the type in which 80% of the industrial population of Germany is housed.[17]

The titles of some of the test reports to come from the various sites during late 1943 and 1944 provide some insight into the thoroughness with which the CWS, now fully committed to winning the war with incendiaries, was testing its various incendiaries. As part of an overall test project supervised by the NDRC, the following tests were conducted:

EWT-3b   "Incendiary effect of M47 bombs and U.S. 500-lb General Purpose (GP) bombs on European industrial buildings."

EWT-3c   "Spread of fire within single-story European industrial divisions, mixed HE and incendiary attack."

EWT-3d   "Spread of fire within multi-story fire divisions in mixed HE-1B attacks."

As the titles indicate, the CWS/NDRC team had constructed not only test dwellings, but model factories, shops, and businesses. To determine how much damage could be done by fire, the scientists devised the control measure known as a "fire division." A fire division might vary from target to target, as it depended upon the floor space, contents, and construction of a target structure. A division was that portion of the structure in which maximum destruction could be expected from unchecked fires. The sum damage to a target would then be the aggregate of the damage to all of the fire divisions in the target. With this simple concept in hand, the scientists and U.S. Army Air Forces bombing staffs could estimate the number of incendiary bombs needed to attack a factory, a town, or a city.[18]

This aspect of incendiary research could not have taken place without the expenditure of large sums of money. Crews of carpenters, steelworkers, and masons were hired to erect, equip, and repair or replace buildings as the tests went on. Fortunately for the CWS and the Army Air Force, an aroused wartime Congress ensured that sufficient funds were available for this, and many other, research projects. The remarkable increase in money made available to the CWS during the war is exemplified by the jump in funds allocated for incendiary bomb procurement. From a mere $302,000 in 1941, the CWS bomb budget increased to $305,702,000 in 1944.[19]

Improvements in weapon design and application that can be directly attributed to the field testing carried on in the United States are numerous. Tests conducted in 1943 showed that while the napalm-filled M69 bomb was by far the most effective fire producer, it was unable to penetrate most types of German roofing material. The M50 and M47 incendiary bombs were better for European targets. Improved fillings like thermate were tested. Thermate increased the incendiary effect of the M50 by providing an oxidizing agent to the thermite filling of the original design. The improved M50A2 bomb was thus produced. Many types of fuses and igniters for different bombs were tested against a wide variety of targets. If the U.S. can be criticized for a lack of foresight in the incendiary field before World War II, it must be admired for the energy and ingenuity displayed by its soldiers, scientists, and engineers in their attempts to play "catch-up ball" after 1941.[20]

The improvements in bombs would have had far less impact on the enemy had not the CWS also devised better methods of delivering aerial munitions to the target in response to demands from the Air Force. Soon after the Eighth AF began to employ incendiaries, the problems of wasted space inside bombing aircraft and bomb aimability surfaced. Ingenuity and hard work by CWS officers and soldiers at air bases in England and in the United States solved the first problem. The second shortcoming of incendiary bombs, that of accuracy, would be attacked by combined teams of Army and civilian engineers with great success. The CWS searched for solutions in both areas with considerable zeal, for the technicians realized that an increase in the use of incendiaries largely depended upon the success of their efforts.

The problem of wasted space in the bomb-bays of the standard B-17 and B-24 bombers in use by the Eighth AF arose after the first few missions were flown by air groups with cargoes of M47 incendiary bombs. The bomb-bay of the B-17 bomber had been designed to hold twenty 500-lb H.E. bombs. When twenty M47 incendiary bombs were loaded into a B-17, the overall payload of the bomber was reduced by more than eighty percent, for although the exterior dimensions of the M47 were identical to that of the 500-lb H.E. General Purpose (GP) bomb, its loaded weight was actually only 69 pounds.

This reduction in potential destructive power was resented by air crews who risked their lives to fly over Germany. Obviously, some method would be needed to load more incendiary bombs into each bomber. Since space within the B-17 bomb-bay was a constant, the solution seemed to rest in finding a means of hanging more M47 bombs on each of the twenty pairs of mounting shackles at the bomb "stations" within the bomb-bay. Fearing the U.S. Army Air Forces might call a halt to the experimental bombing missions with incendiaries, CWS Chemical Support Companies attached to the Eighth AF worked feverishly during the summer of 1943 to devise a way of mounting more than one M47 at each station.[21]

By October, their efforts bore fruit. Using metal cables and a simple toggle device, the CWS fabricated a workable, if crude, method of pairing M47 bombs. The "piggy-back" arrangement was applauded by air commanders who could now double the incendiary tonnage carried on each mission. In November 1944 a contract for the manufacture of M47 pairing straps was let with a supplier in the United States and the double bomb method was utilized for the remainder of the war.[22]

While CWS personnel overseas were grappling with the M47 problem, the CWS, NDRC, and industrial engineers were hard at work on another project destined to enhance the accuracy of the 4-lb incendiary, the M50. As early as 1941, the Ordnance Department had produced devices for clustering the small incendiary bombs into a lightweight container that facilitated the shipment of the bombs overseas, their loading aboard bombers, and their release over the target. The early cluster held fifty-eight of the small bombs. Designed to open after being released from the bomber, the ordnance cluster was unsatisfactory for several reasons. Frequently, the cluster did not open at all. At other times, it opened immediately after leaving the aircraft and damaged other airplanes flying in the same formation. These problems, in conjunction with a high dud rate of the bombs, had caused the RAF to refuse their lend-lease shipments of clustered M50s in early 1942 and also threatened to halt subsequent Eighth AF use of M50 incendiaries.

The CWS-led team working during most of 1943 succeeded in producing a new model cluster designated the M17, which held 110 of the M50 incendiaries. Designed to open after being blown apart by a small explosive charge, the clusters could be adjusted to blow open from sixty to ninety seconds after leaving the aircraft bomb-bay. Supplies of the new M17 clusters began arriving in England in October 1943 and contributed to an improved accuracy rate for the M50 bombs, which were to become the mainstay of the Eighth AF incendiary bombing campaigns of 1944 and 1945.[23]

With the development of incendiary bombs and clusters, the CWS faced another related problem during 1943. As in other areas, the lack of prewar development of incendiaries was to result in a dearth of experience in the packaging and shipping of bombs from the United States to overseas areas. Incendiary bombs, particularly those in clusters, proved to be especially vulnerable to damage during shipment. Attempts during 1943 to ship bombs in crates made of unseasoned timber resulted in high failure rates of igniters when the bombs were dropped on targets in Germany. Investigation of the problem revealed that the high moisture content in the green wood cases had corroded the delicate fuse mechanism of many bombs. Consequently, a great deal of money was spent trying to hurriedly develop a metal shipping container for incendiaries.

No sooner had this problem been addressed than CWS personnel serving with the Eighth AF began complaining about M47 bombs that were arriving in England with defective napalm filling. Tests revealed that the paint used on the exterior of the M47 bomb was causing an adverse chemical reaction during filling operations. The napalm gel, reacting with the paint around the filler plug in the bomb casing, was breaking down and returning to its original components. The paint was changed, but not until three shiploads of bombs were condemned as unfit for use. Once again, prewar unpreparedness had caused problems that influenced wartime performance.[24]

Civilian scientists and the CWS counterparts continued to improve incendiary bombs and related equipment. By early 1944, their efforts had provided the Army Air Force with the incendiaries needed to carry on the air offensive in Europe and, later, in the Pacific. The considerable progress made in the short period 1941–1944 was possible only because the developers of incendiary bombs had access to almost unlimited support in money, manpower, and materials. Had U.S. experimentation with incendiary bombs continued after World War I, the program during World War II would have been much less wasteful. One official Army historian addressed this problem, saying:

> The reason that so many [bomb] models were designed and then discarded somewhere along the development line is that incendiary bombs, as a means of mass destruction, were new in World War II and the necessary characteristics were not well defined.[25]

With the majority of the developmental problems solved, the CWS was able to shift into mass production of improved bombs in early 1944. Stocks of these bombs were increased during the spring of 1944 as the heavy bombers of the Eighth AF concentrated upon the mission of sealing off Normandy from the rest of France in preparation for the planned invasion of the French coast. H.E. bombs were used almost exclusively as the strategic bombers attempted to demolish the rail lines, roads, and bridges that might serve as reinforcement routes for the German defenders of the Channel coast. Only after D-Day, 6 June 1944, did the heavy bombers of the 8th Bomber Command resume a full schedule of raids against German industrial targets. After Allied troops were ashore in France, U.S. airmen found a new use for napalm: the close support of ground troops by fighter aircraft dropping fire bombs.

TACTICAL AIR SUPPORT: THE NAPALM FIRE BOMB

The evolution of the fire bomb as a close air support weapon is a story of imagination and improvisation. As recorded in the unit histories and mission reports of the Ninth [tactical] Air Force, fighter pilots of the Ninth AF began the practice of jettisoning partially filled external fuel tanks during missions over France prior to D-Day. To avoid landing at their home bases with the volatile aviation fuel still suspended from the fighter's wings or belly, thus risking a fire should the tanks break loose on landing, the pilots often tried to drop the tanks on enemy barracks, vehicles, or artillery positions. The fuel which splashed from the ruptured external pods (often made of pressed paper) was ignited by firing tracer bullets into the area where the fuel had landed. The resulting fire was usually quite spectacular and sometimes did considerable damage to anything flammable in the immediate vicinity. Thus, a practice begun primarily as a safety precaution provided the germ of an idea for a new flame weapon.[26]

Noting the effectiveness of these improvised "bombs," fighter unit commanders suggested to CWS Colonel Harold J. Baum (Kellogg's successor at

Eighth AF) that expendable drop tanks might be fitted with some sort of detonator that would ignite the fuel upon impact. Tests conducted by fighter pilots and members of Colonel Baum's staff during May 1944 demonstrated the potential advantages of a fire bomb that could be dropped by a fighter aircraft working in close coordination with ground troops. With a little practice, most of the pilots participating in the tests could spread burning gasoline over a circular target 100 meters in diameter. Colonel Baum requested that the CWS send a number of thermite hand grenades to England for use as igniters for the bombs. With a thermite grenade attached to each end of the fuel tank, and a pressure-sensitive detonator to explode the grenade, Baum's test pilots were able to ignite over eighty percent of the test bombs dropped.[27]

The addition of a thickening agent like napalm or the British gel Perspex was a natural second step. The thickener caused the jellied gasoline to stick to surfaces and to burn more slowly, thereby making the blaze more damaging to humans or flammable materials. Although the fire bombs were never to enjoy much success against "hard" targets like concrete emplacements, tanks, or railroad stock, the success of the test bombs against "soft" test targets (light vehicles, wooden structures, and clothed dummies) was sufficient for Colonel Baum to contract with a British firm for the production of fuel pods for fire bombs pending the arrival of an increased number of U.S.-made external tanks.

The fire bombs, usually made from 75-, 100-, or 165-gallon belly or wing tanks, were used increasingly as the Allied armies encountered stiff German opposition in the bocage region inland from the Normandy invasion beaches. With the *Luftwaffe* frequently absent from the sky, U.S. fighter planes previously dedicated to bomber escort were supplied to the ground commanders in large numbers and provided timely support to the U.S. spearheads pushing into France's Brittany Peninsula after the St. Lô breakout. American fighters equipped with napalm assisted ground troops assaulting the Siegfried Line and tried (unsuccessfully) to burn out German defenders in the heavily fortified city of Metz. Twin-tailed P-38 fighters were among the first aircraft which appeared over the beleaguered town of Bastogne when the weather cleared on 23 December 1944 and inflicted numerous casualties when they attacked German convoys with fire bombs. The use of napalm by the fighter aircraft of the Ninth AF attracted a good bit of attention from higher headquarters, and the airmen were directed to prepare a summary of "lessons learned" concerning the fire bomb.[28]

Colonel L. N. Tindall, director of the Ninth AF Research Section, compiled a staff study in response. The study contains a wealth of information on the use of fire bombs. Tindall's report addresses the problems inherent in formulating tactical doctrine for new weapons. The questions of when, where, and how to drop napalm were answered only after a year of trial-and-error employment. Reading through the recorded instances in which fire bombs were used successfully and those in which the bombs were wasted on inappropriate targets or dropped in the wrong fashion, one can sense the lack of clearcut instructions for those airmen charged with employing the new weapon.[29]

Numerous reports from ground and air observers remark upon the failure of napalm when dropped on targets in damp forests, or employed against enemy troops in heavily fortified positions. Fighter pilots of the Ninth AF were generally enthusiastic about the new fire bombs, perhaps because of the spectacular nature of the smoke and flame produced by a strike. However, the impressive fireball often obscured the fact that the bomb had not neutralized the target. Pilots dropping the fire bombs were required to execute a rather shallow dive on approaching the target. When enemy antiaircraft fire was present, the pilot's aim was often thrown off in the midst of his approach with the resulting poor target effect. Also, pilots sometimes employed fire bombs against targets that should have been engaged with H.E. bombs. Colonel J. L. Ryan of the 7th Armored Division commented upon one such instance:

> The large force of Germans in the woods to our direct front were attacked by four P-38's carrying napalm. These woods were wet with rain. The napalm seemed to have no effect whatsoever. Even after strafing the spot in the woods where the flame pods were dropped, no fire or smoke was observed.[30]

On some occasions, however, napalm drops were very successful. When used against German light vehicles or troops in relatively unprotected positions, napalm bombs were superior to H.E. and had a noticeable effect on German morale. A 29th Infantry Division officer observed a napalm strike by P-38 fighters against a German defensive position and reported:

> Mortar positions were holding up American advance on south side of Hill 367.... Thirteen P-38's loaded with 2 x 165 [gallon] napalm tanks employed against position. Sixteen napalm hits on or near position. Position occupied with few casualties. Surgeon stated that a large number of enemy were killed; their bodies practically disintegrated by heat and flame.[31]

Tactical air support missions flown in France, at Bastogne, and along the Siegfried Line taught the fliers that the best tactic was to use a mix of H.E.

and napalm bombs against most targets. These lessons were applied as American troops pushed into the heart of Germany, with U.S. fighter units polishing their delivery techniques on columns of retreating German troops. The equipment and tactics of close air support with napalm that evolved in Europe would find their way to the far Pacific, where tactical fighter units had a pressing need for the fire bomb.

THE FINAL ROUND IN EUROPE: AMERICANS BOMB THE CITIES

As World War II drew to a close in Europe, the Army Air Forces used more incendiaries than ever before. In August 1944 the Army Air Force Test Board at Eglin Field, Florida, concluded that, where there was any chance of starting a fire, incendiary bombs would do more damage to enemy structures than H.E. From January through March 1945, the heavy bombers of the Eighth and Fifteenth Air Forces regularly bombed the cities of Nuremburg, Magdeburg, Darmstadt, and Berlin with heavy concentrations of M50, M47, and the new large (500 lb) napalm bomb, the M76. Albert Speer, upon being questioned after the end of the war, compared the effect of incendiaries to H.E. bombs on Berlin:

> The difference between the effects of high-explosive and incendiary bomb attacks was to be seen in Berlin. Here the American Air Force carried out several attacks on the centre of the city exclusively with H.E.... These did not have the effect of an incendiary attack of comparable size. Fire was a more effective means of destroying workers' dwellings than high explosives....[32]

Responding to Russian requests for assistance during the great Soviet offensive of 1945, the British/American Combined Chiefs of Staff directed the RAF and USAAF to bomb major cities in eastern Germany which lay within the Russian zone of advance. Incendiaries played a large role in the Allied attacks on the cities, many of which were crowded with refugees fleeing the Russians. The flurry of concern that arose after the ancient cultural center of Dresden was firebombed on 14–15 February 1945 was countered by U.S. and British claims that, while the large number of civilian deaths was unfortunate, the city itself was a viable military target. The Eighth AF commander, General Eaker, offered a pragmatic rationale for the incendiary attacks, saying:

> I deeply regret that British and American bombers killed 135,000 people in the attack on Dresden, but I remember who started the ... war and I regret even more the loss of more than 5,000,000

Allied lives in the necessary effort to completely defeat and utterly destroy Nazism.[33]

The apparent change in the American attitude toward incendiary bombs and area bombing in general was significant. The U.S. air commanders, realizing that German industry had been decentralized in response to earlier bombing of factories, came to look upon cities in much the same light as the British. Large-scale area bombings carried out by U.S. aircraft during the final stages of the war in Europe would presage by a few months a massive bombing campaign conducted by American bombers on the other side of the globe. Even as Berlin fell, the Army Air Force was conducting a fire-bombing campaign that would help to bring Japan to her knees.[34]

CHAPTER 6

Flame Throwers in the Pacific: 1942–1945

During the dark days following the Pearl Harbor attack, some U.S. troops stationed in the path of the Japanese offensive found themselves the victims of flame weapons. As General MacArthur's weary forces retreated into the hills of the Bataan Peninsula, Japanese troops employed flame throwers to burn out last-ditch defensive positions manned by U.S. soldiers. Thus the war in the Pacific would begin with the enemy having a distinct advantage in flame warfare.

Colonel Stuart A. Hamilton, the Chemical Officer on General MacArthur's staff in the Philippines, sent two captured Japanese portable flame throwers and a report of Japanese flame tactics to Edgewood. In his February report, the colonel explained how the Japanese were using their weapons to burn away the heavy foliage that concealed American and Philippine positions, then turning the flame on the outnumbered defenders. In this and later communications, Hamilton requested that flame throwers be provided for the Americans.[1]

After his release from a Japanese prison camp at the end of the war, Hamilton submitted a full report of the activities of the CWS on Bataan and Corregidor. Lacking any flame throwers, he wrote, the CWS officers attempted to fabricate them by using chemical decontamination sprayers. Failing in this, young staff officers and enlisted volunteers manufactured large numbers of Molotov cocktails from empty bottles. Traveling to the front lines, they attempted to halt Japanese tanks with the homemade fire bombs. These heroics had little effect on the Japanese advance. Hamilton was one of the CWS officers captured by the enemy when U.S. forces on Corregidor finally surrendered on 6 May 1942. As he later said, Hamilton hoped until the last that an American submarine might deliver flame throwers, so that the Americans could fight fire with fire, if only for morale's sake. He had just enough men left to destroy much of the toxic gas so carefully husbanded on Corregidor before the war—gas that was never used.[2]

81

No American troops used flame throwers in combat for almost a year. Then, on 16 January 1943, the Chief of the CWS received word that American engineer troops had used a flame thrower in combat during December 1942. To those proponents of flame warfare who had waited hopefully for some vindication of their faith in this weapon, the report came as a blow. The flame thrower attack had resulted in the death of two men—both Americans. Almost nothing had gone right in this first attempt to use American flame throwers against the Japanese. The report stated that on 6 December 1942, a U.S. infantry unit fighting on the southeastern peninsula of New Guinea near the village of Buna had been blocked for several days by a tenacious Japanese defensive position anchored in well-concealed pillboxes. The infantry commander, greatly concerned by the high casualties caused by the Japanese, called for engineer flame thrower support. Troops of the 114th Engineer Combat Battalion had several early model flame throwers on hand and agreed to assault the Japanese position. A cursory check of the flame weapons revealed that quite a bit of deterioration of hoses, seals, and other fittings had occurred in the tropical jungle climate. After a hurried cleaning, the engineers brought the weapons up to the infantry position. No time was taken to conduct a rehearsal of the assault or even make a last-minute test of the flame throwers.[3]

The Americans began their assault by crawling to within fifteen yards of the Japanese bunker. Corporal Wilber G. Tirrell, the lead flame gunner, had hidden his flame thrower in a gunny sack in an effort to conceal his weapon from the Japanese. On a signal, Tirrell hoisted the weapon onto his back and stepped from cover. Accompanied by an infantry squad, he advanced to a position directly in front of the first pillbox and pulled the trigger. Instead of the gushing flame he expected, a weak ten-foot squirt of flame dribbled out. The whole American group was exposed to the Japanese, who lost no time in opening fire with their machine gun. The Americans went down, one by one. Tirrell managed to survive by playing dead until nightfall, then crawled away. Several days later, the same engineer unit met with equally disastrous results in a second attempt to use their flame throwers. They soon made it known that they had no further use for the "worthless" incendiary weapon.[4]

In analyzing this action, several points were clear. First, the weapons had not received the care and maintenance demanded by the moist tropical climate. Second, the flame weapons had not been checked *just prior* to their use. Finally, the inexperienced engineers and infantrymen had exposed themselves to the Japanese fire on the assumption that the flame thrower was going to work. Clearly, improvements in maintenance procedures and employment technique were needed.

Better news was to arrive in February. Reports which slowly filtered back to Edgewood from the fighting on Guadalcanal indicated that Army and Marine troops had used flame throwers to good effect in overcoming Japanese resistance.[5] Marine combat engineers had cleaned out three Japanese bunkers with flame throwers on 15 January 1943. Those Japanese that managed to avoid immediate death from the bursts of flame were gunned down by Marine riflemen as they ran screaming from their holes with their hair and clothing ablaze. Cheered by this success, Major General J. Lawton Collins, the commander of the Army's 25th Infantry Division, also on Guadalcanal, directed that the Division Chemical Officer conduct a one-week school on flame thrower tactics and maintenance for each of the division's infantry regiments.[6]

By mid-1943, several more accounts were to be placed in the CWS combat action file. In July 1943, American forces fighting on New Georgia in the Solomon Islands had used flame throwers with considerable success against Japanese defenders. Captain James F. Olds, one of the more aggressive Chemical Warfare Service officers fighting in the Pacific, had spent most of his time on New Georgia selling the infantrymen on flame throwers. This paid off in an increasing number of calls for flame thrower support as the campaign progressed. On 26 July 1943, Captain Olds led a carefully planned assault by six flame throwers against a strongly entrenched enemy position. Concealed by smoke screens, Olds' party crept close to the enemy positions and unleashed a torrent of flame from the flanks of the Japanese defenses, roasting the surprised defenders.[7]

As Americans advanced in three areas of the Pacific during 1943 (south, southwest, central), the inherent value of the portable flame thrower began to outweigh its shortcomings. It was a weapon that lent itself to the dirty, close-quarters fighting that usually characterized Pacific island combat. The Japanese, imbued with the *Bushido* spirit, generally refused to surrender in spite of fierce American attacks. The flame thrower seemed to be the only weapon they feared. Often, however, the Americans found that their enemies refused to surrender even in the face of certain death from burns. The GIs and Marines moved forward slowly and at great cost in a theater that was of secondary importance to all but those fighting there.

With the spread in the use of flame throwers in the Pacific, the CWS staff at Edgewood increased the amount of training in flame warfare given to CWS troops. In 1943, a special ten-hour course began at Camp Sibert, Louisiana, for troops slated for movement to CWS units in the combat zones. The course dealt with the maintenance and tactical application of flame throwers and was based on lessons already learned in Pacific fighting. Many of the graduates of this course found themselves assigned to infantry units upon their arrival in the Pacific. By September 1943, the CWS Chief lent his personal support to the formation of a special test company at Camp Sibert. This unit was equipped with flame throwers and demolitions and trained intensively until February 1944, practicing assaults on Japanese-style defensive positions. The experimental work done at Camp Sibert provided much of the material included in a CWS field manual dealing with flame thrower assaults.[8]

These attempts to train troops in the United States set a pattern that was to remain unchanged throughout the war. Unfortunately, by the time the CWS replacements reached the battle areas, they often found that tactics, terrain, and equipment had changed as doctrine continued to evolve through combat application. The CWS, like other branches, was never able to solve the problem of time-lag between training and combat. Time, distance, and the convoluted reporting channels used by CWS officers in combat left the development of tactical doctrine and weapon improvement to the men in combat. The CWS staff attempted to react quickly to suggestions and requests from the combat zones, but was often hamstrung by delays in procuring improved weapons.[9]

To those soldiers in action on the Pacific Islands during 1943, the need for the new M1A1 flame thrower with its improved fuel was obvious. A flame gunner operating an M1A1 could direct a concentrated stream of napalm-thickened fuel through the firing ports of a bunker or pillbox with a high degree of accuracy. Once inside, the flames used up all of the available oxygen and those enemy soldiers not burned by the flames quickly suffocated. The older M1, still used by many combat units during 1943, was good for burning off vegetation that concealed enemy positions, but could not deliver a concentrated stream of fire. It *sprayed* flame. Because of this, the flame gunner armed with an M1 had to get very close to his target to neutralize it. Casualties among flame thrower personnel were high, morale suffered, and experience was lost as trained operators were killed or wounded. Realizing the pressing need for the improved model, the CWS went all out to manufacture and procure the M1A1 and to expedite its shipment to the combat forces.[10]

More units were sent to the Pacific to engage in the island-hopping offensives, and the CWS faced a new problem: Since late 1942, the Corps of Engineers had been responsible for using and maintaining the growing number of flame throwers available to combat units. In theory, this plan should have worked reasonably well. In practice, however, the engineers were far too busy with their primary missions of building air strips, roads, and harbor facilities to maintain and use the flame throwers effectively.[11]

As combat commanders became increasingly aware of the capabilities of the flame thrower, they requested engineer flame support more frequently.

If trained engineer troops were not available, infantry commanders were prone to strap a flame thrower on the back of an infantryman and after a two-minute class on its operation, send him off with a quick pep talk. Many a confused eighteen-year-old private faced the enemy remembering only the admonition to "Burn those damn Japs!" Sometimes he succeeded; often he did not. Authority and responsibility for flame thrower operations were becoming entangled in a triangular web as the Infantry, the Engineers, and the CWS all tried to use the weapon.[12]

The CWS and the War Department met this problem in several ways. In late 1943, the War Department staff deleted all flame throwers and flame thrower support equipment from the table of organization and equipment (TOE) of combat engineer battalions. The portable flame thrower became a Class IV (Special Purpose Items) item of supply. In this way, the flame throwers would be maintained at division level, where their distribution to line units, maintenance, and replacement would be supervised by the Division Chemical Officer. The weapons could be drawn by units before embarking upon a campaign and used throughout the action. This step enhanced the assault commanders' ability to provide themselves with adequate flame support and officially recognized the infantry role in flame warfare.[13]

In an effort to provide as much guidance as possible to the infantry units, CWS teams toured the combat areas, training officers and enlisted men to care for their flame throwers. The CWS established semipermanent schools in Hawaii, Australia, and in Port Moresby, New Guinea. These schools, during the last two years of the war, trained large numbers of soldiers and Marines in flame warfare tactics and in the "tricks of the trade" required to maintain their temperamental weapons in the moist climate. Several CWS support units moved to the Pacific to provide expert repair service for flame throwers and their mixing units, pumps, and compressors.[14]

As the CWS organization expanded in 1943–1944, more Chemical Warfare Service officers were sent overseas. This freed other officers for combat units, where CWS officers assisted in tactical training and took part in many flame thrower assaults. Those units with aggressive chemical officers had the most successful records of flame thrower attacks. With the threat of gas warfare somewhat remote, it would have been easy for CWS officers to relax, doing as little as possible. It is to their credit that so many CWS officers overseas demonstrated exceptional energy, originality, and persistence in their support of infantry, armored, and engineer units. The intelligence and innovative nature of CWS soldiers often led to the employment of CWS equipment in ways that sustained the combat strength of their supported units. The CWS gas units provided shower points, insect control, and environmental support.[15]

The Marines and Army joined forces in November 1943 to assault Bougainville, a heavily defended island in the Solomons. From the standpoint of flame warfare, this campaign was significant for several reasons. First, the action demonstrated that crude as the American flame throwers might be, they were probably better than those used by the Japanese. Aside from reports of Japanese flame throwers on Bataan and the capture of several flame throwers on Guadalcanal, there had been no documented reports of their use against Americans.[16]

In December 1943, the Japanese again attempted to kill American troops with flame throwers. Fighting fire with fire, the Japanese attacked a patrol of Americans armed with M1A1 flame throwers. The leader of the American group was the CWS officer of New Georgia fame, Captain Olds. He recorded this experience in an article which appeared in the *CWS Bulletin*. In his words:

> Suddenly, two Jap flamegunners appeared out of the underbrush.... Standing upright and with no hesitation, the Japs fired from their flanking position before we had a chance to move. A stream of oil covered my head and right shoulder and doused Kearns' left side. Fortunately, the Jap flame fuel failed to ignite. Before the Japs could get in a second burst they were cut down.[17]

The unreliability of the Japanese weapons and their increasing difficulty in resupplying isolated garrisons probably helped to prevent any extensive use of flame throwers by the Japanese.

Of significance, too, in the Bougainville fighting was the formation of provisional flame thrower units by the infantry regiments which made up the Americal Division. Two of these volunteer units saw action in March and April 1944 during extremely bitter fighting. The success of the units was attributed to teamwork and high *esprit de corps*—both developed prior to the invasion and honed in the heat of battle. The formation of "flame thrower platoons" in the Southwest Pacific and "assault teams" in the South Pacific became *de rigueur* throughout the area in 1944. These units, generally composed of volunteers, were especially trained and equipped to deal with enemy emplacements by using flame throwers, explosives, automatic weapons, and nerve.[18]

While the fighting in the South and Southwest Pacific areas saw an increased use of flame weapons, the single most impressive use of flame throwers during 1943 was in the Central Pacific on the coral island of Tarawa. When the Second Marine Division assaulted Betio, the largest of several small atolls forming the Tarawa complex, the amphibious attack was resisted by fanatical defenders who had spent several years fortifying their small outcropping. Capitalizing on the rugged coral which formed a natural defense against bombs or high-explosive shells, the Japanese had constructed sturdy bunkers covered with steel plate, large coconut logs, and concrete to reinforce their positions. They were still digging in when the American invasion fleet appeared on 19 November 1943.

When the Marine assault waves landed, a torrent of enemy fire crashed down upon them. Advancing against this storm of fire was impossible and Marines took what cover they could near a seawall that protected the beach. At this point the flame thrower came into its own. The Marine Corps, always the poor relations of the U.S. Navy, had managed to beg sixty M1A1 flame throwers from the Army in preparation for the assault on Tarawa. As the fighting along the seawall evolved into a hand-to-hand struggle, it became evident that only those Marine Corps units that had managed to get their flame throwers ashore were going to advance. It was a slow, costly assault, but better than dying on the narrow beach. The units that had lost their flame throwers during the run into shore melted away.[19]

The Marine after-action report for Tarawa stressed the utility of flame throwers, saying:

> The importance of the portable flame thrower in all phases of Operation GALVANIC [assault of Tarawa] cannot be overemphasized. Flame throwers were largely responsible for the success enjoyed by units that breached the Japanese sea wall defenses on 20 November 1943. Flame throwers proved to be extremely valuable in attacking [Japanese] pillboxes via firing ports and entrances. In the future it is proposed by this Corps that all units making a landing should [be] equipped with flame throwers on the basis of one (1) per rifle platoon.[20]

As a direct result of the Tarawa experience and the increase in the availability of flame throwers to Pacific combat units, both the Army and Marine Corps increased the number of flame throwers that were allocated to units scheduled to conduct future assaults.

The reaction of the American public to the Tarawa battle was mixed. Most Americans were horrified by the U.S. casualties sustained on Betio and there developed a general toughening of public opinion about the conduct of the war. The *New York Times* minced no words in its description of the battle, and words like "Jap" and "Nip" were common.[21] But while most of the American populace felt no pity for the Japanese burned in their holes on Betio, some few complained about the use of flame throwers. The Army

Chief of Staff, General George C. Marshall, felt constrained to answer complaints he had received. On 3 February 1944, in a speech to an American Legion gathering, he said, "Vehement protests I am receiving against our use of flame throwers don't indicate an understanding of the meaning of our dead on . . . Tarawa."[22]

During late 1943, the CWS began to compile data on flame thrower casualties. By asking how and why a flame thrower killed, a more lethal weapon and better tactics might be devised. CWS and Army Medical Corps officers studied the corpses of Japanese soldiers who had been killed by American flame throwers. The results were informally presented in several articles in the *Chemical Warfare Bulletin* in early 1944. Formal autopsy reports were forwarded to the Chief of the CWS. There was, in all of the reports, some question as to whether the victims had died of oxygen starvation or because of the massive trauma occasioned by the flame and a corresponding shock to the central nervous system. Articles for public consumption stressed that the flame thrower was not inhumane, for a man hit by a large burst of flame might die almost instantly, whereas one struck by a bullet or a high explosive shell could linger in terrible pain for hours before expiring. These efforts to humanize the flame thrower were not successful.[23]

The flame thrower had achieved its initial success in 1915 largely because of the terror it had inspired. While mechanical improvements had rendered it more lethal by 1944, it still derived much of its effect from the very human fear of being burned. As was shown on many occasions during World War II, U.S. assault troops supported by flame throwers often charged with more élan. They, too, were affected by their respect for flame.[24]

Criticism of the flame thrower came from both military and antiwar groups. One leading CWS officer wrote after the war that the American use of flame had surprised him. Being very familiar with all types of poison gas, he could name several that killed quickly and painlessly. He could not understand why the U.S. refused to utilize gas for humanitarian reasons, but did not hesitate to burn its enemies.[25]

In spite of continuing problems caused by faulty weapons, and untroubled by moral questions about flame warfare, U.S. commanders used flame extensively in every major Pacific operation of 1944. In the Marianas, Palaus, and Philippine island groups, Army and Marine Corps troops perfected their flame thrower tactics and wrestled with the problems caused by the climate and the undependable ignition system of the M1A1. The troops discovered ways to light the flame fuel if it was not ignited at the flame gun's nozzle. Tracer bullets, white phosphorus shells, or hand grenades were often used to set target areas on fire.[26]

Combat units were pleased to see the arrival in mid-1944 of the newest model flame thrower to be developed by the CWS and NDRC, the M2-2. The new weapon embodied many of the improvements suggested by the fighting forces. The single greatest improvement over the M1A1 was an ignition system that proved to be far more reliable than the old battery-spark models. The M2-2 had a waterproofed revolving cylinder which worked much like a revolver. When an operator pulled the trigger of the flame gun a substance not unlike a match head was struck and produced a spark which fired the flame fuel at the nozzle of the flame gun. Although some units were still using the older M1A1 at war's end, most of them had received the new M2-2.[27]

THE ARMORED FLAME THROWER IN THE PACIFIC

The most ambitious project undertaken by CWS personnel in the Pacific during 1944 was an effort to provide the combat forces with an effective tank-mounted flame thrower. As American forces pushed closer to Japan, they began to encounter terrain that differed markedly from the tropical jungles of the South Pacific. More open ground made mounted operations feasible. In this new tactical environment, which offered less concealment, the man-packed flame thrower became a liability to the soldier carrying it.

The Japanese, recognizing the danger embodied by the flame gunner, sought out the operators, and casualties among flame thrower teams continued to rise. The Marines had recognized the need for more protection in flame operations in 1943 and tried to modify M1 flame throwers so that they could be mounted in the bow machine gun port of M5 light tanks. The experiment was initially successful, but the Marines discovered that constant vibrations from the tank's engine caused the delicate M1s to malfunction.[28]

A flame weapon specifically designed for a tank was needed; not a makeshift field expedient. The CWS at Edgewood Arsenal, with some help from the NDRC, but very little from the Armored Force, had been trying to develop a tank-mounted flame thrower in the United States. The Armored Force, with its attention centered on tank-to-tank combat in Europe, was unenthusiastic about weapons that might reduce the tank's traditional weaponry or ammunition-carrying capacity. For this reason, most of the CWS efforts in the United States were directed toward the development of "auxiliary" flame guns. These models replaced one of the tank machine guns or were mounted like periscopes. Although they could conceivably protect the tank crew from infantry attacks, these "auxiliary" weapons had only limited range and fuel capacity.[29]

A lack of CWS success in the United States led the CWS staff in Hawaii to begin their own flame tank program. Led by one of the most vigorous and capable officers in the CWS, Colonel George F. Unmacht, the Chemical

Section of the U.S. Army Headquarters, Pacific Ocean Areas, began to develop test weapons that could be mounted on the light and medium tanks employed by Army and Marine units in the Pacific. Colonel Unmacht was one of many CWS officers whose field improvisations made up for the lack of planning and preparedness. The great distances separating them from Edgewood Arsenal and the needs of their combat commanders demanded proactive performance.[30]

Requests from the Marine Corps for assistance in the construction of mechanized flame throwers provided the impetus for the project in Hawaii. The Marine Corps, always aggressive, had become the chief proponents of flame weapons in the Pacific. Often, the flame thrower took the place of artillery in the lightly gunned Marine divisions. Trained from their inception to serve as shock, or assault, troops, the Marine Corps found that the flame thrower fit nicely into their concept of tactics.[31]

The Marines, like the Army, were concerned with the casualties suffered in their headlong assaults on Pacific island strongholds. Especially after Tarawa, they wanted mechanized armored flame projectors. With Army and Navy help, the Marines in Hawaii modified several large Ronson flame throwers borrowed from the Canadian army in 1944 and mounted them on armored amphibious vehicles in time for the assault on Peleliu. Although numerous breakdowns of the vehicles caused problems, the flame projectors functioned quite well. The Americans were able to burn out Japanese defenses dug deeply into cliff faces with large weapons with much longer ranges and greater fuel capacities than the man-packed models. Most importantly, casualties for the operators of the flame throwers were minimal.[32]

Heartened by the Peleliu operation, the Marines asked for help in devising a flame projector that could be mounted in the standard M4 medium tank. With the invasion of the Japanese bastion of Iwo Jima scheduled for early 1945, the CWS staff under Colonel Unmacht worked feverishly to fill Marine and Army requests for a powerful flame thrower mounted in a medium tank. Colonel Unmacht's CWS staff devised a weapon that fired from the tank's cannon barrel. Mounted in the standard Sherman tank, this flame thrower was produced by a combined team of Army, Navy, and Marine technicians. Because the main gun barrel was retained, and no fuel trailer was used, the flame tanks produced in Hawaii were indistinguishable from regular M4 tanks until they ejected a 100-yard stream of napalm. They could carry 250 gallons of flame fuel in their interior tanks.[33]

Eight of these tanks were tested during the invasion of the volcanic island of Iwo Jima in February 1945. Marine tankers found that the tank's armor protection, long range, and large fuel capacity greatly assisted in the destruction of Japanese defenses while reducing American casualties. Both the armored flame throwers and the new M2-2 portable flame throwers saw extensive action.[34] On Iwo, the Japanese fought fanatically as always. A message from a Japanese officer to his commander contained complaints about the heavy losses to the American flame weapons, but ended with the promise that his soldiers would "Continue to inflict as much damage as possible upon the enemy until we are annihilated." Faced by such an adversary, the Marines turned more and more to the flame thrower.[35] Once the Iwo Jima campaign was won, U.S. troops faced an even greater test: the conquest of Okinawa.

THE FINAL ASSAULT—OKINAWA: 1945

The American invasion of Okinawa on 1 April 1945 was the culmination of three years of experience in amphibious warfare and six months of careful planning for the conquest of this major Japanese bastion. Situated in the Ryukyu Islands, Okinawa guarded the approaches to Japan itself. Its capture would provide the Allies with a much-needed base for the continued aerial bombardment of Japan and a staging area for the anticipated assault on the Japanese home islands. Two amphibious corps, one Army (24th) and one Marine (5th Amphibious), would assault Okinawa. This mighty amphibious force, commanded by Army General Simon B. Buckner, was designated Tenth Army.

Among the units forming the Tenth Army was a new type of American tank battalion. Specially equipped with fifty-four flame tanks fabricated in Hawaii, the 713th Armored Flame Thrower Battalion was designed to support the ground forces on Okinawa. Landing on 19 April 1945, the 713th was committed to combat almost immediately. During the next seventy-five days of almost continual action, the unit was officially credited with killing 4,788 Japanese troops. Not a single member of this unit was killed by enemy fire while fighting inside the tanks. Although they had been somewhat skeptical of the flame tanks before the invasion, the tankers developed a high degree of confidence in their equipment.[36]

Operating in conjunction with the Army and Marines, the flame tanks were joined by infantrymen with portable flame throwers, regular tanks firing high explosive ammunition, and tanks of the 711th Tank Battalion mounting auxiliary flame projectors. These combined teams assaulted the innumerable fortifications and caves that honeycombed the island. To deal with these caves, the 713th had brought several long fire hoses to Okinawa. Earlier campaigns had shown that some means of carrying flame fuel from a tank to areas not accessible to the vehicle would pay off in more enemy dead and fewer friendly casualties. These hose extensions, attached to the tanks and pumping napalm from the tank's reservoir, were used throughout the later stages of the campaign. One of the best examples of their effectiveness was provided by Captain Tony Niemeyer of the 713th, when, on 10 July 1945, he lugged 200 feet of the hose from his tank up a cliffside and killed over seventy-five Japanese.[37]

One article in an American magazine extolled the virtues of backpack and vehicle-mounted flame throwers and reflected widespread U.S. feelings toward the Japanese by saying, "There are few arguments about fire; it saves U.S. lives and kills Japs."[38]

By the end of the Okinawa campaign, the flame tanks of the 713th were credited by many as being the single most valuable weapon of the fighting. Continued development of the flame tank was urged and large numbers of improved models mounting the flame gun coaxially with the main gun were developed for the invasion of Japan.[39]

Even as soldiers and Marines trained for the final push, Japanese cities were being laid waste by a weapon that eventually killed more people than the two atomic bombs so often credited with ending the war. The Japanese population was having the war delivered to their very doorsteps by low-flying B-29 bombers. Most of the giant aircraft carried but one kind of bomb in their bays: fire bombs.

CHAPTER 7

Target Japan:
Incendiary Attacks in the Pacific

The greatest American use of aerial incendiaries during World War II came during the final year of the war in the Pacific Theater. Using fire bombs that had undergone extensive development in the United States and Europe, Army, Navy, and Marine fliers developed delivery techniques best suited to the demands of the varied and difficult tactical situations they faced. Aggressive aviators in U.S. tactical fighter squadrons and in long-range bomber units turned increasingly to fire bombs as a means of defeating Japanese army units in the field and destroying the industrial base of the Japanese homeland.

The effectiveness of the incendiaries employed was as varied as the targets, bombing techniques used, and skill of aircrews involved. The incendiaries proved most valuable when employed *en masse* by B-29 bombers attacking Japanese cities. The clouds of fire bombs dropped on the Japanese home islands wreaked havoc unequaled even by the atom bombs dropped on Hiroshima and Nagasaki.[1]

The awesome scenes of destruction that attended the wholesale fire bombing of Japan in 1945 were prefaced by a daring, if very minor air raid conducted almost three years before. The first U.S. incendiary bombs to fall upon Japan were dropped by planes under the command of Lieutenant Colonel James H. Doolittle. In an attempt to demonstrate America's ability to undertake some type of limited offensive action against the Japanese during the grim days of early 1942, the small group of B-25 bombers led by Doolittle struck at Tokyo, Kobe, Nagoya, and Yokohama on 18 April 1942. Along with high explosive bombs, Doolittle's force dropped clusters of M54 thermite incendiaries on carefully selected industrial targets. The M54, a stop-gap fire bomb in a steel case, had been designed to provide the U.S. and British air forces with a small incendiary until the new M50 magnesium-cased bombs could be produced in numbers. Although the damage done by this daring raid was mainly psychological, the first U.S. fire bombing served as a precursor of the mighty effort of 1945.[2]

The role of U.S. incendiary bombs in the Pacific was not restricted to massive strategic bombing assaults upon Japanese industry. Before U.S. heavy bombers began attacking Japan proper, Army and Marine fighter planes were using large numbers of fire bombs in tactical support of ground forces battling the Japanese army throughout the broad reaches of the Pacific. The experience gained by U.S. tactical air support units during 1944–1945 was valuable and long lasting. Tactical concepts and flame weapons were developed that would be used by the U.S. Air Force for the next thirty years in conflicts in Korea and Vietnam.[3]

FIRE BOMBS IN TACTICAL SUPPORT

Like their contemporaries in Europe, pilots in the Southwest and Central Pacific commands began experimenting with jellied gasoline in drop tanks early in 1944. In Hawaii, Colonel George F. Unmacht was instrumental in the early testing of expendable M4 75-gallon fuel tanks filled with napalm and gasoline. Unmacht, the driving force in flame thrower development in Hawaii, firmly believed that tactical aircraft could neutralize enemy positions by burning them, as was already being done with flame throwers. He also maintained that the job could be done more effectively by an aircraft carrying large amounts of napalm than by a man armed with a flame thrower.[4]

Colonel Unmacht, like Colonel Kellogg in England, was part soldier, part scientist, and part salesman. One of only ninety-two Regular Army officers in the CWS at the time of the Pearl Harbor attack, Unmacht had begun his long military career by enlisting in the Iowa National Guard in 1903. He secured a commission in the Corps of Engineers in 1912 and served overseas with the new CWS in World War I. Throughout World War II, he energetically directed the efforts of the young officers, most of whom were reservists, that comprised his staff in Hawaii. The knowledgeable career officer and his talented reservists and wartime volunteers formed a winning combination that consistently applied innovative procedures in problem solving.[5] He was determined that the CWS would make a contribution to the war effort despite the fact that its primary weapon, lethal gas, was not being employed.

Not content to rely strictly on Army support, Unmacht worked energetically with Navy and Marine air units based in Hawaii when Army air units were not available to test the fuel tank bombs and fuses that his staff was developing. The efforts of Unmacht and his staff led to the early standardization of the M4 napalm bomb in April 1944. The M4 bomb was simply a combination of the M4 external fuel pod equipped with a simple ignition mechanism. Despite its simplicity (or perhaps because of it), the

M4 proved to be a highly effective fire bomb that was favored by Marine Corps and Navy pilots.[6]

The new fire bomb, made of pressed paper and readily available to USAAF units throughout the Pacific, was authorized for use by the Seventh AF headquarters after tests showed that the tank could be dropped with acceptable accuracy on enemy targets. Having scored a success with the small bomb, the CWS team continued development. With Air Force assistance, larger wing tanks and belly pods were procured for test purposes. Some tanks, mostly 100- and 165-gallon sizes, were fitted with aluminum or plywood fins in an attempt to improve the aerodynamic characteristics of the experimental bombs. One such tank, a 165-gallon wing pod manufactured for use by the Lockheed P-38 fighter, could be given "... complete flight stability by the attachment of plywood fins...."[7]

The first combat test of tactical fire bombs in the Pacific came when Marine and Army fighters dropped M4 bombs in support of the invasion of Tinian, in the Marianas, on 24–30 July 1944. The aviators enthusiastically reported that the napalm had been most successful against Japanese trenches, foxholes, and when used to burn off dense vegetation concealing hidden gun positions. In their after-action reports, the aviators suggested an improved igniter and called for a larger fire bomb. Colonel Unmacht, after reading the reports, was anxious to subject the modified 165-gallon bomb to a combat test. He was able to do so when a request arrived from the Fifth AF supporting General MacArthur's forces in the fall of 1944.[8]

The large tanks were first used on 22 October 1944 by P-38s of the 12th Fighter Squadron. The target of the attack was a heavily defended Japanese oil storage area located at Boela, off the western tip of New Guinea. The U.S. aircraft swept over the Japanese defenses surrounding a fuel oil tank farm at low altitudes, dropping their 165-gallon fire bombs on trenches, motor parks, and gun installations. The fire that blanketed the enemy positions soon spread to fuel oil tanks ruptured by explosives. A massive conflagration followed, wiping out Japanese fuel supplies for the entire area.[9]

By the end of 1944, tactical fighter units in the Pacific had become increasingly able to provide close air support with fire bombs, similar to the type of support being given to U.S. ground forces fighting in the ETO. The Marine Corps, long a leader in close air support for its ground forces, again put air-delivered napalm to use during the assault on Iwo Jima in February 1945. Flights of Marine fighters, directed to their targets by forward air controllers on the ground, dropped M4 bombs as well as larger 100-gallon belly bombs on the entrenched Japanese. Although some problems with ignition were reported because of the soft volcanic sand in Iwo (bombs sometimes burrowed into the sand without detonating), the overall reports on fire bombs were good. A number of Marine Corps units cited the bombs in their after-action reports, stating that they often caused Japanese troops to break from cover in an attempt to evade the napalm blaze. Once in the open, the running enemy could be killed with small arms fire.[10]

The Army Air Force borrowed freely from the Marine Corps experience and showed an inventiveness of its own when, in March 1945, C-47 cargo aircraft "bombed" Japanese positions near Manila with 55-gallon drums of napalm-thickened gasoline. The large puddles that spread from the burst drums were ignited by fighter planes dropping M4 bombs. M69 napalm bombs, designed for use by long-range bombers, were also employed successfully by B-25 bombers attacking the bypassed Japanese stronghold of Truk. The USAAF bombers dropped their loads of M69 bombs on storage sheds, repair facilities, and barracks, creating major fires that defied Japanese firefighting efforts.[11]

The largest tactical fire bombing attack of the Pacific war took place in May 1945, near the vital Ipo Dam in the hills north of Manila. General MacArthur, fearing that retreating Japanese forces might destroy the dam which provided recently liberated Manila with its drinking water, ordered ground troops to seize the dam and the surrounding area as soon as possible. Should the Japanese deny water to the city, typhus, malaria, and a host of other ills were inevitable.

During the first two weeks of May 1945, the U.S. 38th and 43rd Infantry Divisions made little headway in a drive to clear the rugged area around the dam of enemy troops. With casualties mounting daily and attacks bogged down because of the mountainous terrain and dense undergrowth, ground commanders turned to the Fifth AF for assistance. A study of the Japanese-held area suggested that a large-scale fire bomb attack might help, even if it only succeeded in burning off the luxuriant vegetation that concealed the dug-in enemy positions. Fifth AF crews were assisted by the personnel of the Air Chemical Section operating at recently retaken Clark Field in preparing a number of napalm bombs for the mission. By 15 May, the ground personnel had made ready over 3,000 napalm bombs ranging in size from the 75-gallon M4 up to the 165-gallon wing tank bomb.[12]

The bombing of Ipo Dam lasted from 16 to 18 May. Between 200 and 250 Fifth AF fighters took part in each day's strikes. Selected enemy strongpoints were blanketed with napalm bombs dropped by the aircraft which flew over the target area in waves, four to eight airplanes abreast. The flights of planes were directed to their targets by forward air controllers on the ground and by others airborne in light spotter craft. After several waves of fighters had passed over, dropped their napalm, and departed, other aircraft arrived to bomb and strafe the Japanese running wildly about the area in an attempt to flee the flames burning large tracts of jungle. Following the three days of flame attacks, the infantry again took up their advance. The two divisions were able to mop up the area with only minimal casualties, moving into positions formerly held by the Japanese. In the words of the 38th Division commander, the GIs walked in "standing up." This success at Ipo Dam led to continued employment of napalm by the Fifth AF during the remaining battles in the Philippines. Napalm contributed to U.S. success at Mariquina, the Bosboso River, and during the assault on the village of Santa Fe.[13]

The last major employment of tactical fire bombs in the Pacific occurred as the Tenth Army, composed of two amphibious corps, one Army, one Marine, assaulted the Japanese bastion of Okinawa in the Ryukyus. During the period 19 April–12 June 1945, Army and Marine aircraft carried out numerous low-level napalm attacks against the suicidal defenders of the large island fortress. Often working in concert with ground troops employing portable and tank-mounted flame throwers, the planes swooped low to release their fire bombs in an attempt to burn out enemy troops in caves and pillboxes. On Okinawa, deep caves were successfully attacked by the expedient tactic of dropping napalm pods without igniters on enemy positions, giving the fuel a chance to dribble into air shafts and gun ports, then setting the fuel alight with a second strike of fire bombs. As in the past, napalm was lauded by ground commanders in their after-action reports. With the conquest of Okinawa completed, commanders of tactical fighter units conducted strenuous training with napalm bombs in anticipation of the scheduled invasion of the Japanese home islands. Those islands and their populace were even then reeling from the assault of U.S. strategic bombers armed with incendiary bombs, which were the product of the intensive efforts of American scientists and engineers.[14]

RESEARCH AND DEVELOPMENT: PAY-OFF IN THE PACIFIC

While CWS and USAAF personnel were testing makeshift fire bombs for tactical support use in the Pacific, teams of soldiers and civilians continued to improve incendiary bombs at bases in the continental United States. The work done by CWS and NDRC technicians resulted in marked improvements in the incendiary bombs and related equipment employed during the final assault on Japan by strategic bombers. The continued effort by the CWS in the incendiary field responded to the belated realization by the Army Air Force that incendiary munitions could materially enhance the bombing campaigns against Germany and Japan.

By mid-1943, the USAAF Plans and Operations Staff, A-3, had compiled a study entitled *Japan: Incendiary Attack Data*. Using procedures originally employed by the Royal Air Force, the Air Staff planners divided all major industrial areas of Japan into a number of subordinate target zones. Based on prewar photos and current intelligence, the staff further divided the zones into many fire divisions. Although the United States forces would not be in a position to bomb the Japanese home islands until air bases in China and in the Central Pacific were established, the long-range study provided a basis for an increase in incendiary bomb procurement for 1944 and 1945.[15]

After receiving a copy of the USAAF study, the Requirements Section of the CWS Combat Operations (Air) Staff ordered an increase in the tempo of incendiary bomb testing with the M69 napalm bomb. As noted earlier, the M69 had been little used during Eighth AF raids over Germany because of the bomb's low roof-penetrating ability. However, when employed in tests against Japanese-style structures, the 6.2-pound bomb did quite well. Prior to the U.S. attack upon Japan, this bomb was improved in several ways. Thanks to research conducted in the United States, bomber commanders overseas were provided not only with a highly destructive incendiary bomb, but also with sound doctrine in the form of instructions regarding the optimal means of employing this type of incendiary. Developmental work on the M69 and its heavier (10-lb) counterpart, the M74, took place at mock Japanese villages constructed at Eglin Field, Florida; Dugway Proving Ground, Utah; and Edgewood Arsenal, Maryland. Work began in 1942 and continued until the end of the war.

The research and development teams initially emphasized providing the M69 with improved flight characteristics. The first models of the small bomb, lacking any tail fins, tended to tumble end-over-end as they fell through the air. Early M69 bombs often failed to explode because the detonator was located in the nose cap of the bomb. If the cylindrical bomb landed on its side or tail there would be no ignition of its filler. This problem had caused the RAF to refuse the M69 when it was offered as lend-lease. The addition of small metal tail fins seemed to enhance stability of the M69 but this idea was discarded because the space required by fins materially reduced the number of bombs that could be packed in an M19 cluster. The stabilization problem was solved in 1943 when cloth streamers were attached to the tail of the bomb. When the bomb popped out of the M19 cluster, the streamer would deploy, much like a parachute. As the bomb fell earthward, the streamer created enough wind drag to keep the M69 in a nose-down attitude. Detonation on impact was thus assured and roof penetration was optimized.[16]

The M69 was designed so that the detonator (igniter) set off the main gelled-gasoline filler when the bomb hit a hard surface. As the filler ignited, burning napalm gel shot out of the tail of the bomb casing like the flame jet of a small flame thrower. Early models of the bomb could expel a flame jet for only about thirty meters, or until the stream hit an obstruction like a wall. NDRC scientists, after conducting numerous tests on nozzle design, were able to improve the M69 so that, by the time it was employed against Japanese buildings, each bomb could expel a stream of flame for 60–100 meters with sufficient force to penetrate lightly constructed buildings. Before the last missions were flown over Japan, the efforts of technicians in the U.S. had resulted in the M69X, a napalm bomb that not only shot fire, but exploded as well, thus turning the casing of the bomb into shrapnel that could disrupt fire fighting efforts in the target area.[17]

The 10-pound M74 incendiary bomb grew out of the research already conducted on the M69. Using essentially the same bomb casing, CWS engineers were able to increase the amount of incendiary filling carried in each bomb by eliminating the cloth streamers from the bomb's tail. The M74 was provided with an "all-ways" fuse at each end so that it would ignite regardless of whether it landed up, down, or sideways. M74 bombs began reaching the Pacific just as the strategic bombing campaign against Japan began and by the end of that campaign were being used as often as M69 bombs.[18]

Although small incendiary bombs in clusters would account for most of the incendiary tonnage dropped on Japan, the USAAF also conducted experiments with improved versions of the older M47 napalm bomb and the 500-pound M76 napalm "block-burner." Chemical warfare officers attached to the Seventh AF in Hawaii contributed to the improvements in larger napalm bombs when they devised a new toggling system that allowed ground crews to hang six of the 69-pound M47s from each bombing station in a B-29. These large bombs were used by pathfinder aircraft to mark the boundaries of the target areas with large fires, and they contributed to the general blaze that ensued after the main body of bombers dropped small incendiaries in great numbers.[19]

Not nearly as successful as the M47 was an idea advanced by Dr. Louis F. Fieser, the developer of napalm. Intrigued by the proclivity of bats to seek roosting sites in dark places, Dr. Fieser suggested, in 1943, that the CWS develop tiny incendiary time bombs that could be attached to bats. The captive bats would then be flown in long-range bombers to areas over Japan and released. In their search for dark havens, the bats would carry their little fire bombs into Japanese buildings. After a set time, the bombs would ignite, thus starting many small fires in the highly flammable Japanese cities.

For eighteen months, Mexican laborers trapped bats in the deep caverns near Carlsbad, New Mexico, to provide test animals for Army, Navy, and Marine scientists, who had developed tiny incendiary time bombs that were attached to the bats with surgical clips. In spite of a number of failures in test drops of bats from Army bombers, the program continued until almost V-J Day, when the bat bomb joined incendiary leaves and aeroflame in the "Not Adopted for Operational Use" file at Edgewood Arsenal.[20] Despite some time-consuming tangential ventures in the R&D field, the CWS, NDRC, and USAAF enjoyed significant success in developing the weapons needed to unleash a massive blow upon Japan. With weapons and crews available to fly from hard-won air bases on Pacific islands, the scene was set for what proved to be the last chapter of the war in the Pacific. By late 1944, Japan faced the beginning of the end.

THE LAST CHAPTER: JAPAN IS BURNED

"After the first B-29 raid with fire bombs, fear [among the Japanese] became so great that workers began remaining at home merely because they were afraid to be caught in war plants when another raid might strike."[21]

Swiss Red Cross Official
Nagoya, Japan—1945

The strategic assault against Japan would be led by long-range aircraft striking at Japanese factories, as U.S. submarines destroyed much of the raw material needed to feed the factories while it was still at sea, en route to the home islands. To ensure that the strategic air assault would receive the attention and support required, the commanding general of the Army Air Forces directed that a new strategic air force be created. The Twentieth AF, composed of the 20th and 21st Bomber Commands [B.C.s], was established on 1 March 1944 for the sole purpose of orchestrating the all-out air offensive. Under the direction of General Henry H. Arnold, who would act as an "executive agent" from his seat in USAAF headquarters, the Twentieth AF was equipped with the new B-29 bomber and was to strike at Japan from bases in China and on Pacific islands.

Long-range plans called for the two bomber commands to employ daylight precision bombing techniques that had been practiced in Europe. The 20th B.C., after staging through India, began operating from bases in China early in 1944. While the crews became accustomed to the VLR (very long range) B-29, the 20th B.C. conducted a number of shakedown operations, bombing targets in Formosa, Burma, and Malaya. Most missions were flown with H.E. bombs, but there was some experimentation with incendiaries. Colonel Curtis LeMay, the commander of the 20th B.C., urged the employment of incendiaries and personally led several incendiary strikes over Formosa. By the end of 1944, the other operational unit of the Twentieth AF, the 21st B.C., was flying missions from recently captured air fields on Saipan, Tinian, and Guam.[22]

The island-based 21st B.C. was composed of three B-29 Wings: the 73rd, 313th, and 314th. The wings were supported by a host of ground elements, to include a CWS service company, a unit which would work around the clock when the 21st B.C. began incendiary raids against Japan. Brigadier General Haywood S. ("Possum") Hansell commanded the great collection of airpower. Hansell, a veteran of bomber operations in the ETO and one of General Arnold's most brilliant planners on the USAAF staff, insisted that his bomber units follow precision bombing procedures so laboriously developed by the Eighth AF during 1943–1944. His devotion to strict formation flying and high-level daylight bombing conformed to the view held by the majority of the bomber commanders of the time. He was determined to "make the system work." Hansell's adherence to the accepted doctrine would prove to be his undoing.

Bombing missions conducted during November, December, and early January were not very successful. Post-strike analysis revealed that industrial targets bombed by the B-29s, which flew in formation at altitudes up to 30,000 feet, were not being destroyed. High winds and cloud cover over targets blew bombs off course and denied bombardiers clear sightings of aiming points. Formation flight creates a heavy drain on fuel and the extended ranges over which the B-29s were operating took their toll, and a number of aircraft were forced down in the ocean from lack of fuel when returning from missions. Although the American press was reporting favorably on the B-29 campaign, staff members of the USAAF headquarters knew better and began to urge a change in bombing tactics and, perhaps, of commanders.

Convinced that Japan was especially vulnerable to fire damage, members of General Arnold's staff urged Hansell to begin large-scale incendiary raids. Citing the work done during the compilation of the study *Japan: Incendiary Attack Data*, messages from Washington ceased to suggest and began to direct the use of incendiaries, at least on a trial basis, by December 1944. In response to these orders, Hansell staged several incendiary raids, using M69 and M47 napalm incendiaries. Generally, results of these raids were not encouraging. Bombing was conducted from high altitudes with the result that the M19 clusters of incendiaries spilled their contents into turbulent winds high above the designated target zones. The small bombs blew off course and failed to ignite any major fires.

Hansell returned to precision bombing with H.E. in late December. His targets for January were aircraft production sites, assembly plants, and military installations. Determined to prove his point, Hansell directed his wing commanders to apply maximum effort toward striking their primary targets for each mission. Except for an occasional successful mission, the results continued to be mediocre, at best. Despite the B-29's many improvements in bomb capacity, flight stability, and range, the efforts of the Twentieth AF as a whole were not pleasing to General Arnold. Especially galling was the failure of the 21st B.C.[23]

For General Hansell, as it has for many other commanders throughout history, the lack of tangible proof of success meant the end of the road. On 20 January 1945 he was relieved of command. His replacement was a newly minted brigadier from the 20th B.C. in China, Hansell's personal friend Curtis LeMay.[24]

Initially, LeMay continued to follow Hansell's policies regarding daylight bombing; but the new commander also directed his staff to analyze the failure of the bombing campaign. After a series of modifications in the standard high-level techniques had failed to materially enhance the unit's success, LeMay largely took matters into his own hands. Displaying considerable fortitude, he scrapped all of the battle-tested formulas for success and announced a totally different procedure for bombing Japan.

The new tactics, which would prove to be so successful, called for an end to fuel-consuming formation flying. Individual aircraft would take off, fly to the target, bomb, and return under loose control. Instead of bombing during daylight at 20,000 feet, the B-29s would go in at night, flying as low as 5,000 feet. To increase the bomb tonnage carried by each plane, LeMay ordered the big bombers stripped of much of their armor and nearly all the weapons mounted in turrets which studded the B-29. The weight saved would be devoted to increased bomb loads. Lastly, the overwhelming majority of the bombs carried by the B-29s would be incendiaries: M69, M47, and the large M76 "block burners."[25]

LeMay's decision to employ incendiaries came about as a result of his past experience with them in the ETO and in China. He realized that, unlike many of the large German industrial targets, much of the Japanese industrial base had been dispersed throughout a number of major cities. By 1944, military equipment, weaponry, and a host of related items needed by Japanese forces were being manufactured in small shops located in residential areas. This system, so reminiscent of nineteenth-century European "cottage industry," was obviously designed to disperse the operations of a single manufacturer over a large area.

The Japanese system of fragmenting and dispersing their war industry had worked well while the Americans were attempting to bomb single sites from high altitudes with conventional bomb techniques. However, if a Japanese city were subjected to area bombing tactics with incendiaries, the small industrial shops would become quite vulnerable. Although a fair percentage of Japanese manufacturing was carried out in modern, fire-resistant buildings, a great part of the overall output depended upon the small "feeder" stations, which were installed in flimsy wood and paper shops identical to the surrounding residences. Spurred by pressure from Twentieth AF headquarters in Washington, LeMay concluded that to neutralize enemy industry, the 21st B.C. would have to destroy the Japanese cities.[26]

During the first week of March 1945, small groups of 21st B.C. aircraft tested LeMay's concept against carefully selected targets in Japan. The results, while not spectacular, were encouraging. LeMay determined to give low-level incendiary bombing a full-scale test.

The 73rd and 314th Bomb Wings carried out the first large incendiary raid against Japan. The target was Tokyo. Taking off at sunset on 9 March 1945, the bomber force arrived over Tokyo just after midnight. Flying between 6,000 and 7,000 feet, the large, loose formations were not disturbed by the relatively few remaining Japanese interceptor aircraft. As the "sky train" of B-29s passed over the southern portion of Tokyo, over 1,665 tons of bombs, ninety percent of them incendiaries, landed among the flimsy dwellings and manufacturing sites below.[27]

The raging fires started by M69 bombs were fanned by winds which reached speeds of more than 100 mph as the thousands of flammable structures in each fire division began to explode into flame. A general conflagration ensued that was similar to the *Feuersturm* that had raged through Hamburg. The heat and wind, combined with exploding munitions dropped by the bombers, defied the ineffectual, if heroic, efforts of the Tokyo fire department. Some 15.8 square miles of buildings were burned to the ground.

The official CWS history describes in sanitized terms the effect of the attack upon the inhabitants of the area:

> Some people were able to escape through the wide fire lanes, but many others were encircled by the flames and died of suffocation and burns. Those who fled to the canals faced death in the scalding water [which often boiled from the heat] or were crushed by the terrified mob which crowded in on top of them. This raid alone caused the death of an estimated 83,793 people and almost 41,000 more received injuries. Over one million people lost their homes.[28]

Back at their island bases, members of the two bomb wings pored over aerial photos taken after the raid to analyze the damage and decide whether different tactics might be called for in raids scheduled on other Japanese targets. General LeMay directed that the bombs be spread over a larger area and that aircraft formations be more dispersed for the next mission. His decision was based on the conclusion that bombs had been wasted in the Tokyo strike when follow-on flights dropped incendiaries into an area already burning. As

LeMay's aviators readied themselves for the next mission, Japanese English-language radio announcers attested to the effectiveness of the first strike on Tokyo by denouncing the U.S. effort as "slaughter bombing."[29]

The second large incendiary mission took place when Nagoya was bombed on 11 March. In this fire raid, 1,790 tons of bombs were dropped and a great deal of smoke gave evidence of fire below as the bombers roared over the target zone. When post-strike photos were taken, however, the staff of the 21st B.C. on Guam could see that only 2.05 square miles had been destroyed. Unfortunately for the Americans, the widely dispersed bombing pattern ordered by LeMay had started many small fires, but these were too dispersed to join and form a large conflagration. In addition, few "appliance" fires had been started by M47 bombs. [Appliance fires were those of a magnitude calling for attention by firemen equipped with modern mechanized equipment.] The 21st B.C. staff decided that a tighter bombing pattern and more large incendiaries would be used on the next target. As always with incendiaries, trial-and-error seemed to be the major means of developing tactical practice from which doctrine grew.[30]

Osaka and Kobe were the next major cities to be bombed, on 13 and 16 March, with good results. On 19 March, the B-29s returned to Nagoya, destroying another 3.5 square miles of buildings in an area adjacent to the first target struck on 11 March. The efforts of the 21st B.C. were buttressed by bombers of the 20th B.C. in May 1945 when the B-29s were withdrawn from China because of supply problems and a surprisingly successful offensive by Japanese forces which captured several air bases being used by the 20th B.C. With the support of these additional forces, LeMay conducted seventeen maximum effort incendiary raids (and many smaller raids) prior to the explosion of the atomic bomb on 6 August 1945. During the seventeen major raids, 6,960 B-29 sorties were flown, carrying a total bomb tonnage of 41,592 tons. U.S. losses were low. For various reasons, 136 B-29s failed to return to base after missions, a figure which constituted a loss rate of only 1.9 percent.[31]

The effects of the incendiary bombing upon Japan were disastrous. Japanese officials reported that, in Tokyo alone, 87,538 persons had been killed and 60,079 wounded in raids that occurred prior to 25 May 1945. Statements by several highly placed Japanese officials attest to the effectiveness of the mass incendiary bombs. Prince Konoye said, "Fundamentally, the thing that brought about the determination to make peace was the prolonged fire bombing by the B-29s."[32]

As Japanese civilians mourned the loss of friends and family in the gutted cities visited by the fire-bombing B-29s, press releases in the United States hailed the accomplishments of LeMay's airmen. The tone of a *Time* magazine article represented that of a number of pieces dealing with the U.S. fire bombing of Japan:

> A dream came true last week for U.S. Army aviators: they got a chance to loose avalanches of fire bombs on Tokyo and Nagoya, and they proved that, properly kindled, Jap cities will burn like autumn leaves.[33]

The mood of the American public was anything but sympathetic toward the Japanese. In the words of Samuel R. Shaw:

> The ferocity of the Pacific fighting had already persuaded many, if not most, Americans that the most savage efforts were justified in order to reduce the [U.S.] casualties when faced with the fanatical conduct of the Japanese. What was known by early 1945 of the treatment of American prisoners and foreign noncombatants in the areas that had been recaptured also acted to dull any feelings of restraint that some [Americans] might have felt.[34]

Immediately after the Japanese surrender, members of the United States Strategic Bombing Survey staff began to analyze the effects of the strategic bombing of Japan. With regard to the overall effectiveness of the aerial offensive, the authors of one survey volume stated:

> It is the Survey's opinion that certainly prior to 31 December 1945, and in all probability prior to 1 November 1945, Japan would have surrendered even if Russia had not entered the war, and even if no invasion had been planned or contemplated.[35]

In light of the obvious effectiveness of the U.S. incendiary bombing of Japan, various historians have raised questions concerning the need for dropping two atom bombs on Japan. The simple question, "Could the United States have defeated Japan without the atom bomb?" has no simple answer. This book makes no attempt to address the many questions surrounding the employment of atomic bombs, but will offer the following statement of Secretary of War Henry L. Stimson. When asked, shortly after the war, why the United States had used the atom bomb instead of relying upon continued incendiary bombing, Stimson replied:

> Had the war continued until the projected invasion date of 1 November 1945, additional fire raids would have been more destructive of

life and property than the limited number of atomic raids which we
could have executed in the same time period.[36]

The second great world conflict finally ended with the signing of surrender terms on board the U.S.S. *Missouri* on 2 September 1945 as several hundred B-29s of the 21st B.C. droned overhead in a mighty display of U.S.
aerial strength. The Americans ruled Japan, the waters around it, and the
skies above for the foreseeable future. The role of incendiary weapons had
steadily grown during the war with Japan, and near the end of the struggle,
incendiaries had wrought massive damage upon the enemy. After beginning
the fight against the Axis with only one incendiary bomb in its arsenal, the
M47, the United States finished the war with the world's largest inventory of
flame weapons. Peace brought satisfaction in a "mission accomplished," but
also introduced great uncertainty about the future of the American armed
forces. What role would be played by the victorious services? Would there
ever be a need for flame weapons in the atomic age? The answer to these
questions lay in the future.

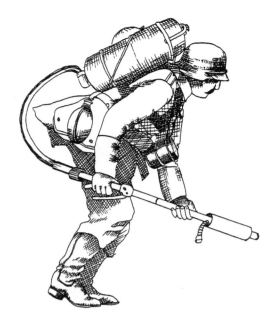

German Assault Engineer with Flame Thrower, circa 1916.

"BUNKER BUSTING," *WAR MONTHLY* 25 (APRIL 1976): 49

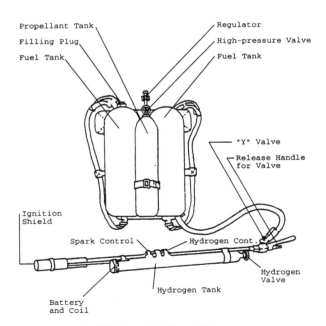

M1A1 Portable Flame Thrower.

LEONARD L. MCKINNEY, "PORTABLE FLAME THROWER OPERATIONS IN WORLD WAR II," CHEMICAL CORPS HISTORICAL STUDY NO. 4 (EDGEWOOD ARSENAL, MD.: HQ CHEMICAL CORPS, 1958), P. 57 (MIMEOGRAPHED)

British "Crocodile" Flame System Mounted on a Churchill Tank. USA

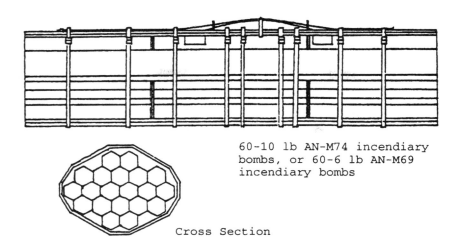

60-10 lb AN-M74 incendiary
bombs, or 60-6 lb AN-M69
incendiary bombs

Cross Section

Aimable Cluster (M19) for M69 Incendiary Bombs.

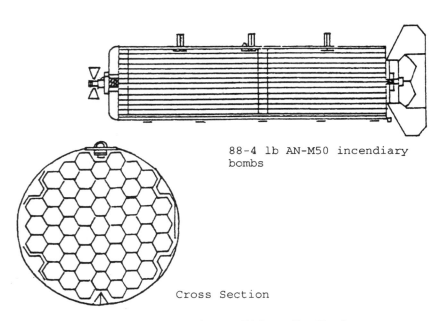

88-4 lb AN-M50 incendiary
bombs

Cross Section

Aimable Cluster (M17) for M50 Incendiary Bombs.

BOTH CLUSTER DEVICES SHOWN IN *JAPAN: INCENDIARY ATTACK DATA* (WASH., D.C.: ASST. CHIEF OF AIR STAFF,
INTELL. A-2, OCTOBER 1943), APPENDIX 7, PP. 6–8, FILE 425, 228.01, HC-EA

Loading M17 Clusters of AN-M50 Incendiary Bombs into a B-24 Bomber. USAF

Attaching a Napalm Fire Bomb to the Belly of a Ninth AF Fighter. USAF

U.S. Troops Train with M1A1 Flame Throwers at Camp McCoy, Wisconsin, 1943. USA

Soldier with Japanese Flame Thrower, Captured on Bougainville. USA

Marine with M1A1 Flame Thrower Surveys Japanese Victims of a Recent Flame
Attack. USMC

Japanese Soldier after Flame Attack. USMC

U.S. Infantryman Firing the M1A1 Flame Thrower on Saipan. USA

Soldier Firing a New M2-2 Flame Thrower on Luzon. USA

Flame Tank of the 713th Armored Flame Thrower Battalion. USA

Tank-Infantry Assault against Japanese on Okinawa. USA

A Marine F4U Corsair Drops Napalm on Japanese Position on Peleliu, 1944. USMC

Ground Crewmen with 165-Gallon Wing Pod Bomb— Note Tail Fin. USAF

Loading M-19 Aimable Clusters on Board a B-29 of the 21st B.C. USAF

Incendiary Clusters
and Fragmentation
Bombs in the Bomb
Bay of the B-29.
USAF

Marine with M2-2 Flame Thrower in Vietnam. USMC

Marine Flame Tank in Vietnam. USMC

Epilogue

Happy throngs danced exuberantly in New York City's Times Square when the final Japanese surrender was announced. The crowd felt not only unrestrained joy, but also unlimited confidence in the overwhelming might of the U.S. armed forces. This obvious reaction to the success of American arms obscured for most of the celebrants the unpleasant memories of 1942, when an Allied victory had not seemed assured. Few of the revelers were aware of how narrow the margin of victory had been in the early months of the American involvement or how much the armed forces owed to the extraordinary performance of the American industrial and academic communities during World War II. Without the prodigious contributions of a fully mobilized civilian sector and almost unlimited financial support, the armed forces would not have overcome their prewar unpreparedness in time to have an effect.

All over the United States, households were welcoming home returning servicemen who were anxious to get on with their lives. So eager were the victors to put the war behind them that a very real danger existed of forgetting the woeful unpreparedness of the United States in the years before World War II. The United States was running the risk of repeating military problems and failures as the rapidly demobilizing forces grew smaller and less capable after 1945.

One of the most basic missions of the military in peacetime is to assume the eventual resurgence of conflict and to plan for American involvement. Military planning staffs in the shrunken, postwar U.S. armed forces did not simply concentrate upon the war just completed, but also looked to the future during the late 1940s. Questions concerning the kinds of weapons that might be required in some future conflict continually arose, and were addressed by those who largely based their assumptions about coming wars on information gleaned during previous experience. The age of computer-based simulations, virtual reality, and sophisticated force structure analyses had not yet arrived. Unable to test positive policies, the staff planners were often forced to define success as "not making the same mistake again."

In grappling with questions about weapons and doctrine development, the staff officers of the postwar Army and newly created Air Force would have done well to review the history of flame weapons as a "case study" of reactive development. There, for them to see, was a record of short-sightedness, financial restraints, lack of doctrinal concepts, interservice rivalries, and moral questions pertaining to the flame weapons eventually employed by the United States during World War II.[1]

Reviewing the short history of U.S. flame weapons, the postwar researcher would have found little to suggest that, prior to 1940, the U.S. Army had ever seriously considered the use of flame weapons despite the fact that such weapons had been introduced during World War I. Although the Chemical Warfare Service had been charged with developing incendiary weapons as part of its charter in 1920, the tiny CWS *never* did so until years after World War I ended. With the development of toxic gasses as its primary mission, the CWS *never* initiated tests of flame throwers or incendiary bombs because of financial constraints and the perception of many CWS officers that the incendiary weapons were little more than "horror" devices. The proclivities of the very influential first commander of the CWS, General Fries, also militated in favor of gas research to the exclusion of flame. Looking further, one notes that no demand for flame weapons of any type was forthcoming from the combat branches of the Army during peacetime, although the chiefs of these branches must surely have known that European armies continued to test and improve their flame weapons. Why had not the desirability of at least a limited research and development program been recognized?[2]

Herein lies the primary failing of the U.S. Army in the field of weapons and doctrine development prior to World War II. Small, fragmented, financially strapped, the Army struggled to pay its bills and to keep old equipment functioning. In addition to its financial woes, the Army sorely lacked an adequate system for identifying future requirements for weapons and the doctrine needed to guide the employment of new weaponry. Depending almost entirely upon the military attachés for information regarding foreign developments in new weapons and ideas, the Army staff was only partially successful at collating information from overseas, disseminating this intelligence to the Army at large, testing new concepts in conjunction with the combat and service branches, or procuring new equipment to support operational testing. Worrisome, too, was the very basic question of whether *doctrine* should be devised to enhance innovative tactical *concepts,* or whether *tactics* ought to be modified to exploit *technological improvements* in weapons.[3]

These problems were not solved prior to World War II. During the war, the dilemma was ameliorated by the infusion of vast sums of money into the business of weapons development. To a large extent, the Army could afford the luxury during the war years of evading the painstaking task of carefully analyzing different weapons to select the best from among a few test prototypes. Thanks to enormously swollen budgets, the Army was able to buy large numbers of many different models of a particular weapon, test them all, then discard as scrap those which did not meet hastily conceived standards. The problem of identifying, resourcing, and developing the weapons and doctrine needed for future conflicts is still with us, of course, and the U.S. military finds itself facing many of the same types of constraints that operated prior to World War II.[4]

Although clearly not as critical to prewar development as the lack of an integrated Army-wide system for analyzing future weapons requirements, the moral aversion Americans felt toward flame weapons also had a negative impact. The Geneva Protocol of 1925 attempted to outlaw all those weapons which, if used, would cause unnecessary suffering to their victims. Although the United States Government did not ratify this treaty, it supported the Protocol in principle. Only when the German army and air force began to use flame weapons after September 1939 did the Engineers, Armored Force, and Air Corps express serious interest in incendiaries. Had the Germans not utilized flame weapons, there is little reason to believe that the Allies would have initiated the first use of flame. Fire, like poison gas, would have remained a weapon threatened as a retaliatory measure.[5]

Although there were a few scattered protests over the use of flame throwers by American troops during the war, the public seems to have generally supported any measure that was capable of ensuring success over the enemy (with the exception of toxic gas). By the end of the war, troops displayed a casual disregard for life that characterizes the attitudes of those who have seen a great deal of violent death. Only *after* the war did some U.S. fighting men begin to question the employment of incendiary weapons. Most of the veterans interviewed for this study considered flame weapons of all types to be necessary implements of modern warfare, especially those who had fought against often fanatical Japanese defenses.[6]

Peacetime military planners of the postwar Army might well have wondered why it took the United States more than three years to field a variety of fairly effective flame weapons after the decision was made to develop such weapons. Why was it that the flame thrower and aerial incendiary found such widespread acceptance in the Pacific Theater, but only comparatively minor use by U.S. forces fighting in Europe? Need it take almost four years to acquaint combat troops with the potential value of such a specialized type of weapon? Questions like these challenge today's military leaders, who must anticipate requirements for a wide range of military operations. Military forces are regularly committed to peace support operations (peacemaking or peacekeeping), disaster relief, and regionalized combat. United States forces being deployed to other parts of the globe must expect to attend a "come as you are" affair. These questions are all the more immediate today as the United States can no longer depend on a prolonged period in which to build up its war-fighting strength.[7]

The answers to the questions posed in the previous paragraphs may be found not only in the shortcomings of the prewar Army, but in the fragmented structure of the greatly enlarged Army that fought World War II. During that great conflict, the Chemical Warfare Service, one part of the vast support force known as the Army Service Forces, was required to serve several masters. CWS officers, especially those stationed in overseas areas, were expected to send reports of their activities to the Chief of the CWS. These CWS officers also served on the staffs of overseas commanders as the resident chemical officers, and as such were responsible to the combat commanders. In order to requisition supplies, the CWS had to apply through Army Service Forces, CWS, and sometimes Ordnance Department channels.

Some CWS officers, thanks largely to personal zeal, were able to persuade their field commanders to devote scarce combat assets to the business of testing CWS incendiary weapons. However, the majority of CWS officers overseas found it difficult to overcome the prewar prejudices or ignorance of commanders with regard to flame weapons. One has only to read the reports sent from various field commands by CWS personnel to sense the frustration felt by many of these technicians on battle fronts around the world. The delay in flame employment can be blamed in part, then, on defective organizational concepts that often cut across service and branch boundaries.[8]

In addition to organizational deficiencies, the Army was hamstrung by its own doctrine. The devotion of the Army Air Forces to high-level, pinpoint bombing with High Explosive bombs serves admirably as an example. In spite of persuasive British arguments in favor of incendiary bombing raids, only a few commanders in the U.S. Eighth AF were willing to devote bomb-bay space to incendiary bombs prior to 1944. Determined to make their prewar doctrine of high-level bombing work, the majority of U.S. heavy bomber commanders followed practices established prior to Pearl Harbor until finally convinced of the destructiveness of incendiary bombs.[9]

The Armored Force, like the USAAF, was opposed to flame weapons on tanks because the flame weapons might reduce or eliminate the tank's ability to engage other tanks. The history of failure that attends CWS attempts to devise an efficient flame thrower for tanks must be attributed in the main to a lack of support by the U.S. tank forces in Europe. In the European Theater, only the British and the Russians used vehicle-mounted flame throwers effectively, demonstrating the value of their prewar interest in flame weapons.[10]

In the Pacific, however, the various branches of the services overcame their differences and worked together to promote flame weapon development and employment. In Pacific ground combat, the flame thrower was frequently regarded as the most valuable weapon on the field. When, in the closing chapter of the Pacific War, U.S. bombers abandoned precision bombing in favor of large-scale attacks against Japanese population centers, incendiary bombs were employed with telling effect. The incendiary bombing of Japan was described by the Japanese as "slaughter bombing." It was, in fact, just that. By 1945, the belligerents largely abandoned most of the restraints that had previously served to limit destruction of civilian life and property in wartime.[11]

Once it determined to bring fire to the enemy population, the United States did so with all the might inherent in its widely diversified and tremendously expanded military and industrial systems. As noted in one official history of the CWS, incendiary weapons had become, by the last year of the war, the most important part of the CWS arsenal.

> More time, manpower, and money were expended on flame throwers and allied developments than in any other field of chemical warfare with the single exception of incendiary bombs.[12]

The United States ended the war with a great number of new and improved incendiary weapons still in the planning stages or already in production. With the coming of peace, production was halted and the weapons on hand were stored for future use or sold for scrap. Despite the demonstrated effectiveness of flame weapons, the U.S. would make no effort to improve the weapons already developed until the Korean emergency created a need, once again, for flame warfare.

FLAME WEAPONS IN THE POSTWAR WORLD: FROM KOREA TO KUWAIT

Most of the flame weapons used in this United Nations–sanctioned "police action" aimed at ejecting the North Koreans and their Chinese allies from the Republic of [South] Korea were supplied by the United States. World War II vintage incendiary bombs and flame throwers were taken out of storage and used by the United States forces and their UN associates throughout the three years of combat. Tactics varied little from those employed during the last year of fighting in the Pacific, and proved to be successful in assaulting dug-in Communist troops. Navy and Marine fighters aggressively employed napalm and the Air Force used incendiary munitions with telling effect against manufacturing sites in North Korea.[13]

The continued successful use of those flame weapons already on hand during the Korean War and limited budgets for the development of conventional weapons in the next ten years discouraged development of newer fire weapons, and the United States would still be utilizing World War II technology when it became involved in its long struggle in Vietnam.

When Marine Corps units landed at Da Nang in 1965, they took portable and tank-mounted flame throwers with them. One of the initial Army units to deploy to Vietnam, the 1st Infantry Division, was subsequently equipped with a small number of M113 personnel carriers on which flame throwers were mounted. In the Mekong Delta, the Navy employed flame throwers mounted upon armored, shallow draft boats manned by the Riverine Force. Despite some successful use of flame throwers, the heat, humidity, and inhospitable terrain with which ground forces had to contend discouraged their widespread use. As the equipment failed, it was usually not replaced. Instead, the commanders of ground units relied upon tactical air support dropping napalm to destroy enemy forces with which they were engaged.[14]

The ability of the Air Force to accomplish this mission represented acquired skill. Unlike the Marines, the Air Force had not emphasized close air support of ground troops and had to learn these techniques during the air advisory effort of the early 1960s when U.S. airmen coached Vietnamese fliers during Operation FARM GATE. The effective use of napalm against ground targets in heavily wooded terrain required not only trained aircrews but knowledgeable controllers on the ground or aloft in light planes. The use of napalm was criticized by the foreign press ("... American napalm [is] one of the most cruel and barbarious weapons. This is graphically confirmed in its war against Korea (32,000 tons) and in Southeast Asia (500,000 tons) ...") and by antiwar activists in the United States. But for troops in contact, it was highly regarded not only for its casualty-producing effects, but because it burned away vegetation concealing enemy positions.[15]

The Vietnam War saw the last tactical employment of napalm by the United States until January 1991. Then, Marine airmen tapped stocks of obsolescent incendigel bombs in order to fly several missions during the Gulf War. Their target? Iraqi forces that threatened to ignite oil-filled trenches to defeat U.S. ground attacks. Just as today's "smart bombs" have replaced iron bombs for the destruction of precision targets, so have sophisticated antipersonnel, Fuel-Air Explosives, and armor-defeating munitions replaced napalm as the first choice to aircrews charged with the elimination of enemy ground forces. The U.S. armed forces still maintain the capacity to employ flame weapons effectively if called upon to do so. [The Army, in fact, still has a four-shot launcher filled with encapsulated flame gel projectiles.][16]

While the United States retains a limited stock of flame weapons, fire warfare, in and of itself, certainly provides no guarantee of future victory. If this history of U.S. flame weapons of World War II underscores one critical theme, it is the need to anticipate potential requirements for weapons and tactics in future conflicts.

LOOKING TO THE FUTURE

In many ways, today's U.S. military planners are faced with the same *types* of questions regarding weaponry that bedeviled the peacetime Army staff prior to World War II. To understand why the United States did not enter World War II properly equipped with incendiaries, one needs to appreciate the kind of "informed stargazing" required of military staffs. As one scholar who has addressed the problem of weapons development in peacetime puts it:

> ... the pace of development of any weapon during the between-war years is chiefly determined by the extent to which its mission or operational function is known and defined. When there is no effective system for determining doctrine, the pace of development is necessarily slow.[17]

The critical need for doctrinal guidance is recognized by most of the world's military forces, but especially by the United States. One useful paper written by the Army General Staff states:

> Joint and Army doctrine are the driving forces that determine how the Army organizes, trains, and equips its forces. When we rethink our warfighting doctrine, we influence directly our training, leader development, force design, and equipment acquisition programs. Doctrine bridges intellectual, physical, and technological change. It synthesizes and harmonizes our ideas about future war and links the institution to individual Army soldiers and leaders, helping them to understand the nature and reasons for the changes that are taking place around them. The Army invests heavily to ensure that the different arms, services, skills, and specialties understand the environment in which their efforts make the difference between success and failure in battle. Doctrine is the medium through which this

sense of belonging is conveyed and enforced. Our doctrine and our professional ethic help us to contain and control the simultaneous and contradictory requirements for continuity of purpose, growth, and change.[18]

Current Army leaders are taking advantage of lessons that can be gleaned from history. There are many references made today to paradigm shifts that are taking place. With the end of the bipolar cold war conflict, much of the doctrine that shaped American military forces for the forty years that followed World War II is under review. A number of similarities exist between today's inquiry and the dynamic changes wrought in U.S. forces on the eve of their entry into the Second World War. Just as General George C. Marshall conducted maneuvers on a scale never before experienced by the U.S. Army in order to facilitate the exploration of new ideas and to test new equipment, the Army again conducted a conceptual version of the "Louisiana Maneuvers" during the period 1991–1995 to establish a climate in which positive change could take place.

Given the speed at which the world itself is changing, there is a growing realization among U.S. military leaders that the services must "change the way they change." The intent of the Louisiana Maneuvers (LAM) of the early 1990s was to sustain the force—to energize and guide the intellectual and physical change in the Army—while simultaneously preparing for a host of possible contingencies. The LAM served as a laboratory for thinking about professional responsibilities to the nation, for practicing roles and missions, for developing and exploring options, and for assessing and directing progress. By harnessing the power of the microprocessor and stretching the state of the art in computer-supported simulations, the Army hopes to focus its assessment of its institutional effectiveness, provide direction for change, and orient key leaders on the accomplishment of critical missions with the resources available. As stated in a recent official publication: "How the Army manages change is as important as change itself in meeting the challenges of the new century." The process by which the Army will modernize its forces to take full advantage of the information age is referred to as "Force XXI." The Army is determined to look beyond the next decade, to lay the groundwork for "the Army After Next."[19]

Principal support for this effort is coming from the Army's Training and Doctrine Command, which has instituted a number of "Battle Laboratories" at service schools to consider the future role of advanced technology, weapons, organizations, and soldiers in the twenty-first century.[20]

The menace of weapons in the hands of unstable powers, questions about future roles of conventional air, land, and sea forces, and the rapidly growing power of the emerging states all provide serious questions for those charged with weapons and doctrine development. Faced by the probability of great destruction in the event of a nuclear attack, and awed by the immense historical account of man's ability to apply lethal weapons, we might conceivably forsake warfare as a means of settling international arguments. International bodies like the United Nations may develop genuine authority. General Douglas MacArthur's prophecy may yet come true: "Sooner or later, if civilization is to survive, . . . war must go."[21]

But we know that the world remains a heavily armed and dangerous place, with battles between national, ethnic, and supranational forces abounding. Strategists regularly revise their estimates of the scale and intensity of present and anticipated conflicts. Those who have been placed in positions of authority and trust must continue to examine history for insights that can assist them in avoiding the dangers that beset them.

If, by reading this history of the development of organizations, weapons, and doctrine under the press of wartime necessity, modern leaders are able to recognize similarities between the past and our present state, they may be better prepared to provide the direction so critical to our nation and to the world. Lacking this direction, we may, once again, have to meet our own trial by fire.

APPENDIX I

Flame Throwers of World War II*

TYPE	NOTES
Germany	
Flammenwerfer (FlaW) Model 35, portable	Weight—79 lb; Range—30 meters; Fuel Capacity—2 gal (Hereafter: W; R; FC)
FlaW M42, portable	W—40 lb; R—35 meters; FC—7.5 gal
Einstoss FlaW (Abn)	W—24 lb; R—32 meters; FC—4 gal
Panzerkampfwagen (PzKw) Mk. II	R—40 meters; FC—200 gal; mounted on fenders, two small nozzles (Sd. Kfz. 122)
PzKw Mk. III	R—60 meters; FC—225 gal; mounted in main turret (Model L)
Sd. Kfz. 251	R—45 meters; FC—100 gal; mounted in half-track
Japan	
Type E, portable	W—31 lb; R—35 meters; FC—3.5 gal
Type 96, M1936	R—45 meters; FC—128 gal; five flame throwers mounted in open turret
Type 98, M1943	R—UnK; FC—140 gal; six flame throwers mounted three to a side
United Kingdom	
Lifebouy, portable	W—82 lb; R—36 meters; FC—6 gal; an improved version of the WWI weapon

---

* The information contained in Appendix I is drawn from Malvern Lumsden, *Incendiary Weapons* (Cambridge, Mass.: M.I.T. Press, 1975), pp. 74–80; and from *TM-E 30–451, Handbook on German Military Forces* (Wash., D.C.: GPO, 1945), pp. VIII 88–VIII 91.

TYPE	NOTES
United Kingdom, cont.	
Akpak, portable	W—80 lb; R—36 meters; FC—5.5 gal
Ronson, mechanized	R—45 meters; FC—65 gal; Canadian
Wasp, MK I, mech	R—90; FC—320 gal; mounted in Bren gun tracked carrier
Crocodile, Mk VII, mech	R—125/140 meters; FC—400 gal; fuel trailer behind Churchill tank
United States	
M1, portable	W—72 lb; R—15 meters; FC—5 gal
M1A1, portable	W—65 lb; R—45 meters; FC—5 gal; fired thickened fuel, improved M1
M2-2, portable	W—65 lb; R—45 meters; FC—5 gal; new ignition system
M3-4-3, auxiliary mech	R—75/100 meters; FC—50 gal; mounted in place of bow machine gun
POA/CWS mech	R—75/100 meters; FC—250 gal; flame gun replaced 75-mm main gun
Satan M3, mech	R—60/80 meters; FC—140 gal; USMC M3 light tank with Canadian Ronson FT
LVTA Ronson, mech	R—50/75 meters; FC—110 gal; Canadian Ronson mounted on amphibian tractor
USSR	
ROKS—2, portable	W—60 lb; R—35 meters; FC—3 gal
LPO, portable	W—55 lb; R—70 meters; FC—3.5 gal; fired thickened fuel, equipped with three disposable fuel cells, still in use
OT—34, mech	R—120 meters; FC—45 gal; mounted in a periscope mount on T-34 tank

APPENDIX II

Incendiary Bombs of World War II*

TYPE	NOTES
Germany	
1 kg *Elektron*	Magnesium case, thermite filler, improved version of WW I bomb
25 kg thermite	Steel-cased, thermite filler
50 kg, C-50, *sprenebrand*	H.E. component added to blow thermite bomblets away from point of impact
220 kg, C-500 *Flam*	TNT burster, thickened oil filler (thickener usually polystyrene)
ABB-500 cluster	500 kg cluster loaded with 440 1-kg magnesium/thermite bombs
Japan	
1 kg phosphorus	Tin-plated case, red phosphorus filler
60 kg	H.E./incendiary; picric acid and crepe rubber pellets
70 kg	Magnesium-cased; filler was oil and asphalt
United Kingdom	
INC-4 lb	250 grams of filler composed of gasoline thickened with aluminum soaps
I-30, Mk 1	3.5 liters of thickened gasoline and thermite
Lc-250 lb	Napalm or IM filler

---

* The information contained in Appendix II is drawn from Malvern Lumsden, *Incendiary Weapons* (Cambridge, Mass.: M.I.T. Press, 1975), pp. 74–80.

TYPE	NOTES
United Kingdom, cont.	
INC-4000 lb	Benzene and synthetic rubber filler
SBC 250 lb cluster	Loaded with 90 INC-4 incendiary bombs
United States	
M-47	Napalm or IM filler; weight 69 lb; four modifications; in use until 1969
M-50	4 lb; thermite/thermate in magnesium case
M-54	4 lb; thermite/thermate in steel case
M-69	6 lb; napalm/IM filler, phosphorus igniter
M-69X	Same as above with an explosive charge added
M-74	10 lb; M-69 case without tail streamers; napalm/IM filler; two igniters
M-76	500 lb; napalm filler
M-17 cluster	500 lb; filled with M-50 bombs
M-19 cluster	500 lb; filled with M-69 or M-74 bombs
USSR	
ZAB 100 CK	100 kg; thermite
ZAB 300-100 TS	300 kg; loaded with balls of compressed thermite

Notes

INTRODUCTION

1. Fourth Marine Division D-3 Periodic Report No. 57, 2 Mar. 45, cited in 4th Mar-Div After Action Report [AAR] on Iwo Jima Operation, Record Group 127, National Archives (hereafter shown as RG 127, N.A.). See also George W. Garand and Truman R. Strobridge, *Western Pacific Operations*, vol. 4 of the *History of U.S. Marine Corps Operations in World War II* (Wash., D.C.: Government Printing Office [hereafter shown as GPO], 1971), for reports of USMC operations on Iwo Jima.

2. Richard J. Wheeler, "The 'First' Flag-Raising on Iwo Jima," *American Heritage* 15, no. 4 (June 1964): 103.

3. The Marines employed not only man-packed flame throwers, but tank-mounted flame throwers as well. Marine commanders were very enthusiastic about the performance of the armored flame throwers and called for many more, as they materially reduced the heavy casualties generally suffered by flame thrower operators on foot. See 5th MarDiv AAR, Iwo Jima, vol. 2, p. 731, RG 127, N.A. Napalm bombs, dropped by Marine fighters, were also used on Iwo Jima. See Wesley F. Craven and James I. Cate, eds., *The Pacific: MATTERHORN to Nagasaki, June 1944 to August 1945* (Chicago: Univ. of Chicago Press, 1953), pp. 352–54.

4. For background on the Dresden attacks, refer to David J. C. Irving, *The Destruction of Dresden* (New York: Holt, Rinehart, and Winston, 1964), chap. 1. Also, see Wesley F. Craven and James L. Cate, eds., *Europe: ARGUMENT to V-E Day, January 1944–May 1945* (Chicago: Univ. of Chicago Press, 1951), pp. 725–27; and Alexander McKee, *Dresden, 1945: The Devil's Tinderbox* (New York: E. P. Dutton, 1982). An unpublished study completed by a student at the U.S. Army War College concludes that the Allied bombing of Dresden was the application of weapons of mass destruction by a combatant bereft of concerns over civilian casualties. See Richard A. Conroy, "Operation THUNDERCLAP: The Bombing of Dresden" (Carlisle, Pa.: USAWC, 1989), pp. 35–40.

5. *Effectiveness of Third Phase Air Operations in the European Theater* (U.S. Army Air Forces Evaluation Board in the ETO, August 1945), pp. 230–56 and 314–18, File No. 168.7045–52, Albert F. Simpson Historical Center (hereafter shown as AFSHC.) Also, "Monthly Chemical Warfare and Activity Reports," Eighth Air

Force Chemical Section, 1 July 1944–30 June 1945, Inclosures 28, 29, and 32, AFSHC, File 730.85.

6. At Dresden, as it had in other target cities, the bombing accuracy fell victim to "creep back" which occurred when succeeding waves of bombers dropped their loads early, thus spreading the bomb carpet back along the approach route to the designated target. For a discussion on the problems of accuracy in bombing large targets, see Charles Webster and Noble Frankland, *Victory*, vol. 5 of *The Strategic Air Offensive Against Germany, 1939–1945* (London: Her Majesty's Stationery Office, 1961), pp. 4, 19, 19n, 130–32.

7. A recent study of the RAF's use of incendiaries is found in Stephen A. Garret's book, *Ethics and Airpower in World War II: The British Bombing of German Cities* (New York: St. Martin's Press, 1993).

8. See Irving, *Destruction of Dresden*, p. 9.

9. An excellent analysis of the effects of the various missions and locales in which flame weapons were employed can be found in the final chapter of Brooks E. Kleber and Dale Birdsell, *The Chemical Warfare Service: Chemicals in Combat* (Wash., D.C.: GPO, 1966), pp. 645–48.

10. General George C. Marshall, "Biennial Report of the Chief of Staff of the United States Army (July 1, 1943, to June 30, 1945) to the Secretary of War," GPO, 1945.

CHAPTER 1

1. Judges 13:20, 14:15; Jeremiah 23:29; Numbers 11:1, 16:35.

2. Judges 15:4–5.

3. Bernard Brodie and Fawn M. Brodie, *From Crossbow to H-Bomb*, 2d ed. (Bloomington, Ind.: The Indiana University Press, 1973), pp. 14–15. An excellent account of ancient flame weapons may be found in J. R. Partington, *A History of Greek Fire and Gunpowder* (Cambridge, England: W. Heffer, 1960), pp. 1–91.

4. Thucydides, *The History of the Peloponnesian War*, trans. Rex Warner (Middlesex, England: Penguin Books, Ltd., 1972), p. 325.

5. Augustin M. Prentiss, *Chemicals in War* (New York: McGraw Hill, 1937), p. 249.

6. Ibid. See also Brodie and Brodie, pp. 4–15.

7. Look to the *Encyclopedia Britannica*, 11th ed., new vol. 31, s.v. "Fireships" and "Greek Fire," for an encapsulated treatment of incendiaries in the ancient and medieval periods.

8. On fire ships, see Lynn Montross, *War Through the Ages* (New York: Harper & Bros., 1946), p. 334. Information on the Prussian flame device was extracted from an article by Charles Theune entitled "The Flame Thrower" in the German *Artilleristische Monatshafte* (Jan.–Feb. 1921). Translated by the Military Intelligence Division of the U.S. War Department, it is contained in the Records of the Chief, Chemical Warfare Service, RG 175, File #470.71/1164, N.A.

9. James M. Spaight, *Air Power and the Cities* (London: Longmans, Green, 1930), pp. 169–73. In 1854, Lord Dundonald argued that the use of flame-generated toxins in the Crimea would, in fact, be humane in that it would reduce casualties among French and British soldiers attacking Russian positions. The linkage here between toxic gasses and fire warfare is important in

light of the later rationale for the organization of chemical warfare branches in twentieth-century armies. Note: Dundonald never carried out the experiment, apparently feeling (quite properly) that he was being made the dupe by Palmerston.

10. Robert V. Bruce, *Lincoln and the Tools of War* (Indianapolis, Ind.: Bobbs-Merrill, 1956), pp. 171–73. Bruce reports that:

> ... Lincoln watched, while two thirteen-inch shells were exploded, each tossing fire forty or fifty feet in the air and carpeting the ground over a fifty-foot radius with a blaze that lasted ten minutes.

11. Ibid., pp. 237–42.
12. Bruce, in previous note 10, discusses the civilians' reaction in Charleston, S.C. The response of civilians to fire bombing during World War II is reported by Martin Caidin, *The Night Hamburg Died* (London: New English Library, 1966). The United States Strategic Bombing Surveys conducted after World War II cover not only physical damage to target cities, but civilian casualties as well. See USSBS Report No. 193, *Fire Raids on German Cities* (Wash., D.C.: GPO, 1947); USSBS Report No. 79, *The Effect of Strategic Bombing on German Morale* (Wash., D.C.: GPO, 1947). Also, USSBS Report No. 190, *Effects of Incendiary Bomb Attacks on Japan—A Report on Eight Cities* (Wash., D.C.: GPO, 1947).
13. Morris Greenspan, *The Modern Law of Land Warfare* (Berkeley: University of California Press, 1959), pp. 11–16.
14. "A Code for the Government of Armies in the Field, as Authorized by the Laws and Usages of War on Land, Printed as Manuscript for the Board Appointed by the Secretary of War [Special Orders, No. 399] To Propose Amendments or Changes In the Rules and Articles of War....," February 1863. Cited by Alex Roland, *Underwater Warfare in the Age of Sail* (Bloomington, Ind.: The Indiana University Press, 1978), p. 159.
15. Roland, *Underwater Warfare*, pp. 180–81.
16. Ibid., p. 182.
17. Alistair Horne, *The Fall of Paris* (New York: St. Martin's Press, 1965), pp. 391–94.
18. Greenspan, *Law of Land Warfare*, pp. 360–61. See also Malvern Lumsden, *Incendiary Weapons* (Cambridge, Mass.: M.I.T. Press, 1975), p. 20. Also published by the Stockholm International Peace Research Institute under the title *Napalm and Incendiary Weapons* (Stockholm: 1972).
19. Theodore Ropp, Duke Univ., Durham, N.C., letter to author, October 1978, p. 2.
20. This information on German development of the early-model flame throwers is taken from the previously cited article by Charles Theune entitled "The Flame Thrower," pp. 2–4.
21. Hermann Redemann was to command the German flame unit throughout the war. He rose to the rank of colonel. After the war, retired at his permanent grade of major, he conducted a running battle with the Chief of the U.S. Chemical Warfare Service over the value of the flame thrower.
22. Theune, p. 3.
23. A letter from Hermann Redemann to Brig. Gen. Amos A. Fries, the CWS Chief in the 1920s, provides a great deal of information about the German flame engineer troops. See Redemann to Fries, Records of the War Dept., General and Special Staffs, RG 165, MID #2612–64, N.A.

24. Brig. Gen. Sir James E. Edmonds, *History of the Great War, Military Operations, France and Belgium,* vol. 4, 1915 (London: Macmillan & Co., Ltd., 1928), cited by Henry Sorensen, "Flame Warfare," *Canadian Army Journal,* vol. 2, nos. 5&6 (Aug.–Sept. 1948), p. 31.

25. Ibid., p. 32.

26. Arthur B. Ray, "Incendiaries," Chemical Warfare Service Mongraph No. 43 (Wash., D.C.: Chemical Warfare Service, A.E.F., 1919), p. 13. The "thermite" listed as an ingredient in so many incendiary bombs of World Wars I and II was a mixture of finely ground aluminum or magnesium with oxygen-containing compounds. It did not need air to burn, since the oxygenated compounds in thermite would supply the oxygen needed for combustion. Temperatures of about 5,400 degrees were generated when this mixture was ignited by a detonator.

27. "Agents," bk. 2 of the course material, CWS School (Edgewood Arsenal, Md.: CWS, Dept. of Technique, 1925), pp. 55–60.

28. Ray, "Incendiaries," pp. 10, 24.

29. "Agents," pp. 58–59.

30. "Chemical Warfare Service Materials Used by the Air Service," *Chemical Warfare* 8 (January 1922): 2. This article in a service journal published by the fledgling U.S. Army Chemical Warfare Service drew nearly all of its material from official technical publications of the British and French air arms. At the time the article was published, the U.S. CWS did have some Mark III incendiary bombs in storage, but there was no plan to utilize them as incendiaries.

31. On the British effort in flame warfare during World War I, see Charles H. Foulkes, *Gas! The Story of the Special Brigade* (London: Wm. Blackwood & Sons, 1934), pp. 165–68. Also, Leo Finklestein, "Flame Throwers," pt. 1, pp. 14–15, in vol. 15 of the "History of Research and Development of the Chemical Warfare Service in World War II" (mimeographed), Historical Collection, Edgewood Arsenal, Md. It is filed in a voluminous collection of material that the CWS historians maintained on flame throwers during and after WWII (hereafter referred to as 314.7 File, HC-EA). Finally, look to Sorensen, above, pp. 32–33.

32. Finklestein, p. 14.

33. Alden S. Waitt, "Assault Troops Silence Pillboxes with Fire," *Popular Science Magazine* 141, No. 2 (Aug. 1942), p. 40.

34. Finklestein, p. 15.

35. Leonard L. McKinney, "Portable Flame Throwers in World War II," U.S. Army Chemical Corps Hist. Study no. 4 (Dec. 1958), p. 10 (mimeographed), CWS 314.7 File, HC-EA.

36. Finklestein, pp. 7–13.

37. Theune, pp. 4–6. See also Alden H. Waitt, *Gas Warfare* (New York: Duell, Sloane, and Pierce, 1942), p. 116.

38. The controversy over the effectiveness of the weapon and the danger to its operators will be discussed at some length in chap. 2. By 1917, all three armies (French, British, and German) conducted regular schools for flame thrower operators and emphasized combined arms teams in the assault.

39. Lt. Col. John M. Palmer, memo for the Chief of Staff, AEF, Subj.: Gas and Flame Service, Offensive and Defensive, 30 July 1917, in the "History of the Chemical Warfare Service, American Expeditionary Forces, General History, App. 2"

(unpublished official history). This document is retained by the Historian's Office, Aberdeen Proving Ground, Md.

40. General Order #8, AEF, 5 July 1917. *The United States Army in the World War: Bulletins*, HQ, AEF (Wash., D.C.: GPO, 1948), p. 23.

41. Brooks E. Kleber and Dale Birdsell, *The Chemical Warfare Service: Chemicals in Combat* (Wash., D.C.: GPO, 1966), p. 4. For a first-hand account of life in the 1st Gas Regiment, look to William L. Langer, *Gas and Flame in World War I* (New York: Knopf, 1965).

42. Bureau of Mines, Army Medical Department, Ordnance Department, Signal Corps, and Corps of Engineers.

43. The work done at American University during 1918 is recorded in a "Summary of the Development of Liquid Flame Projectors and Fuel at American University," *Pyrotechnics Monograph, Research Division, American University Experiment Station*, vol. 39 (Wash., D.C.: GPO, 1918), pp. 125–37.

44. McKinney, "Portable Flame Throwers . . . ," p. 11. Also, see Benedict Crowell, *America's Munitions* (Wash., D.C.: GPO, 1919), p. 220; and Finklestein, "Flame Throwers," p. 17.

45. This account is contained in a letter from Maj. Gen. (Ret.) Amos A. Fries to Maj. Gen. Wm. N. Porter, CWS, September 12, 1942. Records of the Chief, CWS, RG 175, Box 234, N.A.

46. Ray, "Incendiaries," pp. 13–17. Also, "CWS Materials Used by the Air Service," pp. 4–6.

47. *The London Times, History of the War*, vol. 10 (London, 1917), p. 425.

48. Commanded by Maj. Charles S. Whittlesay, the American force was made up by fragments of four rifle companies, from the 307th and 308th Infantry Regiments, which had been cut off by German troops after a too-quick advance in the Argonne Forest.

49. Thomas M. Johnson and Fletcher Pratt, *The Lost Battalion* (Wash., D.C.: Infantry Journal Press, 1943), p. 36.

CHAPTER 2

1. For more detailed information on the CWS during the period November 1918–June 1920, see Leo P. Brophy and George J. B. Fisher, *The Chemical Warfare Service: Organizing for War* (Wash., D.C.: GPO, 1953), pp. 11–18; and Kleber and Birdsell, *Chemicals in Combat*, pp. 24–25.

2. The fight for a permanent CWS is covered in the official CWS histories but a more interesting treatment may be found in Frederic J. Brown, *Chemical Warfare, A Study in Restraints* (Princeton, N.J.: Princeton Univ. Press, 1968), pp. 77–78.

3. Act of June 4, 1920 (Public Law 242), chap. 227, sec. 12a, 66 stat. 768.

4. Brophy and Fisher, *Organizing for War*, p. 26. The table on this page lists the military personnel strength of the CWS from 1918 to 1946. By 1921, the CWS was composed of only 79 officers and 442 enlisted men. It hit bottom in 1923 with a strength of 64 off. and 363 EM. Compare this to the high of 1943—8,103 off., 61,688 EM.

5. The newsletter, entitled aptly enough *Chemical Warfare*, was the forerunner of the *Chemical Warfare Journal*. For a discussion of the actions of anti-gas pressure

groups, see Lumsden, *Incendiary Weapons*, pp. 20–24, 72–73. Prior to June 1921, the CWS was financed with funds already appropriated for other purposes. The first funds, provided specifically for the CWS, were appropriated by the 67th Congress. See Act of June 30, 1921 (Public Law 27), chap. 33, 67 stat. 92. For the smaller amount appropriated for the following year, see Act of June 30, 1922 (Public Law 259), chap. 253, 67 stat. 746.

6. Act of June 4, 1920 (Public Law 242), ch. 227, sec. 17b, 66 stat. 768. Also War Dept. General Order 54, sec. 3c, 28 Aug. 1920.

7. Lt. Col. Amos A. Fries, Chief, CWS, to T. B. Gilbert, Subj.: Flame Throwers, 28 June 1920. Chief, CWS Records, RG 175, File 470.71/1065, N.A.

8. See Amos A. Fries and Clarence J. West, *Chemical Warfare* (New York: McGraw-Hill, 1921), p. 3. Fries' book suffers from the lack of footnotes, bibliography, or index. The reader is left to assume that Fries has some basis in fact for his contentions.

9. Ibid., pp. 305–12, 401. The comments made by Fries regarding flame throwers sound a great deal like those made earlier by S. J. M. Auld in a book that is also devoid of annotation or bibliography. In *Gas and Flame* (New York: George H. Doran, 1918), p. 194, Auld said:

    > Service in the Guard Reserve Pioneers is apparently a form of punishment. Men convicted of offenses in other regiments are transferred there either for a time, or permanently, and are forced under threat of death to engage in the most hazardous enterprises. . . .

    In the case of incendiary bombs, Fries had said in a 1922 CWS report, "Purely incendiary materials are generally of much less importance [than smoke]." Cited by Leo P. Brophy, Wyndham D. Miles, and Rexmond C. Cochrane in *The Chemical Warfare Service From Laboratory to Field* (Wash., D.C.: GPO, 1959), p. 167.

10. The power wielded by the Chief of a service (in this case the Engineers) is aptly treated in an official Army history of the Corps of Engineers. See Blanche D. Coll, Jean E. Keith, and Herbert D. Rosenthal, *The Corps of Engineers: Troops and Equipment* (Wash., D.C.: GPO, 1958), pp. 4–6. Also look to Brophy and Fisher, *Organizing for War*, pp. 26–30. Fries continued to lead an active life until his death in 1963. Becoming very alarmed over the growth of Soviet military strength, Fries wrote and published a polemical diatribe entitled *Communism Unmasked* in 1937. In it, he identifies Nazi Germany as the main bulwark protecting the world from Communism.

11. "Smoke Screens," *Chemical Warfare* 8 (15 January 1922): 5–6.

12. Alex Roland, *Underwater Warfare in the Age of Sail*, pp. 179–80.

13. Maj. A. Gibson, CWS, to New Jersey State Firewarden, Trenton, N.J., Subj.: Flame Throwers, 16 August 1922, File #470.71/1250; and Lt. Col. C. R. Alley to A. P. Miller, Subj.: Flame Thrower, 8 February 1932, File #729.2/67, both found in RG 175 N.A. Also see Maj. A. Wilson, CWS, to J. Tomaszewski, Attaché Polish Embassy, Wash., D.C., Subj.: Flame Throwers, 2 June 1933, File #1304-J-14, RG 165, N.A.

14. Fred L. Israel, ed., *Major Peace Treaties of Modern History* (New York: Chelsea House, 1967), vol. 2, "The Treaty of Versailles, June 28, 1919," Arts. 271, 172, 180, pp. 1367–71. The Austrians and Hungarians, former allies of Germany,

were also denied the further use of flame throwers. See Israel, vol. 3, "The Treaty of St. Germain, Sept. 10, 1919," art. 135, p. 1582, for Austria. For the treaty with Hungary, see vol. 3, "The Treaty of Trianon, June 4, 1920," art. 119, p. 1906. In each case, the flame weapons were to be turned over to the representatives of Britain and France—who continued to test and improve their flame throwers during the 1920s and 1930s. Redemann's criticism of Fries' treatment of flame throwers found in a letter from Hermann Redemann to Brig. Gen. Amos A. Fries, Chief, CWS, Thru: Maj. Herman H. Zornig, U.S. Army, Military Attaché, U.S. Embassy, Berlin, Feb. 29, 1928, File #MID 2612–64, N.A. A copy is also found in RG 175, File #470.71/32, N.A.

15. Redemann to Fries, p. 1, of translation by Zornig.

16. Brig. Gen. Amos A. Fries to Hermann Redemann, Thru: Military Attaché, U.S. Embassy, Berlin, Subj.: Flame Throwers, 1 June 1928, File #461/4788, RG 175, N.A.

17. The parochialism of the CWS at this time is discussed by Kleber and Birdsell in *Chemicals in Combat*, pp. 25–27. For statistics on U.S. gas casualties during World War I, look to the "Report of the Surgeon General," pp. 443–1173 in vol. 1 of *War Department Annual Reports*, 1920 (Wash., D.C.: GPO, 1921). The report shows, on page 452, that among U.S. troops hospitalized as gas casualties, only 1.73% died. The mortality rate among those troops suffering gunshot/shrapnel wounds was much higher (8.26%).

18. Constance M. Green, Harry C. Thomson, and Peter C. Roots, *The Ordnance Department: Planning Munitions for War* (Wash., D.C.: GPO, 1955), p. 260.

19. Maj. William N. Porter, CWS, for the Chief of CWS, to the Assistant Chief of Staff, G-2, War Dept., Subj.: Lecture Outlines, 16 June 1930. RG 165, File #MID 303-W-44. The French lesson outlines were shipped to the CWS and can be found in RG 165, Box 145-4, File #MID 2314-C-90, N.A.

20. An excellent explanation of the various missions of the CWS during the 1920s and 1930s may be found in Brophy, Miles, and Cochrane, *From Lab. to Field*, pp. 29–34; and in Leo P. Brophy and George J. B. Fisher, *The Chemical Warfare Service: Organizing for War* (Wash., D.C.: GPO, 1959), pp. 18–45.

21. Index to Official Publications Pertaining to Chemical Warfare (Edgewood Arsenal, Md.: HQ, CWS, 1934). Currently in the historian's file collection, Aberdeen Proving Ground (APG), HC-EA. This author, in searching through the large collection of lesson outlines, course schedules, etc. that remain from the Chemical Warfare School courses of the 1930s, could find not one case in which more than the most cursory attention was paid to incendiary weapons, although the development of incendiaries was still a CWS mission. There are no requests from the Infantry or Engineer branches for flame weapons in the files of the CWS Chief during the 1920s or 1930s.

22. For information on British and French developments in flame weaponry during the twenty years following World War I, see Leo Finklestein's monograph, "Flame Throwers," pp. 19–21. Another source on British developments in this field is Sir Donald Banks, *Flame Over Britain* (London: Sampson Low, Marston, & Co., 1947), pp. 62–63.

23. Lumsden, *Incendiary Weapons*, pp. 24, 72–73. See also Peter D. Trooboff, *Law and Responsibility in Warfare: The Vietnam Experience* (Chapel Hill, N.C.: U.N.C. Press, 1975), p. 24. Trooboff comments upon the customary rules of

international law and the fact that the legality of flame weapons was not successfully challenged during the years prior to World War II.

24. I. B. Holley, Jr., *Ideas and Weapons* (Princeton, N.J.: Princeton Univ. Press, 1953), p. 15.

25. Green, Thomson, and Roots, *Planning Munitions for War*, p. 256.

26. Giulio Douhet, *The Command of the Air*, trans. by Dino Ferrari (New York: Coward-McCann, 1942), as quoted by I. B. Holley, Jr., in *Ideas and Weapons*, p. 15.

27. Professor Zanetti's remarks are cited by Brooks E. Kleber in "The Incendiary Bomb," *Armed Forces Chemical Journal* 7 (October 1953): 24.

28. L. Wilson Greene, "Prewar Incendiary Bomb Development," *Chemical Corps Journal* 2 (October 1947): 25.

29. As the commander of the Fifth AF supporting MacArthur's troops in the Southwest Pacific, Kenney directed his aviators to use incendiaries on Japanese targets previously bombed only with H.E. and had good results. He is also credited with applying the still-experimental technique of low-level skip-bombing with medium bombers which resulted in the sinking of sixteen Japanese ships in March 1943 during the Battle of the Bismarck Sea. For information about this innovative airman, see Craven and Cate, eds., *The Pacific: Guadalcanal to Saipan, August 1942 to July 1944. The Army Air Forces in World War II* (Chicago: Univ. of Chicago Press, 1950), pp. 147–50, 319–23.

30. Ibid., pp. 26–30. See also Alfred E. Gaul and Leo Finklestein, "Incendiaries," vol. 18 of the *History of Research and Development of the Chemical Warfare Service in World War II* (1 July 1940–31 December 1945) (Edgewood Arsenal, Md.: HQ, CWS, 1952), pp. 29–30 (mimeographed); and the *Edgewood Arsenal Technical Report*, no. 312, 31 August 1939, passim. Both located in File #228–01, HC-EA, APG.

31. Augustin M. Prentiss, *Chemicals in War* (New York: McGraw-Hill, 1937), pp. 248–61. Prentiss later rose to the rank of brigadier general during World War II, serving in the United States and in Europe.

32. Greene, "Prewar Incendiary Bomb Development," p. 28. Also, Brophy, Miles, and Cochrane, *From Lab. to Field*, p. 168; and Kleber, "The Incendiary Bomb," p. 24.

33. After-Action Report, Subj.: Inspection of Incendiary Munitions, for the Chief, CWS, 13 October 1936, File #425, HC-EA, APG. This trip must have generated some interest in incendiaries, for the following year, a CWS officer, Lieutenant Colonel Augustin M. Prentiss, authored a book in which he foresaw a "large and useful role" in the future bombing of cities. See *Chemicals in War* (New York: McGraw-Hill, 1937), p. 261.

34. The 4.2-inch mortar was developed from the British 4-inch (Stokes) mortar. It could fire accurately at ranges from 300 meters to 4,000 meters. The importance of the 4.2-inch mortar in CWS tests with a phosphorus shell during the late 1930s was attested to by former CWS officer Robert M. Colver, Duke University, Durham, N.C., 5 November 1975.

35. Lt. Col. Haig Shekerjian, CWS, to Asst. Chief of Staff, G-2, War Dept., 16 March 1937, RG 165, File #MID 2612–130, N.A.

36. Col. G. H. Paine, FA, to Asst. Chief of Staff, G-2, War Dept., 7 December 1938, and First Indorsement to Chief, CWS, RG 165, File #MID 2612–130/2/3. Also in RG 175, File #740.71/14, N.A.

37. Henry Sorensen, "Flame Warfare," *Canadian Army Journal* 2 (August 1948): 18.

CHAPTER 3

1. Paul W. Thompson, "How the Germans Took Fort Eben Emael," *Infantry Journal*, vol. 51, no. 2 (Aug. 1942): 26. Also see Thompson, "Engineers in the Blitzkrieg," *Infantry Journal*, vol. 47 (Sept.–Oct. 1940): 429–32. It should be noted that the Germans left routine construction and road maintenance work to their Labor Service troops and to the Todt organization, a paramilitary construction organization that organized engineers and laborers in countries subject to German rule.

2. For information on German flame weapons, see Leonard L. McKinney, "Portable Flame Thrower Operations in World War II," pp. 30–32, and McKinney, "Mechanized Flame Thrower Operations in World War II," Chemical Corps Historical Study No. 5 (Feb. 1951), pp. 14–17 (mimeographed), 314.7 File HC-EA, APG. Typical of the reports coming to the U.S. from Europe was the report of the U.S. military attaché in Berlin, Subj.: Display of German Flammenwerfers at Leipzig Fair, 1940, RG 165, Box 1450, MID #2314-b-595, N.A. Also, look to a *Handbook on German Military Forces*, TM-E 30-451 (Wash., D.C.: GPO, 1945), p. VIII-88 and p. VIII-91 which describe the Model 1935 and the tank-mounted German flame throwers.

3. For many of these suggestions (some pertaining to assault equipment) see File 352.11, Engineer School Library Archives, Fort Leonard Wood, Mo. An excellent source of information on the Engineer Corps chief and his staff is in Blanche D. Coll, Jean E. Keith, and Herbert D. Rosenthal, *The Corps of Engineers: Troops and Equipment* (Wash., D.C.: GPO, 1959), pp. 5–20.

4. Coll, Keith, and Rosenthal, *Engineers: Troops and Equipment*, pp. 7–20.

5. Chief of Engineers to the Adjutant General, War Dept., 24 July 1940, Records of the Adjutant General's Office, 1917, RG 407, File #470.71/6, N.A. (Hereafter "The Adjutant General's Office" will be shown as "TAGO.")

6. 2d Ind. to Ltr., C/E to AG, 30 July 1940, RG 175, File #470.71/52, N.A.

7. 3d Ind., Disposition Form, G-4 Supply Div., WD, Subj.: Flame Throwers for Individual Use, 9 Aug. 1940, RG 165, File #31745/10, N.A. (Hereafter, "Disposition Form" will be shown as "DF.")

8. For a copy of General Chaffee's request, see DF, G-4 Supply Div., WD, Subj.: Mechanically Transported Flame Thrower, 25 May 1940, RG 165, File 31745, N.A.

9. Ibid., 2d Ind., 30 May 1940, File #31745/2.

10. DF, G-4, WD, Subj.: Flame Throwers for Indiv. Use, 9 Aug. 1940, RG 165, File #31745/10, H.A.

11. Chief, Technical Division, CWS, to Industrial Safety Office, Kincaid Co., Inc., New York, N.Y., with CWS Purchase Order No. 41-A470E/C, and War Department Concurrence Memo No. 41-28-3/CWS/2, 11 September 1940, File 470.702212, RG 175, N.A. These drawings, material specifications, and safety limitations for pressure valves appear to reflect the haste with which they were prepared. Replete with smudges and erasures, the CWS specifications left much to the imagination of the Kincaid design engineers. The sale of the last Boyd No. 3 flame thrower for scrap in 1919 is chronicled in Finklestein, "Flame Throwers," pt. 1, pp. 12–13.

12. British flame throwers of the early war years are described by Donald Bank, *Flame Over Britain* (London: Sampson Low, Marston, 1946), pp. 61–72. See also

Brophy, Miles, and Cochrane, *From Laboratory to Field*, p. 144, for information on the Model E1.

13. "E1" referred to the fact that it was an experimental model and the first of its type.

14. Report of the Engineer Test Board, Report No. 621, 16 May 1941, Records of U.S. Army Commands, RG 338, File #21753/7, N.A. Also found in the Archives Section, Engineer School Library, Fort Leonard Wood, Mo.

15. The DF designating the infantry as primary test agency was sent to the Chief of Infantry on 7 May 1941. It is included as Appendix "A" of the Final Report of the Infantry Test Board, Report No. 1225, 20 June 1941, Records of U.S. Army Commands, RG 338, Box 1051, N.A.

16. Reproduced in Appendix "B" of Inf. Board Report 1225. Also found in the Records of the Chiefs of Arms, RG 177, N.A.

17. Inf. Test Board Rept. 1225, pp. 6–15. An example of insufficient testing prior to field issue is the case of the U.S. M16 rifle in 1966.

18. App. "G," Inf. Test Board Rept. 1225.

19. President, MCEB to the Maj. Gen. Commandant, USMC, Subj.: Demonstration of the E1R1 Flame Thrower, 9 Aug. 1941, USMC Central Files, RG 127, Job 62A2371, Box 25, File #2000-15, N.A.

20. For a full account of the standardization of the M1 flame thrower, see CWS Technical Division Report 1069 (June 1945), pp. 12–22, CWS 314.7 File, HC-EA, APG.

21. The wartime service of the NDRC has been recorded in James P. Baxter, III, *Scientists Against Time* (New York: Little, Brown, 1952) and William N. Noyes, ed., *Chemistry* (Boston: Little, Brown, 1948). Also see Lincoln R. Thiesmeyer and John E. Burchard, *Combat Scientists* (Boston: Little, Brown, 1947). For specific information about the work done by Division 11 in the incendiary field, look to vol. 3 of the *Summary Technical Report of Division 11, NDRC* entitled "Fire Warfare" (Wash., D.C.: GPO, 1946), pp. 95–103.

22. The work done on the flame thrower nozzle (CWS project 41-10) is illustrated in vol. 3 of the *Summary Report of the NDRC-Division 11*, "Fire Warfare," p. 3.

23. ACS, G-4 to Chief of Staff of the Army, Subj.: Standardization of Portable Flame Thrower, M1, 22 August 1941, Records of the HQ, Army Ground Forces, RD 337, File 470.71/31745-3, N.A. (Hereafter "Army Ground Forces" will be shown as "AGF.")

24. Secretary of War to the AG, Subj.: Tactical Doctrine for, and Technique of, Employment of Flame Throwers, Sept. 3, 1941, Records of the HQ, AGF, RG 337, File #470.71/43052, N.A.

25. The AG to the Chief of Engineers, Subj.: Tactical Doctrine for Flame Throwers, Sept. 5, 1941, Records of the HQ, AGF, RG 337, File #470.71/(9-3-41) MC-C, N.A.

26. Chemical Warfare Training Circular No. 72, U.S. War Department, Dec. 22, 1941, Records of the AGF, RG 337, File #470.71, N.A. This circular was superseded in May 1943 by a technical manual (TM 3-375) entitled *Portable Flame Throwers, M1 and M1A1*. Kincaid's M1 assembly line was modified to ensure greater productivity in addition to the triple shift. See McKinney table "Flame Thrower Operations World War II," pp. 47–48, 117–119, and 213. Quartermaster, HQ USMC, to Chief, CWS, Subj.: Request for Shipment of Flame

Throwers, M1, Portable, 10 Nov. 1941, RG 175, File #400.312/429, N.A. The CWS had also experimented with a large emplaced flame thrower for beach and air field defense. For information on the CWS emplaced flame projector project, see McKinney, "Portable Flame Thrower Oper.," p. 25.

27. 1st Ind. to G-4 DF, dtd. 25 May 1940, Subj.: Military Requirements for Mechanized Flame Throwers, 28 May 1940, Records of TAGO, RG 407, File #471.6, N.A.

28. The Chief of the CWS had asked that a medium tank be provided for testing purposes at Edgewood Arsenal. The Armored Force could not comply, so CWS technicians went to Fort Knox. See letter from Chief, CWS, to President of the Armored Force Test Board, 5 Nov. 1940, RG 175, File No. 470.71/40, N.A.

29. Military attaché report to ACS, G-2, WD, 19 Mar. 1941, RG 165, MID #3842, N.A.

30. CG, Armored Force to AG, WD, Subj.: MID Report 3842, 21 July 1941, Records of TAGO, RG 407, File #470.71, N.A.

31. J. E. Moss to Maj. Gen. John K. Kerr, Chief of Cavalry, Mechanized Division, 27 May 1940, RG 177, File #470.71/14, N.A.

32. A report of the abortive test is contained in Charles T. Mitchell, "Development of Mechanically Transported Flame Throwers," Technical Division Report 373, Nov. 1943, pp. 9–10, CWS 314.7 File, HC-EA.

33. Report of the Armored Force Test Board, "Mechanized Flame Thrower, E2," Report No. 58, 13 Sept. 1941, RG 175, Box 4263, N.A.

34. Problems experienced in flame tank development are recorded by E. P. Sherman, "History of NDRC Flame Thrower Development," in Noyes, *Chemistry*, pp. 420–30. Sherman says, "The biggest problem was to obtain a definite assignment from the Army amid the endless discussion of whether mechanized flame throwers were really needed. . . ." CWS difficulties with the Armored Force are cited in *Lab. to Field*, p. 151. The U.S. Chemical Warfare Committee, composed of civilian and military scientists and engineers, was sent to England in an attempt to promote uniformity in U.S. and British flame weapons. In spite of this group's efforts, there was little progress in this regard. *Lab. to Field*, pp. 45–46.

35. Fiorello H. LaGuardia and John J. McElligott, *Wartime Fire Defense in London . . .* (Wash., D.C.: U.S. Conference of Mayors, 1941).

36. On German fire bombs, see the *Handbook on German Military Forces*, pp. VIII–92; also the *Course Outline, USAAF ANSCOL Course* App. 34, p. 4, File #228.01 HC-EA, APG. This course material on incendiary bombs states that while incendiaries made up only about 25 percent of the total German bomb load dropped on London, the British judged the incendiaries to have done 90 percent of the total damage. The Air Corps request is recorded in an extremely valuable document compiled by Capt. William H. Baldwin, CWS. Entitled "Development of Incendiary Bombs," it is based on interviews and Baldwin's personal experience while at Edgewood Arsenal, 1940–1945. Now located in File #228.01, HC-EA, APG.

37. See chronology based on notes and interview by Capt. Wm. H. Baldwin, CWS. Entitled "Development of NaPalm," this set of interview notes is found in File #228.01, HC-EA, APG. Along with the notes entitled "Development of Incendiary Bombs" mentioned previously and the "Development of NaPalm," Baldwin prepared an excellent background outline entitled "Development of Incendiaries." These three sets of working papers, full of typographical errors and misspellings, bring to life many of the individuals who labored to perfect the CWS incendiaries during World War II.

38. *From Lab. to Field*, p. 163 and pp. 186–87 in a section entitled "Incendiary Oddities." Also, James S. Carson, CWS Tech. Div. Memorandum Report 482, "Incendiary Bomb M2 (Leaf)," dated 17 December 1942, File 425, 228.01, HC-EA, APG.

39. The letter alerting General Baker to the impending shift in responsibility is now located in RG 175, N.A. See Asst. C/S, G-4, to Chief, CWS, Procurement of Incendiary Bombs, dtd. 3 September 1941, File #471.6/340–351. The order making this official was War Dept. GO No. 13, 24 November 1941. Luckily for the CWS, the general staff transferred sixty-nine million dollars from Ordnance to CWS to cover the cost of the bombs. See Brophy, Miles, and Cochrane, *From Lab. to Field*, pp. 342–43.

40. For background reading on the U.S. decision not to use poison gas, see Kleber and Birdsell, *Chemicals in Combat*, pp. 652–56.

41. Col. Stuart A. Hamilton to Chief, CWS, Subj.: Japanese Flame throwers, 19 Feb. 1942, Chief, CWS Records, RG 175, File #470.71/281, N.A. Also found in the compilation of "Reports of CWS Activities, U.S. Forces in the Philippines," HQ, Army Chemical Center (Nov. 1946) (mimeographed), in file #2389, USAMHI, Carlisle Barracks, Pa. Later, evidence of Japanese flame throwers used against the Marine defenders of Wake Island was uncovered. See Frank O. Hough and Verle E. Ludwig, *Pearl Harbor to Guadalcanal*, vol. 1 of *U.S. Marine Corps Operations in World War II* (Wash., D.C.: GPO, 1967), p. 142.

42. Commentary on attitudes derived from interview with Leonard Cohen, USA Ret., Edgewood, Md., 10 Mar. 1975.

43. Memo, CWS Munitions Development Div. for Chief, CWS, Subj.: Report of Conference on Mechanized Flame Thrower (CWS Project 4-3-8.1), 30 Mar. 1943, CWS 314.7 File. On emplaced flame throwers, see Memo, G-4 Requirements Div., WD, to Chief, CWS, Subj.: Emplaced Flame Throwers, 14 Sept. 1942, Records of TAGO, RG 407, File #470.71/10, N.A. Also, McKinney, "Port. F. T. Operations," p. 25.

44. Chief, CWS to CC, AGF, Subj.: Requirements for Flame Thrower, portable, M1, June 3, 1942, RG 175, File #470.71/137, N.A.

45. 1st Ind. to CWS 470.71/137 above, HQ, AGF to Chief, CWS, June 23, 1942, RG 175, File #470.71/1372r, N.A.

46. FM 3-5, *Tactics of Chemical Warfare*, 20 July 1942, sec. 6, "Engineer Troops," pp. 76–78, and TM 3-375, *Portable Flame Throwers, M1 and M1A1*, May 1943. Also, see FM 5-135, *Operations of Engineer Field Units*, 23 April 1942.

47. C.O., 4th Engineer Motorized Bn. to CG, AGF, 24 Sept. 1942, indorsed to Chief, CWS, 30 Sept. 1942, Records of AGF, RG 337 and RG 175, File #470.71/724ie, N.A.

48. McKinney, "Port. F. T. Operations," p. 35. See also Baldwin, "The Development of Napalm," pp. 2–3.

49. *Summary Tech. Rpt. of Div. 11, NDRC*, vol. 3, pp. 7–15, 192–227. See also Brophy, Miles, and Cochrane, *From Lab. to Field*, pp. 167–69.

50. *Summary Tech. Rpt. of Div. 11, NDRC*, vol. 3, pp. 199–206. For a first-hand account of the work at Harvard, see Louis F. Fieser, *The Scientific Method* (New York: Reinhold, 1964), pp. 180–93.

51. Memo for Record, Subj.: History of M1A1 Portable Flame Thrower, Office of the Chief, CWS, Nov. 11, 1942, RG 175, Box 1457, File 470.71/2260, N.A.

52. Finklestein, "Flame Throwers," pt. 1, pp. 127–34. Over 14,000 M1A1s were manufactured during World War II, principally by the Kincaid Co. and the Beattie Manu. Co., Little Falls, N.J. Brophy, Miles, and Cochrane, *From Lab. to Field*, p. 367.

53. Chap. 2 of Brophy and Fisher, *Organizing for War*, contains a number of diagrams depicting the expansion of the CWS during this period. Appendix A, page 398, shows an increase in CWS military personnel strength from that of 993 officers and 5,591 enlisted men in December 1941 to a figure of 5,192 officers and 40,990 enlisted men one year later. For some grasp of the proliferation of CWS units, see Appendix H, pp. 424–71.

54. Brophy and Fisher, *Organizing for War*, chap. 3, pp. 49–62. This short chapter, entitled "Crystallizing the Wartime Mission," shows that the CWS was still concerned with how and when to employ poison gas. The role to be played by flame weapons was still unknown and the development of such weapons still a sidelight of the CWS effort and perceived mission.

55. Baldwin, "Development of NaPalm," pp. 3–4, alludes to a number of personal and staff rivalries that arose in 1942 and, in the end, adversely affected CWS progress. An insight to the importance of sound organization prior to war is provided in a letter to the author by Theodore Ropp, Duke University, 6 October 1978.

CHAPTER 4

1. After Action Report, S-3, 16th Armored Engineer Bn., 1st Armored Division, TORCH Operation—1st Phase, 16 Feb. 1943, CWS 314.7 File, HC-EA, APG.

2. Chem. Off., Western Task Force, to Chief, CWS, 21 Dec. 1942, RG 175, File #470.71/2349, N.A. Also, see McKinney, "Portable Flame Thrower Oper.," pp. 181–82. The M1A1 flame throwers received by the forces in North Africa were among the first M1A1s shipped overseas. In all, 14,000 M1A1 flame throwers were manufactured in 1942 and 1943 by the E. C. Brown Co., an agricultural sprayer firm.

3. McKinney, "Port. Flame Thrower Oper.," pp. 182–84. Also, Lt. Gen. George S. Patton, "Notes of the Sicilian Campaign, 10 July–11 August 1943," p. 38; and After Action Report, Chem. Off., European Theater of Operations [ETOUSA] to Chem. Off., HQ, Army Ground Forces [AGF], Subj.: Use of flame thrower in Sicilian Operation, 18 Nov. 1943. Both the Patton report and the Chemical Officer's report are located in the 314.7 File, HC-EA, APG.

4. Minutes of Meeting, Conference of Chemical Officers in Seventh Army, 28–29 Aug. 1943; and Routing Slip, Chem. Off., North African Theater of Operations [NATOUSA] to G-4, Engineer Command, NATOUSA, 14 Nov. 1943, Subj.: Flame Thrower Allocation. Both located in CWS 314.7 File, Mediterranean Notes Section, HC-EA, APG.

5. Final Report, CWS Spare Parts Contact Team in the Mediterranean Theater of Operations [MTO] to Chief, CWS, Subj.: M1A1 Flame Thrower Utilization, 2 Mar. 1944, RG 175, File #470.71/437/2, N.A.

6. Fifth Army Training Memo #8, Subj.: Technique and Tactical Use of Flame Throwers, 5 April 1944, reprinted as Appendix 18 of McKinney, "Port. Flame Thrower Oper.," pp. 312–16. Also see "A Military Encyclopedia Based on

Operations in the Italian Campaigns," G-3, HQ, 15th Army Group, p. 189. CWS 228-01 File, HC-EA, APG.

7. On U.S. lack of interest in flame throwers, see Kleber and Birdsell, *Chemicals in Combat*, pp. 594–95. Canadian engineers using light mechanized flame throwers (The "Wasp") and British tankers of the 51st Royal Tank Regiment using Churchill flame thrower tanks (The "Crocodile") joined British infantrymen armed with portable flame throwers in Italy. See A. J. Kerry and W. A. McDill, *The History of the Corps of Royal Canadian Engineers*, vol. 2 (Ottawa: Mil Assoc. of Canada, 1966), p. 257; and Basil Liddell Hart, *The Tanks* (New York: Praeger, 1959), p. 287.

8. For further information on British flame throwers, see Donald Banks, *Flame Over Britain* (London: Sampson Low, Marston, 1947), pp. 114–40; Leonard L. McKinney, "Mechanized Flame Thrower Operations in World War II," Chemical Corps Historical Study No. 5 (Edgewood Arsenal, Md.: HQ, Chemical Corps, 1951), pp. 36–38, 160–61; Liddell Hart, *The Tanks*, pp. 328–9; and a first-hand account by Andrew Wilson, *Flame Thrower* (London: Bantam Books, 1984), p. xii. The U.S. request for flame throwers is in a letter from CG, ETOUSA to G-4, AGF, 17 Sept. 1943, Subj.: Mechanized Flame Throwers, RG 337, File #470.714/212–215. (The request was later reduced to twenty kits.)

9. Kerry and McDill, *History of Royal Canadian Engrs.*, p. 93.

10. "Enemy Capabilities for Chemical Warfare," Special Series #16 (Wash., D.C.: War Dept. G-2, July 1943), pp. 30–35; and "Enemy Tactics in Chemical Warfare," Special Series #24 (Wash., D.C.: War Dept. G-2, Sept. 1943), pp. 55–56, both in File #2389, USAMHI, Carlisle Barracks, Pa. Also, look to a *Handbook on German Military Forces*, pp. VIII, 89–91.

11. On FRAS, see McKinney, "Mech. Flame Thrower Oper.," p. 37. Regarding German flame fuels, look to Herman Ochsner, "A History of German Chemical Warfare in World War II," trans. by H. Heitman (Wash., D.C.: HQ, Chemical Corps, 1948), pp. 231–38 (mimeographed), in File #2389, USAMHI, Carlisle Barracks, Pa.

12. Flame thrower training was conducted at the Assault Training Center, Ilfracombe, England. See ETOUSA Trng. Memo No. 33, 6 Oct. 1943, Subj.: Portable Flame Thrower Assault Tactics; and ETOUSA Trng. Memo No. 10, 5 April 1944, same subject; both in CWS 314.7 File, HC-EA. Each assault division was issued 150 M1A1 flame throwers rather than 24. See the *First Army Report of Operations, 20 October 1943–1 August 1944*, bk. 7, p. 190. Found in the U.S. Army Military History Institute (USAMHI), Carlisle Barracks, Pa.

13. McKinney, "Portable Flame Thrower Oper.," pp. 192–93.

14. CG, 8th Inf. Div. to CG, VIII Corps, 23 Sept. 1944, Subj.: Employment of Vehicular and Portable Flame Throwers; and Chem. Off., 2d Inf. Div. to Chem. Off., VIII Corps, 25 Sept. 1944, Subj.: Use of Flame Throwers during Brest Campaign. Both in the CWS 314.7 File, HC-EA, APG. The efforts of troops from the 11th Inf., 5th Div. at Fort Driant met with the same results, for the same reasons: inexperience and sketchy training. An account of their actions is provided by Stephen E. Ambrose, *Citizen Soldiers* (New York: Simon and Schuster, 1997), p. 137.

15. Joseph H. Ewing, *29, Let's Go!* (Wash., D.C.: Infantry Journal Press, 1948), pp. 138–40; and Report on Montbarey Operation by Col. F. W. Wilkinson,

forwarded to Chief, CWS, by Lt. Col. T. H. Magness, Subj.: Crocodile Flame Throwers, 17 Oct. 1944, with attached 29th Inf. Div. Operations Memo #18, Subj.: Infantry-Tank Coordination, RG 175, File #470.71/20, N.A.

16. A letter from the Commander, Armored Force Test Board to the CG, Armored Command with an indorsement to the Chief, CWS, 3 Feb. 1944, stated the opposition of the Test Board to any type of tank flame thrower that would create a distinctive silhouette or deprive the tank of its main gun. Letter in CWS 314.7 File, HC-EA, APG. Also, Chem. Off. XIV Corps to Chief, CWS, 26 Aug. 1943, Subj.: Report of Mounting Flame Throwers in Tanks, RG 175, File #470.71/277–279, N.A.

17. Kleber and Birdsell, *Chemicals in Combat,* pp. 606–8; McKinney, "Mechanized Flame Thrower Oper.," pp. 184–86; and Chief of the Armored Section, 12th Army Group G-3 Staff, to Chief, CWS, 12 Oct. 1944, Subj.: Flame Throwers, E4-5, CWS 314.7 File, HC-EA, APG. Also see Combat Observer Report to CG, 12th Army Group, 13 Oct. 1944, Subj.: Mechanized Flame Thrower, CWS 314.7 File, HC-EA, APG.

18. Col P. F. Powers, Chem. Off., 12th Army Group, to Brig. Gen W. F. Kabrich, Chief, Tech. Div., CWS, 17 Nov. 1944, Subj.: CWS Activities in 12th Army Group, RG 175, File 470.71, N.A. For information on the E4-5 (M3-4-3), see McKinney, "Mech. Flame Thrower Oper.," pp. 10–23; and Memo for Lt. Col W. H. Kayser, 5 Oct. 1944, Subj.: Current Flame Thrower Development Program, pp. 14, RG 175, File #470.71, N.A.

19. Report on Breaching the Siegfried Line, prepared by the Engineer Section, XVIII Airborne Corps, 28 Jan. 1945, RG 337, File #470.715, N.A.

20. Charles D. MacDonald, *The Siegfried Line Campaign* (Wash., D.C.: GPO, 1963), p. 48.

21. 212th Army Group G-3 Immediate Report No. 4 re: Comments of Lt. Col. Learned, C.O. of 1st Bn, 18th Inf., 1st Inf. Div., 29 Nov. 1944, CWS 314.7 File, HC-EA. Lt. Col. Learned said, "When I need a flame thrower, I usually try to find a German Model 42 as it is lighter, has more range, and you can shoot fuel, then light it."

22. MacDonald, *Siegfried Line Campaign,* p. 263.

23. Operations Div., CWS, to Chief, Technical Div., CWS, 11 Jan. 1943, Subj.: Flame Thrower, Portable, One-Shot. RG 175, File #470.71/B8.2-2, N.A. Also: Chief, Tech. Div., CWS, to CG, U.S. Army Service of Supply, 11 Mar. 1943, Subj.: Military Requirement and Military Characteristics for One-Shot Portable Flame Thrower, RG 175, File #470.71/3203, N.A.

24. After-Action Interview with Capt. James W. Mitchell, p. 106 of bk. 4, "Ninth U.S. Army Operations" (mimeographed), File #2324, USAMHI, Carlisle Barracks, Pa. Canadian armored flame thrower operations are recounted in *The History of the Royal Canadian Engineers,* by Kerry and McDill, pp. 221, 343–45.

25. Ambrose, *Citizen Soldiers,* p. 411. Chem. Off., 9th Army to Chem. Off., 12th Army Group, 30 April 1945, Subj.: Mechanized Flame Thrower Activities. The tendency of Germans to surrender in the face of flame attacks had been reported earlier in a letter from the Chem Off., 30th Inf. Div. to the Chem. Off., 1st Army, with Indorsements, 30 Oct. 1944, Subj.: Report on the Use of Flame Throwers on the Siegfried Line. Both reports are found in CWS File 314.7, HC-EA, APG.

26. Wilson, *Flame Thrower,* p. 111.

CHAPTER 5

1. The Eighth AF was joined by the Ninth AF just prior to D-Day. The Ninth AF was composed chiefly of fighter and medium bomber units. The Fifteenth AF, operating from bases in Italy after 1943, assisted the Eighth AF in the strategic (long-range) bombing of Germany. For more information on the U.S. Army Air Forces in the ETO, see W. F. Craven and J. L. Cate (eds.), *The Army Air Forces in World War II*, vols. 1–3 (Chicago: Univ. of Chicago Press, 1951).

2. J. E. Zanetti, "Strategy of Incendiaries," Chemical Warfare Bulletin [hereafter CWB] 27 (April 1941): 41–44.

3. See Kleber and Birdsell, *Chemicals in Combat*, pp. 150–51, 619–21. A number of message slips and notes from Kellogg to various staff members of the Eighth AF headquarters regarding the arrival of M47 bombs are found in the Eighth AF Chemical Munitions File. Now preserved as File #519.86717 (vol. 1), in the Albert F. Simpson Historical Center [AFSHC].

4. Norman A. Graebner and Martha J. Roby, "Allied Assault on Germany," in *Case Studies of Mass Attacks on Populations*, pp. 57–58. This is vol. 3 of the four-volume study completed in 1965 by the Historical Evaluation and Research Organization [HERO] entitled *Military, Political, and Psychological Implications of Massive Population Casualties in History.*

5. Chief, CWS Supply Division to Chem. Off., Eighth AF, 14 June 1942, Subj.: Material Shipment, RG 175, File #329.75/23, N.A.

6. *Chemicals in Combat*, p. 619. See also the "History of the Chemical Section, Eighth A.F." (mimeographed), CWS 425.01 file, HC-EA, APG. Some information is found in the "Exposition of the Composition, Functions and Activities of the Chemical Section, U.S. Strategic Forces in Europe," 16 June 1944, pp. 78–79, File 519.805, AFSHC.

7. Horatio Bond to Col. R. D. Hughes, Asst. Chief of Air Staff, A-5, Eighth AF, 3 April 1943, Subj.: Incendiary Bombs, File 519.551.7, AFSHC.

8. Col. A. R. Maxwell to Col. L. C. Cabell, Air Staff, A-4, 8 May 1943, Subj.: Informal Comments on Incendiary Bomb Status, 145.81–84, AFSHC. See also Lt. Gen. H. H. Arnold, CG, USAAF, to ACS, Air Staff, Material, Maintenance, and Distribution, 21 April 1943, Subj.: Incendiary Bombs, with two indorsements, 145.81–84, AFSHC.

9. *Incendiary Attacks of German Cities*, Dept. of Bombing Operations, British Air Ministry, January 1943, pp. 66–67, 512.547J, AFSHC.

10. The planning and objectives of Operation GOMORRAH are fully treated on pages 168–70 of Anthony Verrier's *The Bomber Offensive* (New York: Macmillan, 1968). See also *Endeavour*, vol. 2 of the four-volume official history of the RAF in World War II, by Sir Charles Webster and Noble Frankland, *The Strategic Air Offensive Against Germany, 1939–1945* (London: Her Majesty's Stationery Office, 1961), pp. 138–67. Finally, look to Martin Caidin, *The Night Hamburg Died* (London: New English Library, 1966). Some of the major industrial targets were: Blohm & Voss Shipyards, Europaische Tanklager & Transporte, A. G., and the Deutsche Petroleum A. G. refineries.

11. Horatio Bond (ed.), *Fire and the Air War* (Boston: Nat'l. Fire Protection Assoc., 1946), pp. 116, 119. See also Appendix 30, vol. 4 of the *Strategic Air Offensive Against Germany*. This appendix contains an "Extract from the Report by the

Police President of Hamburg on the Raids on Hamburg in July and August 1943, dated 1st December 1943," pp. 310–15.

12. "Interrogation of Albert Speer, former Reich Minister of Armament and War Production, 18th July 1945," App. 37, vol. 4, *Strategic Air Offensive.*

13. CG, 8th Bomber Command, to CG, Eighth AF, 6 Aug. 1943, Subj.: Incendiary Bomb Requirements, 519.8671-7 (vol. 1), AFSHC. Gen. Eaker wrote, "It is requested that all possible efforts be made to expedite the supply of incendiaries as they are of vital importance and the shipment by the most expeditious means is requested." Monthly bomb tonnages are from an "Exposition of the Composition, Functions, and Activities of the Chemical Section, U.S. Strategic Forces in Europe," 16 June 1944, 519.805, AFSHC. Also see *Chemicals in Combat*, p. 623. By the end of World War II, the USAAF had dropped 97,046 tons of incendiaries on European targets. This was about 15% of the total bomb tonnage dropped by the USAAF in the ETO.

14. Maj. Gen. W. N. Porter to Dr. Paul Pritchard, Hist. Off., HQ, CWS, 28 March 1945, Subj.: Incendiaries Opposed by Eighth Air Force, File 425, #228.01, HC-EA, APG.

15. "Report of the Activities of the Technical Division in World War II," Office of the Chief, CWS (Wash., D.C.: Army Service Forces, 1 Jan. 1946), pp. 120–24.

16. Ibid., pp. 98–102. See also Baldwin interviews, "Development of Incendiary Bombs," pp. 6–8.

17. Baldwin, "Development of Incendiary Bombs," p. 7.

18. "Effects of Weapons on Targets," vol. 3, 5 June 1945, OSRD, NDRC Division 11. Fire divisions are explained in App. 10 and 34 of the "ANSCOL Course Material," Army Air Force School of Applied Tactics, Staff & Special Trng. Dept., Orlando, Fla., 13 Nov.–2 Dec. 1944, File 425.03, HC-EA, APG.

19. See chap. 12, entitled "More and More of Everything," Brophy, Miles, and Cochrane, *From Lab. to Field.* Also in the same book, chap. 15 deals exclusively with the procurement of material and the massive construction costs of new research and test facilities. The Secretary of War had provided the Chief of the CWS with *carte blanche* for incendiary development soon after Pearl Harbor when he wrote, "Take all measures necessary to expedite so far as possible the delivery of incendiary bombs." *Lab. to Field*, p. 344.

20. The *best* single source for a full treatment of the cooperative efforts of the CWS, USAAF, and civilians in the field of incendiary weapons is *Fire Warfare*, vol. 3 of the *Summary Technical Report of Division 11, NDRC.* The CWS "Report on the Activities of the Tech. Div." is also good, as the Technical Division worked constantly with the NDRC.

21. "Exposition . . . ," Eighth AF Chem. Sect., pp. 120–28. An excellent source of information on the activities of the CWS units attached to the USAAF in England is a manuscript for a proposed article in a troop publication. See "Fire in Thousand Ton Lots: The Eighth Air Force Wrecks the Reich War Machine with Chemical Warfare Service Incendiaries," Eighth AF Chem. Sect., 1 April 1944, pp. 2–6, File 519.805, AFSHC.

22. *Chemicals in Combat*, pp. 620–21. When the "F" model of the B-17 arrived in England late in 1944, 52 M47 bombs could be loaded in the bomb bay. The B-24 Liberator heavy bomber, also used by the Eighth AF, could carry 48 M47s. See, CG, Eighth AF to CG, 8th Bomber Command, 10 March 1943, Subj.: Use of Incendiary Bombs, with indorsements, 519.225-4, AFSHC.

23. See *Fire Warfare*, chap. 1, for a good discussion of the problems encountered in developing efficient cluster bomb containers. The M17 cluster was improved several times after its initial employment in late 1943.

24. See Fred B. Shaw, Jr., "Packing Incendiary Bomb Clusters: A Container Problem," *AFCJ* 3 (April 1950): 20–21, for a readable treatment of the serious problems facing the developers of bomb clusters and shipping containers.

25. *Lab. to Field*, pp. 190, 344. The rapid expansion of the U.S. incendiary bombing program put great stress on U.S. manufacturers as well as the military. A few examples of the increased demands: In 1941, there was only one producer of thermite, who turned out about 50 tons per month. CWS let a contract with this supplier for 2,000 tons per month. By 1943, the International Silver Co. was making 30,000 M50 bombs per *day*. This plant, and others like it, were trying to meet the U.S./British demand for magnesium bombs for 1943—52,570,284! See Chief, Industrial Div., CWS to CG, Army Service Forces, 20 March 1943, Subj.: Magnesium Bomb Requirements April–August 1943, File 425.4, HC-EA, APG.

26. "Fire, Blaze, and Belly Tank" File, HQ, Eighth AF, Maintenance and Technical Service, 820.8671E, AFSHC. Also, "Test of Improvised Fuel Oil Incendiaries," USAAF Board Project No. (M-5) 172, 6 June 1944, 428.01, HC-EA, APG.

27. Col. N. J. Baum to CG, ETOUSA, with indorsements to Chief, CWS, 16 July 1944, Subj.: Justification for Certain Extraordinary Requirements, 519.86717, AFSHC.

28. "Final Report on Test of Fire Bomb with Thickened Fuel," USAAF Board Project No. (M-5) 229, 26 June 1944, 228.01, HC-EA, APG. Also see Asst. Chief of Staff, A-3, to Research Division, Ninth AF, 14 Sept. 1944, Subj.: Information on Effectiveness of Thickened Gas Bomb-Current Operations, 168.7045-12, AFSHC.

29. Col. L. N. Tindall, Director of Research, Ninth AF, "Use and Effectiveness of Napalm Fire Bomb," 471.06, USSTAF-ETO File, AFSHC. Also, *The Effectiveness of Third Phase Tactical Air Operations in the European Theater*, USAAF Evaluation Board in the ETO, August 1945, pp. 230–56, 314–18, 168.7045–52, AFSHC.

30. Tindall, p. 7.

31. Ibid., p. 5.

32. Green, Thomson, and Roots, *The Ordnance Department: Planning Munitions for War*, p. 468; Speer remarks in *Strategic Air Offensive*, pp. 394–95. For more information on the Allied air offensive against Germany, see the following reports of the U.S. Strategic Bombing Survey: No. 64b, *The Effects of Strategic Bombing on German Morale*; No. 134b, *Physical Damage Division Report (ETO)*; and No. 193, *Fire Raids on German Cities*, which states, on p. 136, "Fires started by IB's caused more damage to the cities surveyed than HE's and damage to Hamburg, Kassel, Darmstadt, and Wuppertal was 70–80% due to fire and only 20–30% due to H.E."

33. General Eaker's statement appears on p. 8 of *The Destruction of Dresden*, by David J. C. Irving. Years after the war, Air Force Chief of Staff General Curtis LeMay was quoted by E. Bartlett Kerr as saying:

> You drop a load of bombs, and if you are cursed with any imagination at all, you have at least one quick horrid glimpse of ... a three-year old girl wailing 'Mutter, Mutter' because she has been burned. Then you have to turn away from the picture if you intend to retain your sanity. And also if you intend to keep doing the work your nation expects of you.

See Kerr, *Flames Over Tokyo*, p. 154.

34. In a recent study of U.S. attacks on enemy cities, the author states:

> Precision doctrine recognized the validity of transportation targets as a means to weaken the enemy's economy, but attacks on marshaling yards in cities were bound to increase the number of noncombatant casualties from errant bombs. In the Pacific, the evolution toward total war went much further. The strategic air campaign targeted factories and military facilities, but normal precision tactics did not seem to work. In order to destroy these objectives, LeMay resorted to incendiary attacks on urban areas that were bound to kill thousands of civilians. If European air commanders were showing less concern for noncombatant casualties in 1945, Pacific air leaders were demonstrating none at all. Proponents of precision bombing had long argued that it was both the most efficient and humane way to fight a war. But once LeMay became convinced that pinpoint tactics were no longer effective, morality alone was not enough to prevent the firebombing of Tokyo.

See Conrad C. Crane, *Bombs, Cities, and Civilians: American Airpower in World War II* (Lawrence, Kans.: University of Kansas Press, 1993), p. 8.

CHAPTER 6

1. Hamilton, "Reports of CWS Activities USFIP," sec. 2, pp. 2–14.

2. Ibid., sec. 2, p. 29; sec. 3, pp. 12–15. See also Alden H. Waitt, *Gas Warfare* (New York: Dueil, Sloane & Pierce, 1942), pp. 116–17.

3. The weapon used at Buna was not an M1, but an E1R1 that the Engineers had acquired during training in the U.S. See Ltr., Chief Cml. Off., U.S. Forces in the Far East (USAFFE) to Chief, CWS, Subj.: Malfunction of Flame Thrower, E1R1, 6 Jan. 1943, RG 175, 319.1/101, N.A.

4. Acting Div. Chem. Off. to CG, 32d Inf. Div., Subj.: "Report of Activities of the 32d Division Chemical Section during the Papuan Campaign," 18 Feb. 1943, CWS 314.7 File, HC-EA.

5. Reporting channels for CWS officers overseas were complex. As representatives of a support branch of the Army, CWS officers on the staffs of combat unit commanders had to submit after-action reports through the combat organization as well as through Service of Supply (later Army Service Forces) channels. Letters to the Chief of the CWS were often sent through regular mail and were often quite slow in arriving at Edgewood Arsenal. For a good discussion of CWS organizational problems overseas, see *Chemicals in Combat*, pp. 637–40.

6. Second Marine Division Operations Report–Guadalcanal, 16 June 1943, App. J, pp. 4–5, USMC Central Files, RG 127, Job 65A5188, Box 13, A19-1, N.A. 25th Div. Trng. Memo #6, HQ 25th Inf. Div., 27 Mar. 1943, as cited in McKinney, "Portable F.T. Operations," p. 230.

7. James F. Olds, Jr., "Flamethrowers Front and Center," *Chemical Warfare Bulletin*, vol. 30, no. 3 (June–July 1944), pp. 5–8. See also Chem. Off., XIV Corps HQ to Chief Cml. Off., USAFFE, Subj.: Portable Flame Thrower Operations on New Georgia, 15 Sept. 1943, 6th Army Records, 470.71, CWS 314.7 File, HC-EA,

APG. During the first six weeks of the New Georgia campaign, flame throwers were employed on fifty-four separate occasions.

8. See Brophy and Fisher, *Organizing for War*, p. 394. Also, CG, Camp Sibert, La. to CG, ASF, Subj.: Final Report on the Operations of the Experimental Company, Jungle Warfare, 22 Jan. 1944, indorsed to Chief, CWS, 15 Feb. 1944, RG 175, File #370.2/147, N.A.

9. The highly trained troops of the Experimental Company were all eventually assigned as replacements to 4.2-inch mortar units in Italy. This type of personnel mismanagement was rife in the wartime Army. For information on training programs and problems, see Robert R. Palmer, Bell I. Wiley, and William R. Keast, *The Procurement and Training of Army Ground Troops* (Wash., D.C.: GPO, 1948]. See chap. 12 of Brophy, Miles, and Cochran, *From Lab. to Field*, for a discussion of weapons procurement problems.

10. John Miller, Jr., in *CARTWHEEL: The Reduction of Rabaul* (Wash., D.C.: GPO, 1959), comments on the inherent dangers for M1 operators. He says, "On New Georgia . . . the flame thrower operators, carrying their bulky, heavy fuel tanks on their backs, were not properly protected by the riflemen and were soon killed," p. 151.

11. McKinney, "Port. F.T. Operations," pp. 219–20.

12. Julian E. Bers, "How to Fight with Flame-Throwers," *Chemical Warfare Bulletin*, vol. 29, no. 1 (Jan. 1943), pp. 62–67. Also, interview with MSGT William A. Campbell, USMC, Quantico, Va., 11 June 1975.

13. U.S. War Dept. Circular No. 204, 23 May 1944, CWS 314.7 File. Also in Archives Section, U.S. Army Engineer School, Ft. Belvoir, Va. Also, see Orbie Bostick, "21 Months in the South Pacific," *Chemical Warfare Bulletin*, vol. 29, no. 8 (Dec. 1943–Jan. 1944), p. 5.

14. CWS Tech. Intell. Team No. 4 to Chief, Cml. Off., USASOS SWPAC, 24 June 1944, Subj.: Report on Use of Chemical Warfare Weapons and Munitions, CWS 314.7 File. Also, William A. Borden, BG, CWS, to Chief, CWS, Subj.: Report of Visit to Pacific of the "Sphinx Mission" (No Date), CWS 314.7 File, HC-EA, APG. On CWS schools, look to the previously cited "History of Chemical Warfare in the Middle Pacific," and *Chemicals in Combat*, p. 230. Units like the 10th Chem. Mntnce. Co. and the 43d Chem. Lab. Co. rendered support to the combat units in the South Pacific and SWPA. See *Chemicals in Combat*, pp. 286–88, 293–94.

15. The contributions of CWS officers in front-line combat are recorded in after-action reports. For example: Memo, CG, I Corps to CG, 6th Army, Subj.: Flame Throwers, 23 June 1944; and XXIV Corps After-Action Report, Ryukyus, chap. 1, pp. 85–86, 1 Apr. 1945; both in CWS 314.7 File, HC-EA, APG.

16. Earlier attacks recorded in Office Journal, CWS Sec., USFIP, 17 Feb. 1942, copy in Sec. B, "CWS Activities in the Philippines during WWII," and in 1st MarDiv Operations Report Guadalcanal, concerning ten Japanese portable flame throwers captured after the battle on the Tenaru River, Aug. 21, 1942, CWS 314.7 File. Reports on Japanese flame throwers used on Wake Island in December 1941 did not surface until after the war.

17. James F. Olds, Jr., "Early Bougainville Experiments," *Chemical Warfare Bulletin*, vol. 30, no. 4 (Aug.–Sept.–Oct. 1944): 7–9. On a few occasions, Japanese were able to use flame successfully against U.S. positions as was the case on 19 Jan.

1945 in the Philippines. Japanese infiltrators attacked Battery A, 147th FA on Luzon and burned five American troops with flame throwers; see Chemical Intelligence Report, HQ, 158th Reg. Combat Team, 19 Jan. 1945, 6th Army Cml. Records. Copy in CWS 314.7 File, HC-EA, APG.

18. Lt. Thomas B. Allen, F.T. Plt. Ldr., 132d Inf. Reg. to Cml. Off., Americal Div., Subj.: Flame Thrower Plt., 3 Nov. 1944. Also, Trng. Memo #15, 33d Inf. Div., Subj.: Assault Teams, 15 July 1944, CWS 314.7 File, HC-EA, APG. For Marines, see 1st MarDiv GO #172, Subj.: Special Weapons Plt., 23 Dec. 1944, RG 127, Job 62A2371, File #2000-15, N.A.

19. Part 1 of "Study of Japanese Defenses on Betio Island (Tarawa Atoll)," D2, 2d MarDiv, 20 Dec. 1943, RG 127, Job 62A2371, Box 42, N.A. On the M1A1 FT loan, see "History of CWS in Middle Pacific," vol. 2, annex 11g, p. 3. When asked later to justify giving Army equipment to the Marines, Col. Unmacht said, "They were gathering dust in an Army warehouse and killed a lot of Japs." On the conduct of the Tarawa battle, see Robert Sherrod, *Tarawa: The Story of Battle*, 3d ed. (Fredericksburg, Tex.: Nimitz Foundation, 1973); and Henry I. Shaw, Bernard C. Nalty, and Edwin T. Turnbladh, *Central Pacific Drive*, vol. 3 of *History of U.S. Marine Corps Operations in World War II* (Wash., D.C.: GPO, 1966), p. 73.

20. V. Amph. Corps Report of GALVANIC Operation-Tarawa, 11 Jan. 1944, p. 6, RG 127, Job 62A2371, Box 41, N.A. Commandant of the Marine Corps to Quartermaster, USMC, Subj.: Increase in Flame Thrower Allocation, 6 Dec. 1943, RG 127, File #2000-40, N.A.

21. *New York Times*, 24 Nov. 1943, p. 20, col. 3; 28 Nov., p. 1, col. 6; 22 Nov., p. 62, cols 1, 2, 5. See also J. S. Twohey (ed.), *Twohey Analysis of Newspaper Opinion*, 9 Dec. 1943.

22. Extract from speech delivered at Mayflower Hotel, Wash., D.C., p. 6, Speech File (Civilian) Archives, George C. Marshall Research Foundation, Lexington, Va. One of the few protest letters was sent to Sec. of War H. L. Stimson by Joseph H. Leib. Forwarded to General Marshall for reply, it is now in RG 407, File 095/11, Box 263, N.A.

23. Orbie Bostick, "Mercy Killers," *Chemical Warfare Bulletin*, vol. 30, no. 1 (Feb.–Mar. 1944), pp. 16–17, and "CWS Studies Flame Deaths," *Chemical Warfare Bulletin*, vol. 30, no. 2 (Apr.–May 1944), pp. 31–32. A more clinical view of flame toxicology is to be found in the "Report of the Symposium on the Toxicological Effect of the Flame Thrower," CWS, Dunbarton Oaks, 29 Jan. 1945, RG 127, Job 62A2086, Box 24, N.A.

24. For a commentary on the effect of flame throwers on American morale, see Robert A. Arthur and Kenneth Cohlmia, *The Third Marine Division* (Wash., D.C.: Infantry Journal Press, 1948), p. 375. The morale value of flame is also addressed in 3d MarDiv Trng. Order 50–44, 19 Dec. 1944, RG 127, Job 63A2135.

25. George F. Unmacht, "Flame Throwing Seabees," U.S. Naval Institute *Proceedings*, vol. 74, no. 4 (Apr. 1948), pp. 425–27. See also, George F. Hopkins, "Bombing and the American Conscience During World War II," *Historian* 28 (May 1966): 464–69. Also discusses flame thrower employment.

26. After-action Report, Subj.: Chemical Warfare Activities during the Leyte Operation, HQ 6th Army, 10 April 1945, CWS 314.7 File, HC-EA, APG.

27. The development of the M2-2 is well covered in *Fire Warfare*, vol. 3, of the *Summary Technical Report of Div. 11, NDRC*, pp. 99–101. See, too, Report of the

Armored Board, "Comparative Tests of Portable Flame Throwers," Project No. 532, 23 May 1944, CWS 314.7 File, HC-EA, APG.

28. MCEB Report, Subj.: Use of Mod. M1 F.T. in USMC tanks, Project #198, 15 Feb. 1944, RG 127, File #200-15, N.A. Also, CG, 1st MarDiv to MCEB Chief, 12 Nov. 1943, Subj.: Installation of flame thrower in light tank, RG 127, File #200-15/2, N.A.

29. Leonard L. McKinney, "Mechanized Flame Thrower Operations in World War II," pp. 80–140, 145–94.

30. Col. Unmacht served as chemical officer in Hawaii from 1943 to 1945. For his account of the flame tank project, see George F. Unmacht, "Flame Thrower Tanks in the Pacific Ocean Areas," *Military Review* 25, no. 12 (Mar. 1946), pp. 44–51.

31. Special Action Report–Tarawa, C.O. 2d Tank Bn. to CG 2d MarDiv, Subj.: Requirement for tank-mounted flame thrower, 14 Dec. 1943, USMC Cent. Files, RG 127, Job 65A4556, Box 11; and 4th MarDiv Operations Report–Saipan, 18 Sep. 1944, RG 127, Job 62A2371, Box 45, both at N.A. Marine assault forces relied on Navy gunfire support during island landings. The high-velocity, flat-trajectory naval guns were often unable to provide the high-angle fire support that was customary in the ETO.

32. Col. G. F. Unmacht to Chief, Technical Div., CWS, Informal Report of adaption of Ronson Mk. IV Flame Thrower to the LVTA1 (No Date); and Report on use of LVT Flame Throwers on Peleliu, C.O. 1st Amph. Tractor Bn. to CG 3d Amph. Corps, 11 December 1944. Both in CWS 314.7 File, HC-EA, APG.

33. The energetic group headed by Unmacht produced 354 tank-mounted flame throwers in one year, trained over 750 soldiers and Marines in their use, and had only one accident. "Flame Throwing Seabees," p. 427. The M4 flame tanks produced in Hawaii were referred to as the "POA-CWS-H1 Mechanized Flamethrower." In addition to articles previously cited, information on this project is contained in Ltr, Col. G. H. Unmacht to Brig. Gen. Alden H. Waitt, Ass't. Chief, CWS, 10 Jan. 1945, RG 175, File #470.71/B8.1-1, N.A. The Marines preferred this model over any then produced in the U.S. See Commandant, USMC, Memorandum for Record, 22 Jan. 1945, RG 127, File #2000, N.A.

34. One Marine division called the flame tanks "the single most important weapon available to this division." 5th MarDiv Action Report–Iwo Jima, 28 Apr. 1945, vol. 1, sec. 9, p. 33. The 5th Amph. Corps CG stated in an indorsement that the flame throwers had been "invaluable." 1st Ind., 24 May 1945. The portable flame thrower, M2-2, was also used to good advantage by the Marines, as demonstrated by Corp. Hershel W. Williams, who was awarded the Medal of Honor in recognition of his feats with an M2-2 on 23 Feb. 1945.

35. Intercepted radio message from C.O., 309th Independent Infantry Bn. to CG, 2d Mixed Bde., 23 Feb. 1945. Copy in "History of the CWS in the Middle Pacific," vol. 2, p. 569.

36. A full history of the 713th Armored Flame Thrower Bn. is contained in a lengthy after-action report covering the period 10 Nov. 1944 to 30 June 1945, Records of TAGO, RG 407, Box 16687, NA.; and Joseph Morschauser, III, "Blowtorch Battalion," *Armor* (Mar.–Apr. 1960), pp. 30–33. Also, interview with former platoon leader in 713th, Col. Richard H. Jones, USAR, Ft. Myer, Va., 20 May 1975.

37. Following the capture of Peleliu, the CG, Pacific Ocean Areas, General Richardson, directed that Colonel Unmacht devise extension hoses for the mechanized flame throwers. This project is described in a letter from Colonel

Unmacht to Brig. Gen. Alden H. Waitt, Ass't. Chief, CWS, on 13 Jan. 1945, RG 175, File #470.71/3038, N.A. Captain Niemeyer was awarded the Silver Star for this feat. GO #170, HQ, 7th Inf. Div., 28 Aug. 1945.

38. See "Attack by Fire," *Time* 45 (4 June 1945): 35.

39. 1st Tank Bn. AAR–Okinawa, 15 Apr. 1945, Job 65A5188, Box 28; and 3rd Amph. Corps AAR-Ryukyus Operation, App. 8, Job 63A2535, Box 25, both in USMC Cent. Files, RG 127, N.A. Also see 7th Inf. Div. AAR, 30 July 1945, File #05-7, Military Hist. Col., U.S. Army War College Library, Carlisle Barracks, Pa.

CHAPTER 7

1. Vol. 5 of the official USAAF history of World War II, entitled *The Pacific: From MATTERHORN to Nagasaki*, provides the reader with an excellent survey of the planning and execution of the strategic air offensive against Japan.

2. See vol. 1 of the USAAF history, entitled *Plans and Early Operations*, pp. 438–44; and *From Lab. to Field*, pp. 174–75.

3. A typical "lessons learned" summary published toward the end of World War II is found in File 730.3085, AFSHC. See *Area Bomb Study Four: Philippine Islands* (HQ, Fifth A.F., 34th Statistical Control Unit, Aug. 1945). Earle J. Townsend discusses the ways in which incendiary bombing tactics in World War II were employed during the Korean conflict in his article, "Hell Bombs Away," *AFCJ* 4 (January 1951): 8–11. Also see the Far East Air Force report, *Report on the Korean War* (Wash., D.C.: Dept. of the Air Force, 1953), pp. 84–87 (mimeographed). Found in File K720.04D, AFSHC. Coverage on the use of incendiaries abounds. For two factual accounts of aerial incendiary use in Vietnam, see Earl H. Tilford, Jr., *Crosswinds: The Air Force's Setup in Vietnam* (College Station, Tex.: Texas A&M University Press, 1993), pp. 51–52. Also, see Moyers S. Shore, II, *The Battle for Khe Sanh* (Wash., D.C.: GPO, 1969), pp. 108–10, 129–33.

4. Colonel Unmacht's staff prepared a full account of CWS activity in Hawaii. Although mentioned in the last chapter, I cite it again because of its importance to this topic. See the "History of Chemical Warfare in the Middle Pacific, 7 December 1941–2 September 1945" (Chemical Office, HQ, Army Forces Middle Pacific) (mimeographed).

5. Kleber and Birdsell, *Chemicals in Combat*, say on page 637 that although Army CWS Reserve officers were often unfamiliar with current Army doctrine at the outset of World War II, they very quickly caught up and earned high praise from most of the senior CWS officers, especially those overseas. Historian Brooks Kleber cites Kellogg and Unmacht as being two officers who were not hobbled by narrow perceptions built up over long years of service in the tiny peacetime CWS. Their flexibility in solving problems extended to their relations with their wartime staffs, which were noted for getting the job done, often by circumventing established procedures. Letter, Brooks E. Kleber to the author, 27 September 1977, p. 3.

6. HQ, CWS, *Report of the Activities of the Technical Division During World II*, pp. 109–10.

7. *Hist. of Chemical Warfare, Middle Pacific*, vol. 4, annex 11g, p. e.

8. CWS Theater of Operations Newsletter No. 19, Inclosure 5, "Fire Bomb Operations," 3 Nov. 1944, File 228.01/12, HC-EA, APG; and AAR, FORAGER

Operation, Task Force 52, pp. 86, 93, 94, and annex D, RG 127, Job 6325.03, N.A. Also see, Organizational History, HQ, 318th Fighter Group, 7th Fighter Command, Seventh AF, 1 July 1944–31 July 1944, 318.11 (FI), AFSHC.

9. History of the Chemical Section, HQ, Fifth AF, 15 June 1944–2 Sept. 1945, pp. 4–7, File 730.805, AFSHC.

10. 4th MarDiv AAR, DETACHMENT Operation, annex C, pp. 6–7, RG 127, Job 2364.07, N.A.

11. *Hist. of Chemical Warfare, Middle Pacific*, vol. 4, annex 11g, pp. 2, 6–7.

12. "Napalm: Fire Bombs Turn Trick Against Holed Up Nips in Luzon," *Impact* 3 (August 1945): 49–53; also, Colonel H. F. Cunningham, Asst. Chief, Air Staff, A-2, "Tactical Use of Napalm by the Fifth Air Force, January–April 1945" (monograph), File 730.805, AFSHC.

13. *MATTERHORN to Nagasaki*, p. 436; *Lab. to Field*, p. 183.

14. *Hist. of Chemical Warfare, Middle Pacific*, vol. 4, annex 11g, pp. 20–21.

15. *Japan: Incendiary Attack Data* (Wash., D.C.: HQ, USAAF, October 1943). Prepared by the Assistant Chief of Air Staff for Intelligence (A-2), this report highlighted Japan's vulnerability to fire. File 425, 228.01, HC-EA, APG.

16. E. W. Hollingsworth, "The Use of Thickened Gasoline in Warfare," *AFCJ* 4 (April 1951): 32; *Report of the CWS Technical Division*, pp. 98–100; and Baldwin Interviews, "Development of Incendiary Bombs," pp. 8–10.

17. See the NDRC's *Fire Warfare*, pp. 82–85; and E. H. Lewis, Major, CWS, "Tests of the M69X Incendiary Bomb at Dugway Proving Ground, Tooele, Utah, 19 September–10 November 1943," File 240.07617-2, AFSHC.

18. *Report of the CWS Technical Division*, pp. 100–101.

19. An excellent account of the employment of large napalm bombs by pathfinder aircraft is found in an unpublished thesis by Joseph L. Laughlin, Colonel, USAF, "The Application and Effect of Napalm," presented at the Air Command and Staff College, the Air University, Maxwell AFB, Ala., March 1948, pp. 38–45. The M76, tested and rejected by the USAAF in the ETO, was popular in the Pacific. Over 38,000 were dropped on Japan.

20. *From Lab. to Field*, pp. 187–88 in a section entitled "Incendiary Oddities." For a less-than-gracious account of Dr. Fieser's bat bomb idea, see Seymour M. Hersh, *Chemical and Biological Warfare: America's Hidden Arsenal* (New York: Bobbs-Merrill, 1968), pp. 62–63. The best treatment of the bat bomb project has been provided by Jack Couffer, one of the members of the test staff, in his book *Bat Bomb: World War II's Other Secret Weapon* (Austin, Tex.: University of Texas Press, 1992).

21. Cited by John H. Munhall, "Were Japs Defeated by CWS 2 Incendiaries?" *CCJ* 1 (October 1946): 41.

22. *MATTERHORN to Nagasaki*, pp. 38–39; *Chemicals in Combat*, pp. 624–27; and "The Giant Pays its Way," from *World War II in the Air: The Pacific* (New York: Franklin Watts, 1962), pp. 253–54. The 20th B.C. refitted in India after phasing out of China, then joined with the 21st B.C. in April and May 1945. 20th B.C. units flew missions over Japan, but primarily were used to bomb Formosa and to provide bomber support for the Okinawa landings.

23. Telephone Conference, Brigadier General Lauris Norstad to Brigadier General H. S. Hansell, Subj.: Conduct of incendiary raid vs. Nakajima plant, Musashiro, Japan, 11 November 1944. Transcript in File 471.07P, AFSHC. For a breakdown

of missions flown see Twentieth AF, "Summary of Bombing and Mining Missions, 24 Nov. 1944–30 June 1945," File 425, 228.01, HC-EA, APG. Arnold's staff, in coming to the conclusion that incendiaries should be employed in large numbers, relied upon a report prepared by the Army Air Forces Board dated 4 July 1944, "A Study of Incendiary Bombs for Employment by the Army Air Forces," Project (M5) 261, File 425, 228.01, HC-EA, APG. The report discussed the types of bombs for use against different targets, determined the mix of H.E. and incendiaries to optimize destruction, and even diagrammed the best formations for the bombers to use.

24. *MATTERHORN to Nagasaki*, pp. 563–65.

25. *Chemicals in Combat*, pp. 627–28. See also T. P. Gahan, Colonel, USAAF, "The Status of Incendiaries in the Army Air Forces," unpublished thesis, the Air University, Maxwell AFB, Ala., March 1947, pp. 9–12.

26. The industrial areas of all Japanese cities bombed by B-29s were inspected and diagrammed in USSBS Report P90, *Effects of Incendiary Bomb Attacks on Japan—A Report on Eight Cities* (Wash., D.C.: GPO, 1947), App. C.

27. "The Giant Pays its Way," p. 254; *MATTERHORN to Nagasaki*, pp. 628–32; and Twentieth AF, "Summary of Bombing and Mining Missions."

28. *Chemicals in Combat*, p. 629; USSBS, *Report on Eight Cities*, pp. 67–68, 94–102.

29. *MATTERHORN to Nagasaki*, p. 640.

30. "Analysis of Incendiary Phase Operations against Japanese Urban Areas, 9–19 March 1945" (HQ, 21st B.C.) (mimeographed), File 760.01 (vol. 7), AFSHC. With respect to the development of doctrine, incendiaries differed little from the host of weapons employed during World War II.

31. "The Giant Pays," pp. 258–60; and Twentieth AF, *Special Report on the Incendiary Attacks Against Japanese Urban Industrial Areas* (Wash., D.C.: GPO, Dec. 1945), File 760.551, AFSHC.

32. U.S. Army Forces, Pacific, *Documents Submitted to the Supreme Commander for the Allied Forces by the Japanese Mission to Negotiate Surrender* (1945) (mimeographed), pp. 4–5. Also, Munhall, "Were Japs Defeated by CWS Incendiaries?" p. 41; and *MATTERHORN to Nagasaki*, p. 756.

33. "Firebirds' Flight," *Time* 45 (19 March 1945): 32. See also, "Fire Bombs Over Japan," *Chicago Sun*, 15 May 1945, sec. B, p. 26, copy in File 425, 228.01, HC-EA, APG.

34. Samuel R. Shaw, "Nonnuclear Attacks," pp. 83–102 in vol. 3 of Hero study on effects of mass casualties.

35. USSBS, *Japan's Struggle to End the War*, Report P2 (Wash., D.C.: GPO, 1946), p. 13.

36. As cited by Egbert F. Bullene, "Chemicals in Combat," *AFCJ* 5 (April 1952): 21.

EPILOGUE

1. Despite the success of U.S. incendiary weapons in World War II, financial constraints forced the U.S. Air Force and the Naval Air Service to delete training with aerial incendiaries from flight training and unit training in 1946. Only the Marine Corps continued to train its pilots in napalm attack techniques during the period 1946–1950. See Theodore P. Gahan, Colonel, Chemical Corps, "The

Status of Incendiaries in the Army Air Forces," unpublished thesis, Air University, Maxwell Field, Ala., 1947.

2. Leo P. Brophy, "Origins of the Chemical Corps," *Military Affairs* 20 (Winter 1956): 217–26; also Green, Thomson, and Roots, *The Ordnance Department: Planning Munitions for War*, pp. 256, 260.

3. In studying the procedures by which bureaucratic governments reach decisions, this writer has found a model for decision making proposed by Graham T. Allison to be a most helpful study guide. Using the U.S. response during the Cuban Missile Crisis as an example, Allison shows how "Rational Policy," "Organizational Process," and "Bureaucratic Politics" all influence final policy decisions. See Allison, "Conceptual Models and the Cuban Missile Crisis," *American Political Science Review* 63 (September 1969): 699–718.

4. A number of historians of the CWS during wartime have talked about the tendency to spend great sums of money in procurement of new weapons to speed developmental testing. See James P. Baxter, III, *Scientists Against Time* (Boston: Little, Brown, 1952); Lincoln R. Thiesmeyer and John E. Burchard, *Combat Scientists* (Boston: Little, Brown, 1947); "Chemical Procurement in the New England States," *CCJ* 2 (October 1947): 48–50; and Gilbert White, "Armor for the Flamethrower: Staff Gave Us 60 Days," *CWB* 30 (August–September–October 1944): 4–7.

5. Lumsden, *Incendiary Weapons*, pp. 24, 72–73; Trooboff, *Law and Responsibility in Warfare: The Vietnam Experience*, p. 24; and especially Frederic J. Brown, *Chemical Warfare: A Study in Restraints* (Princeton, N.J.: Princeton Univ. Press, 1968), pp. 51–96.

6. Interviews with Richard H. Jones, COL, USAR, Ft. Myer, Va., 20 May 1975; William A. Campbell, MSGT, USMC, Quantico, Va., 11 June 1975; and Wilson C. Turnage, COL, USMC (Ret.), Kansas City, Mo., 6 December 1976. Postwar soul-searching prompted bomber pilot–turned poet James L. Dickey to write "The Fire Bombing," found in a collection of his works entitled *Buckdancer's Choice* (Middleton, Conn.: Wesleyan Univ. Press, 1964), pp. 11–20.

7. Roger A. Beaumont and Martin Edmonds, eds., *War in the Next Decade* (London: Macmillan Press, Ltd., 1975). See especially the essay by Roger Williams, "Science, Technology, and Future Warfare," pp. 157–79. Another exceptionally thought-provoking essay is taken from a lecture presented on 3 October 1973 to the Royal United Services Institute by Sir Michael Howard entitled "Military Science in an Age of Peace," *RUSI Journal* 119 (March 1974): 3–9.

8. A lucid and comprehensive discussion of the problems encountered by CWS officers in overseas areas may be found in Kleber and Birdsell, *Chemicals in Combat*, pp. 637–40, in the chapter entitled "The CWS Overseas."

9. Incendiary bombs *were* more destructive to most targets than H.E. In 1944 the British RE/8 staff reported that, "When properly employed, incendiaries were more effective against German cities and industrial targets than High Explosives," cited in NDRC, *Effects of Weapons on Targets*, Project AN-23 Report, June 1945, p. 34. The Strategic Bombing Survey also compared incendiary bombs to H.E. The USSBS reported that even against fire-resistant structures, the M47 incendiary bomb was twice as destructive as the 500-lb H.E. general purpose bomb. See USSBS Report No. 193, *Fire Raids on German Cities* (Wash., D.C.: GPO, 1947), p. 129.

10. It should be noted here that the Soviet army also used flame throwers to good advantage. For a discussion of Soviet flame warfare techniques, see Alexei Kononenko, "Attack on a Fortified Inhabited Point," *Infantry Journal* 51 (May–June 1944): 62–63.

11. Trevor N. Dupuy, ed., HERO Study, vol. 1, p. 65. Dupuy, in his study of attacks against civilian populations, explains this shift in attitude by saying:

> Although at some time in the past legal, moral, ethical, or other considerations have inhibited belligerents from inflicting mass casualties upon civilian populations, restraints which may have seemed strong in peacetime have tended to be less binding during a war. This is particularly true when a war psychology has been developed either through propaganda or the frustration of a long war, or when the people of one belligerent have come to look upon its opponents as beings of lesser human value.

12. CWS, *Report on the Activities of the Technical Division During World War II*, p. 136.

13. For information on the role of flame weapons in Korea, see the following: Walter G. Hermes, *Truce Tent and Fighting Front: The United States Army in the Korean War* (Wash., D.C.: GPO, 1966), which also mentions the Chinese claim that the U.S. was using germ warfare; and Pat Meid and James P. Yingling, [USMC] *Operations in West Korea* (Wash., D.C.: GPO, 1972).

14. Information on the use of flame throwers is in John Cookson and Judith Nottingham, *A Survey of Chemical and Biological Warfare* (London: Shedd and Ward, 1969); Richard A. Falk, ed., *The Vietnam War and International Law*, 3 vols. (Princeton, N.J.: Princeton University Press, 1972); and "Assault on Hill 875," *Time* 90 (1 Dec. 1967): 27. Lest the reader feel that all flame weapons were American, see "The Massacre at Dak Son," *Time* 90 (15 Dec. 1967): 32–34.

15. For information on napalm employment techniques, see Earl H. Tilford, Jr., *Crosswinds: The Air Force's Setup in Vietnam* (College Station, Tex.: Texas A&M Press, 1993), p. 5. I. D. Gravovoy and V. K. Kadyuk criticized the U.S. fire weapons in their book *Incendiary Weapons and Defense Against Them* (Moscow: Voyehizdat, 1983), p. 5. Formerly classified reports published in 1970 provide information on another use of aerial incendiaries. During the early stages of the U.S. air campaign in Vietnam, the U.S. Forest Service assisted the Air Force in a project reminiscent of the cellulose leaves experiments of World War II. Highly classified experiments named SHERWOOD FOREST and HOT TIP were conducted to determine whether incendiaries could defoliate large tracts of forest, thus denying sanctuary to the Communist forces. Although the forests were burned, the tests concluded that defoliation by means of a chemical agent codenamed Agent ORANGE would be more effective and incendiaries were once again targeted against enemy troops and equipment, just as they had been in Korea. See Jay R. Bentley and Craig C. Chandler, eds., *Forest Fires as a Weapon* (U.S. Forest Service, 1970), pp. 2–7.

16. Rick Atkinson, *Crusade: The Untold Story of the Persian Gulf War* (New York: Houghton, Mifflin, 1993), pp. 366–67. Marine Corps capacity to employ Fuel-Air Explosive and napalm confirmed in an interview with Lt. Col. John Cushing, Operations Officer of Marine Air Group 11 during DESERT STORM. Interview on 9 November 1993. The M202A1 multirocket launcher weighs 27 lb. loaded and will project a flame round about 750 meters. The encapsulated flame missile

weighs 3 lbs. The Navy still maintains extensive stocks of Korean-vintage napalm bombs in a storage site in Fallbrook, California. The Navy is making efforts now to sell the napalm bomb filling for use in commercial furnaces. See "Navy Set to Move Napalm Stockpile," *Boston Blade* (22 March 1996): 8.

17. I. B. Holley, *Ideas and Weapons*, p. vii.

18. Army Initiatives Group, Office of the Deputy Chief of Staff for Operations and Plans, "State of America's Army on Its 218th Birthday" (Wash., D.C.: 1993), p. 3.

19. Ibid., pp. 5–6. See also *America's Army—One Team, One Fight, One Future*, the U.S. Army's Posture Statement for FY 1999 (Wash., D.C.: U.S. Army, 1998), pp. 26–29.

20. For an appreciation of the U.S. Army's vision of the future, read FM 3-0, *Operations* (Wash., D.C.: February 2008). Also, look to Gordon R. Sullivan, "America's Army: Into the Twenty-first Century" (Cambridge, Mass.: Institute for Foreign Policy Analysis, 1993), pp. 12–17, 38–41.

21. General Douglas MacArthur cited by Theodore Ropp, *War in the Modern World*, p. 403.

Bibliography

SOURCES

Special Aids to Research

Those interested in the development and employment of incendiary weapons during World War II may wish to begin their inquiry by looking at generally available sources of information on the subject. There is, unfortunately, no single good bibliography that deals exclusively with flame weapons utilized by the United States armed forces. Lacking such a guide, the researcher must depend upon published works that contain well-documented footnotes and suitable bibliographical notes. A recommended starting place would be the three-volume history of the U.S. Army Chemical Warfare Service during World War II. The books are as follows:

Brophy, Leo P., and George Fisher. *The Chemical Warfare Service: Organizing for War.* Washington, D.C.: Government Printing Office, 1959.
Deals primarily with the prewar organization of the CWS and the tremendous changes wrought in this small technical branch by the entry of the USA into World War II. Little information about flame weapons *per se*, but valuable for the picture it presents of organizational problems of the CWS.

Brophy, Leo P., Wyndham D. Miles, and Rexmond C. Cochrane. *The Chemical Warfare Service: From Laboratory to Field.* Washington, D.C.: Government Printing Office, 1959.
Research and development of CWS weapons and material provides the focus for this, the second volume. While the testing of flame throwers and incendiary bombs by the CWS and civilian scientists is thoroughly covered, very little is said in explaining why the U.S. Army neglected incendiary weapons prior to 1940.

Kleber, Brooks E., and Dale Birdsell. *The Chemical Warfare Service: Chemicals in Combat.* Washington, D.C.: Government Printing Office, 1966.
The most important published source in this bibliography. Chapters 14–17 deal exclusively with flame throwers and aerial incendiaries in combat, but critical insight into the role of the CWS overseas is provided throughout this very well-written and carefully annotated history. If the researcher has time for only one book on the subject of U.S. incendiary weapons, this is the one he must read.

149

The official wartime histories of the U.S. Marine Corps and the U.S. Army Air Forces contain a good deal of information about the use of flame weapons by their respective services, but require an index search of each volume. "Incendiaries," "Flame Throwers," "Napalm," and "Weapons" are the most fruitful index topics. Most major libraries will have these multivolume histories. Look to:

Historical Branch, HQ, USMC. *History of U.S. Marine Corps Operations in World War II.* 5 vols. Washington, D.C.: Government Printing Office, 1969.

These five volumes recount the operational history of the USMC prior to Pearl Harbor to the period following V-J Day. The enthusiastic response of Marines to incendiaries and numerous accounts of flame weapon employment are chronicled in each volume.

Craven, Wesley F., and James L. Cate, eds. *The Army Air Forces in World War II.* 5 vols. Office of Air Force History. Chicago: Univ. of Chicago Press, 1952.

Weapons development, the growth of a body of tactical doctrine based on combat experience, and organizational evolution are as important to this five-volume history as strictly operational matters. Well footnoted and served by a carefully constructed index for each volume.

A nicely organized index may also be found in the official British history of the Royal Air Force during World War II. By investigating the role that incendiaries played in the Allied bomber offensive against Germany, the student may gain an appreciation for the development, employment, and effects of aerial incendiaries. See:

Webster, [Sir] Charles K., and Noble Frankland. *The Strategic Air Offensive Against Germany, 1939–1945.* 4 vols. London: H. M. Stationery Office, 1961.

Good indexes and a text remarkably free of jargon. Volume 4, "Appendices," has a number of documents of German origin that speak to the effectiveness of area bombing in general, and to incendiary bombs in particular.

Several other sources of information that may be found in the well-stocked library will shed some light on the past history of fire in warfare and upon the modern concerns being expressed over the morality of flame weapons. Suggested are the *Encyclopedia Britannica.* 15th Edition. Volumes 5 and 29 for good descriptions of "Greek Fire"; and Partington, J. R. *A History of Greek Fire and Gunpowder.* Cambridge, England: W. Heffer, 1960. See also, *Napalm and Incendiary Weapons.* Stockholm: Stockholm International Peace Research Institute, 1972. (Also published by the author, Malvern Lumsden. *Incendiary Weapons.* Cambridge, Mass.: M.I.T. Press, 1975.) The researcher with access to United Nations publications will find a helpful, though incomplete, bibliography dealing with incendiary weapons in Annex 2 of the *Report to the Secretary General: Napalm and Other Incendiary Weapons and All Aspects of their Use.* New York: U.N., 1973.

For those able to travel in pursuit of information on this topic, the archival collections listed in Section 2 of this bibliography (Primary Sources) will prove indispensable to a full appreciation of the difficulties encountered by the American military forces in fielding effective flame weapons. Among the many archival collections examined during the preparation of this book, two stood out as being absolutely essential to the study. These two collections deserve special attention here.

Foremost in importance and wealth of material is the voluminous accumulation of correspondence, reports, monographs, and notes compiled by the authors of the three-volume history of the CWS during World War II. Located at Aberdeen Proving Ground, Maryland, this treasure trove of information was maintained by the Historian's Office, Chemical Warfare Center, until 1976. Upon the retirement of the historian, Dr. Sherman Davis, the files were moved to Washington until recently, when they were returned to Aberdeen Proving Ground. Within this mass of paper, two groups of files are most germane to the topic of flame weapons. File No. 314.7 on flame throwers and File No. 228.1 on aerial incendiaries have been painstakingly indexed and sorted and remain virtually undisturbed. Access to the unclassified material which makes up the bulk of the Edgewood Arsenal collection may be obtained through application to the U.S. Army Research, Development, and Engineering Command, Aberdeen Proving Ground, Maryland.

Second only to the Aberdeen files in importance is the extensive collection of information concerning aerial incendiaries maintained in the archives of the Albert F. Simpson Historical Center at Maxwell Air Force Base, Alabama. Located in the library of the Air University, the Simpson Center has a wealth of after-action reports, correspondence, test reports, British and German intelligence summaries, and U.S. combat narratives. A trip to the Simpson Center is time well spent, thanks in large part to the team of competent and helpful archivists who are anxious to assist the researcher in any way possible.

Before concluding this section on "Special Aids to Research," I must mention the Defense Technical Information Center (DTIC). As a major component of the Department of Defense (DOD) Scientific and Technical Information Program, DTIC contributes to the management and conduct of defense research by DOD personnel and organizations. Universities involved in federally funded research are also eligible to receive DTIC services. The public can apply for access to DTIC through the National Technical Information Service (NTIS). For further information, contact NTIS at 5285 Port Royal Road, Springfield, Va. 22161.

PRIMARY SOURCES

Manuscript and Document Collections

George C. Marshall Research Foundation Archives, Lexington, Va., Speech File

This compilation of addresses given by General Marshall contains an address to the American Legion in Washington, D.C., in which the Chief of Staff defended the use of flame weapons by American troops.

National Archives

Records of the Army Air Forces. Record Group [RG] 18.

A subdivision of this group is the collection of Records of Headquarters, Twentieth Air Force, which contains reports and correspondence between Arnold's Washington headquarters and the 20th and 21st Bomber Commands, the operational branches of Twentieth Air Force.

Marine Corps Central Files, Records of the Commandant, USMC. RG 127.

This collection, subdivided into numerous "JOB" numbers, contains information on Marine use of flame throwers as well as copies of numerous CWS documents provided to the USMC during WWII.

Records of the War Department General and Special Staffs. RG 165.

Staff actions concerning flame throwers are found in the office records of G2, G3, and G4 Sections.

Records of the Chief, Chemical Warfare Service. RG 175.

This record group is arranged chronologically from 1919 to 1947. Of special value is File No. 470.71 during the period 1940–1945, as it contains most of the information in RG 175 about flame throwers.

Records of the Chiefs of Arms. RG 177.

Pre–1942 correspondence, directives, and studies are found in this collection, which is subdivided into the various branches, i.e. Records of the Chief of Engineers or Chief of Infantry.

Records of the Office of Scientific Research and Development. RG 227.

Created in June 1941, as part of the Office for Emergency Management, OSRD exercised jurisdiction over numerous civilian-manned wartime agencies engaged in scientific research. Chief among them, and of primary interest to this study, was the NDRC. Records of the National Defense Research Committee are found here in Record Group 227. See especially the records of Division 11, NDRC, which worked on incendiary weapons and fillers.

Records of the Headquarters, Army Ground Forces. RG 337.

During WWII, the AGF controlled troop units training in the U.S. for overseas combat. Official reports of flame thrower training conducted at various posts is to be found here.

Records of the U.S. Army Commands, 1942–. RG 338.

Some records of flame thrower tests carried out prior to 1942 as well as tests completed during wartime at various U.S. posts are filed in this group.

Records of the Adjutant General's Office, 1917–. RG 407.

This massive compilation of orders, correspondence, and programs contains quite a bit of correspondence about flame weapons after 1940. It is difficult to use this group unless the specific date and addressee of a letter from the AG is known. Correspondence from, or going through, the AG is catalogued and filed by date and addressee.

United States Army

Center of Military History. Ft. McNair, D.C.

This outgrowth of the Office of the Chief, Military History has a large collection of World War II historical studies, among which are historical monographs completed by CWS historians soon after WWII.

Chemical School. Manuscripts and Archives Library. Ft. Leonard Wood, Mo.
 The records of the CWS school and a great deal of material on flame weapons are now available for research at the Chemical School Library.

Command and General Staff College. Manuscripts and Archives Library. Ft. Leavenworth, Kans.
 Full collection of U.S. Army Technical and Field Manuals of World War II on microfilm, to include those on flame weapons. Numerous unclassified reports on flame weapons and combat narratives, as well as unit after-action reports.

Corps of Engineers. Engineer School Archives. Ft. Leonard Wood, Mo.
 The archival collection of the Engineer School Library contains nearly all of the flame thrower test reports submitted by the Engineer Test Board during WWII.

War College. Military History Institute. Carlisle Barracks, Pa.
 These archives contain several references to flame warfare in the personal papers and photographs donated to MHI. The expert archivists and reference librarians make working in these collections a pleasure.

United States Marine Corps

Marine Corps Schools Library Archives. Quantico, Va.
 This archival collection, although poorly organized, contains numerous after-action reports, unit histories, and test reports of the Marine Corps Equipment Board for the period 1942–1945.

United States Government Publications

Chemical Warfare Service and Chemical Corps

Agents. Book II. of Course Material Chemical Warfare School. Edgewood Arsenal, Md.: CWS Dept. of Technique, 1925. (Mimeographed).
 Excellent source of information on World War I incendiary bombs. Indicates a scholarly awareness of incendiary materials at a time when the CWS had no incendiary weapons in its inventory.

Finklestein, Leo. "Flame Throwers," Vol. 15 of "History of Research and Development of the Chemical Warfare Service in World War II." Edgewood Arsenal, Md.: Chemical Corps, 1949. (Mimeographed).
 This is an extremely informative study of the activities of the Technical Division of the CWS, the procurement activities of the CWS, and developmental testing of flame apparatus.

Finklestein, Leo, and Alfred E. Gaul. "Incendiaries," Vol. 18 of "History of Research and Development of the Chemical Warfare Service in World War II." Edgewood Arsenal, Md.: Chemical Corps, 1952. (Mimeographed).
 A very important document. Traces the development and testing of all types of U.S. incendiary bombs during World War II.

German Chemical Warfare Materiel. Chief CWS, HQ, ETO, USA. 1945. Typescript. 250 pages.
    Produced by the Intelligence Division of the CWS in ETO, this hardback has a 10-page section on German flamethrowers and accessories. Part 1, section P.

Index to Official Publications Pertaining to Chemical Warfare. Office of the Chief, CWS. Washington, D.C.: Government Printing Office, 1934.
    No publications listed in this bibliography deal with flame warfare. A fact that reveals much about the CWS in the mid-1930s.

McKinney, Leonard L. "Mechanized Flame Thrower Operations in World War II." Chemical Corps Historical Study No. 5. Edgewood Arsenal, Md.: Chemical Corps, 1951. (Mimeographed).
    Authoritative monograph about the American use of tank-mounted flame projectors during World War II.

McKinney, Leonard L. "Portable Flame Thrower Operations in World War II." Chemical Corps Historical Study No. 4. Edgewood Arsenal, Md.: Chemical Corps, 1958. (Mimeographed).
    This study contains a great deal of information gained from interviews with participants of flame thrower actions as well as numerous reproductions of official documents.

Ocshner, Herman. "A History of German Chemical Warfare in World War II." Trans. by H. Heitman. Washington, D.C.: Chemical Corps, 1948.
    This monograph contains useful text and diagrams concerning German flame weapons and the problems experienced with fuel after 1944.

Principles of Employment of Flame and Incendiaries. U.S. Army Chemical Corps School. Ft. McClellan, Ala.: Dept of the Army, 1955.
    Published as a "Special Text," this manual contains the approved Army doctrine for flame throwers developed during World War II and Korea.

Ray, Arthur B. "Incendiaries." Chemical Warfare Service Monograph No. 43. Washington, D.C.: Chemical Warfare Service, AEF, 1919.
    This monograph, written during and just after World War I, reflected General Fries' views of flame weapons. Only phosphorus was thought to be efficient.

Report of the Activities of the Technical Division During World War II. Washington, D.C.: Chemical Warfare Service, 1946.
    This valuable report compiled during and immediately after World War II recounts the diverse activities of the CWS Technical Division.

"Study Guide—Incendiaries." CWS Pamphlet No. 3. Edgewood Arsenal, Md.: Chemical Warfare School, 1942. (Mimeographed).
    A self-instruction text that borrows heavily on British and German experience with incendiaries from 1939 to 1941.

National Defense Research Committee

Effects of Weapons on Targets. National Defense Research Committee. Vol. 3. Washington, D.C.: NDRC, 1945.
    Report of NDRC, Army, and Navy joint project AN-23 entitled "Studies of Combined HE-1B Attack on Precision Targets." The data demonstrates the increasing sophistication of target destruction procedures utilized during World War II.

Ewell, R. H. "Theory and Tactics of Incendiary Bombing." Washington, D.C.: Government Printing Office, October 1942.
    Prepared by Division 8 of the OSRD, the report on methods and desired results of incendiary bombing is very significant. It preceded by many months the U.S. Army's ability to carry out an effective incendiary bombing program.

Fire Warfare. Vol. 3 of *Summary Technical Report of Division 11, NDRC.* Washington, D.C.: Government Printing Office.
    This study provides a great deal of specific information about research methods, contracts, and manufacturing problems encountered by the CWS and NDRC during World War II.

Standard Oil Development Company. *Use of Flame on Japanese Bunkers.* NDRC Contract OEMsv 390, Report PDN 1700, November 3, 1943.
    Report of tests of different types of flame throwers and fuels conducted at Ft. Belvoir, Va., and Ft. Pierce, Fla.

Statutes at Large

National Defense Act. Amended. Statutes at Large. Vol. 41 (1920).
    Established the Chemical Warfare Service.

Annual Army Appropriations Act. Statutes at Large. Vol. 42 (1931).
    Provided funds for the CWS.

Military Establishment Appropriations Act. Statutes at Large. Vol. 56 (1942).
    Provided funds for the CWS.

Strategic Bombing Surveys

Description of R.A.F. Bombing. USSBS Report No. 4. Washington, D.C.: Government Printing Office, 1945.
    RAF procedures and tactical techniques as well as bombing results are dealt with in detail. This study provides an interesting comparison of British and U.S. bombing procedures.

Effects of Incendiary Bomb Attacks on Japan—A Report on Eight Cities. USSBS Report P90, Washington, D.C.: Government Printing Office, 1947.
    This report contains a vast amount of data on physical damage and loss of life in Tokyo, Nagoya, Akashi, and five other Japanese cities that were fire bombed.

Effects of Strategic Bombing on German Morale. USSBS Report No. 79. Washington, D.C.:
   Government Printing Office, 1947.
   A survey conducted in Germany at the close of WWII. This study outlines the
common physical and emotional trauma experienced by the inhabitants of heavily
bombed cities.

Fire Raids on German Cities. USSBS Report No. 193. Washington, D.C.: Government
   Printing Office, 1947.
   An operational report which recounts the conduct as well as the effect of incendi-
ary bomb campaigns in Germany.

Japan's Struggle to End the War. USSBS Report P2. Washington, D.C.: Government
   Printing Office, 1947.
   Interviews with Japanese leaders at the close of the war revealed the tremendous
damage done to Japanese morale by fire bombing.

Physical Damage Division Report (ETO). USSBS Report 134b. Washington, D.C.: Government Printing Office, 1947.
   The vast damage done by incendiary bombs to German structures is recorded in
this particular report.

Summary Report: European War. USSBS. Washington, D.C.: 1945.
   Best place to start in assessing the effects of the Allied Bomber Offensive. Specific
reports can be checked later.

War Department, Department of the Army, and Department of the Air Force

Biennial Report of the Chief of Staff of the United States Army (July 1, 1943 to June 30,
   1945) to the Secretary of War. Washington, D.C.: Government Printing Office, 1945.
   Gen G. C. Marshall reports of the progress of World War II.

Chanard Incendiary Bomb. Chief of Ordnance, USA War Department, GPO, 1920.
   Eight-page Service Handbook describes the French Chanard incendiary. Contains
description of construction, dimensions, and operation of the Chanard.

Chemical Warfare Training Circular No. 72. Washington, D.C.: War Department, December 1941.
   The first effort to provide engineer troops with a basic tactical doctrine for the
portable flame thrower.

*Documents Submitted to the Supreme Commander for the Allied Forces by the Japanese Mission
   to Negotiate Surrender.* GHQ, U.S. Army Forces, Pacific, 1945. (Mimeographed).
   A translation of Japanese documents presented to General MacArthur. Part 1 lists
all Japanese cities suffering bomb damage in 1945.

"Enemy Capabilities for Chemical Warfare." Special Series No. 16. Washington, D.C.:
   War Department, 1943.
   This pamphlet outlines the chemical warfare equipment of Italy, Japan, and Germany.

"Enemy Tactics in Chemical Warfare." Special Series No. 24. Washington, D.C.: War
    Department, 1944.
    German flame thrower tactics as practiced in Belgium, France, and Russia are
reported in this pamphlet.

Forest Fires as a Military Weapon. Chandler, Craig C., and Jay R. Bentley. U.S. Depart-
    ment of Agriculture, Forest Service, 1970. Initially SECRET. Declassified via
    DARPA in 1983.
    Sponsored by Advanced Research Projects Agency (ARPA) Overseas Defense
Research. Responds to a 1965 request by JCS, which asks OSD to initiate a study to
determine the feasibility of starting large fires to destroy VC sanctuaries.

"Fougasse Flame Throwers." Intelligence Bulletin. Vol. 3, no. 3. Washington, D.C.:
    War Department, 1944.
    Discusses the use of fixed flame projectors by the Soviets and Russians during
World War II.

Handbook on German Military Forces. TM-E 30-451. Washington, D.C.: Government
    Printing Office, 1945.
    Originally restricted matter, this manual contains a great deal of information on
German equipment.

"Handbook of the Incendiary Drop Bombs, Mark I and II." War Department Pam-
    phlet, GPO, 1918.
    Explanation and line drawings of two scatterable bombs. Gives detailed informa-
tion on the construction, nomenclature, and employment of these 40-lb bombs.

History of Chemical Warfare in the Middle Pacific, 7 December 1941–2 September 1945. HQ,
    U.S. Army Forces, Mid-Pacific, 1945. (Mimeographed).
    An excellent chronological, and topical, account of the actions of Chemical War-
fare Service troops and chemical weapons employed in the Pacific during World War
II. Somewhat critical of the efforts of HQ, CWS, at Edgewood Arsenal, Md.

Joint Munitions Effectiveness Manual: Weapons Characteristics. Field Manual (FM) 101-50-
    20. Washington, D.C.: U.S. Army, 1985, w/Change 4, 1992.
    This is the unclassified reference manual for air-to-surface munitions, to include
all incendiary munitions in the USAF inventory. Updated annually, the "JMEM" is a
standard for researchers.

*Joint Munitions Effectiveness Manual: Surface-to-Surface; Weapons, Ammunition, and Fuze
    Characteristics.* FM 101-61-2. Washington, D.C.: U.S. Army, 1989.
    Ground mounted weapons and ammunition are covered in this manual. Basic
information on all surface-to-surface weapons in the U.S. military is found here.

The Law of Land Warfare. FM 27-10. Washington, D.C.: U.S. Army, 1956.
    Still the current Army manual that covers the laws of land warfare. Discusses the
restrictions on the employment of mass-casualty weapons, to include flame
weapons.

Operation of Engineer Field Units. FM 5-135. Washington, D.C.: War Department, 1942.
  Little specific information is provided in this FM. It does point out that engineers may refer to TC No. 72 regarding flame thrower doctrine.

Operations. FM 3-0. Washington, D.C.: U.S. Army, 2008.
  Current U.S. Army tactical and operational doctrine, this manual provides the latest view on the way in which the Army responds to missions across the total spectrum of conflict.

"Operation THUNDERCLAP: The Bombing of Dresden." Conroy, Richard A. Carlisle, Pa.: U.S. Army War College, 1989.
  War College student's study on the utilization of incendiaries as weapons of mass destruction at Dresden in 1945. Author concludes that the Allies had become inured to civilian casualties.

Portable Flame Throwers, M1 and M1A1. Technical Manual 3-375. Washington, D.C.: War Department, 1943.
  This first complete TM for the early flame throwers also provided some information of flame thrower tactics.

Pyrotechnics Monograph. American University Research Station. Washington, D.C.: War Department, 1918.
  An account of the work done at American University on flame fuels during World War I.

"Report of the Surgeon General." *War Department Annual Reports.* Washington, D.C.: Government Printing Office, 1921. Vol. 1, pp. 443–1173.
  Statistics submitted as a final report on casualties and sickness among U.S. Army troops during World War I. No index for the report but not difficult to locate information.

"Supply Action: Flame Throwers, Portable." Supply Circular No. 204. Washington, D.C.: War Department, 1944.
  This provided authority for subordinate commands to delete the flame thrower from the Engineer TOE and to issue them to infantry units.

Tactics of Chemical Warfare. FM 3-5. Washington, D.C. War Department, 1942.
  Section 6, entitled "Engineer Troops," provides basic guidance for using the M1 flame thrower.

The United States Army in the World War: Bulletins. HQ AEF. Washington, D.C.: Department of the Army, 1948.
  This contains the AEF General Order No. 8 that established the forerunner of the CWS, a "gas and flame" regiment.

U.S. Army Air Force School of Applied Tactics. Course Summary, AAFSAT ANSCOL Course. USAAF, 1944. (Mimeographed).
  This course outline clearly shows the increasing role of incendiary munitions in the USAAF by 1944. See especially Appendices 10 and 34.

United Nations Publications

Official Records of the General Assembly. Twenty-Eighth Session, Annexes. New York: U.N., 1974.
The Annex covering meetings of 18 September–18 December 1973 and 16 September 1974 contains the report of the Secretary General on Agenda Item 34. This item dealt with disarmament in general and on napalm/incendiaries in particular.

Resolutions Adopted by the General Assembly During Its Twenty-Seventh Session. Annexes. 19 September–19 December 1972. U.N. Supplement No. 30, 1973.
This resolution (A/8730) concerns the response of the General Assembly to the Secretary General's report entitled "Napalm and Other Incendiary Weapons and All Aspects of Their Possible Use."

Napalm and Other Incendiary Weapons and All Aspects of Their Possible Use. U.N. Publication No. E. 73.1.3, 1973.
A report prepared by direction of the Secretary General. General review of modern flame weapons, their use during World War II and since 1945, and information regarding the toxicology of flame weapons.

Newspapers

"A Mean Attack Implement of the English Air Gangster," *Berliner Allgemeine* (September 18, 1940): 2–3.
A translation forwarded to the G2, U.S. War Department by the U.S. Naval Attaché, Berlin, provides an interesting treatment of propaganda. Even as German bombers dropped incendiaries on British cities, the Germans criticized the British for responding in kind.

"American Jets Attack Suspected Mortar Site." *Richmond News Leader.* 26 July 1966. P. 1, cols. 6, 7, 8.
The role of aerial napalm bombs in the Vietnam War is illustrated by this article, which fills three columns discussing massive U.S. reaction to a suspected VC firing position near Saigon.

"Fire Bombs Over Japan." *Chicago Sun.* 15 May 1945. P. 12, cols. 1–6.
One page devoted to illustrated article covering the incendiary bombing of Japan then in progress.

"Marines Burned Japs." *Washington Post.* 2 Dec. 1943. P. 1, col. 5.
Sensationalist report on Tarawa battle.

New York Times. 22 Nov. 1943, p. 62, cols. 1, 2, 5; 24 Nov. 1943, p. 20, col. 3; and 28 Nov. 1943, p. 1, col. 6.
Articles concerned with fighting on Tarawa and Makin Island.

Books

Banks, Donald. *Flame Over Britain.* London: Sampson Low, Marston, and Co., 1947.

Author was deeply involved in programs of the British Petroleum Warfare Branch during WWII. First-hand account of the development of British flame weapons, but no footnotes.

Couffer, Jack. *Bat Bomb: World War II's Other Secret Weapon.* Austin: University of Texas, 1992.
Written by the youngest member of the highly classified multiservice Project X-Ray. The United States worked for two years (1942–43) to develop minute incendiary bombs which could be dropped on Japanese cities after being attached to bats.

Crane, Conrad C. *Bombs, Cities and Civilians: American Airpower Strategy in World War II.* Lawrence, Kans.: University of Kansas Press, 1993.
Excellent study of U.S. strategic bombing policy and operations in Europe and the Pacific. Provides a complete bibliography for researchers.

Development of International Legal Limitations on the Use of Chemical and Biological Weapons. 2 vols. Washington, D.C.: 1968.
Authoritative study prepared for the U.S. Arms Control and Disarmament Commission by the students and faculty of the Southern Methodist University Law School, Dallas, Texas.

Dion, CPT S. A. *Tanks, Gas, Bombing, Liquid Fire.* New York: Harvey Publishing Co., 1917.
A slim wartime pamphlet written by a Canadian officer. "How to" book for U.S. officers bound for service in AEF. Only one page on German "liquid fire."

Fieser, Louis F. *The Scientific Method.* New York: Reinhold Publishing Co., 1964.
The highly intelligent, somewhat eccentric developer of napalm tells of his work as a member of the NDRC during WWII.

Foulkes, Charles H. *Gas! The Story of the Special Brigade.* London: Wm. Blackwood & Sons, 1934.
Excellent account of British chemical warfare activities in France by the former commander of the Special Brigade.

Fries, Amos A., and Clarence J. West. *Chemical Warfare.* New York: McGraw-Hill, 1921.
Unofficial history of the AEF CWS by its first commander. Severely criticizes the early flame throwers and reflects his official position as Chief of the peacetime CWS. Suffers from the lack of a bibliography and annotation.

Gravovoy, I. D., and V. K. Kadyuk. *Incendiary Weapons and Defense Against Them.* Moscow, USSR: Voyenizdat, 1983. Translated 1985.
Published in Russian as *Zazhigatelnoye Oruzhiye T. Zashchito ot Nego.* Translation by the Foreign Broadcast Information Service, 31 Dec. 1985.

Harris, Arthur. *Bomber Offensive.* New York: Macmillan, 1947.
The former commander of the RAF Bomber Command outlines his rationale behind large-scale incendiary attacks upon German cities in this book. Interesting comments on the "Ethics of Bombing" in chap. 8.

Incendiary Attack of German Cities. London: British A Ministry, January 1943.
Prepared by the Department of Bombing Operations, this lengthy report lays out, in detail, the procedures to be followed six months later during the incendiary attack on Hamburg.

Paszek, Lawrence J. *United States Air Force History: A Guide to Documentary Sources.* Washington, D.C.: Government Printing Office, 1973.
Important guide to various collections of records. Three sections: USAF Depositories, National Archives, Private Holdings.

Thomas, Ann V. W., and A. J. Thomas, Jr. *Legal Limits on the Use of Chemical and Biological Weapons.* Dallas, Texas: SMU Press, 1970.
Discusses the present status of international law as it relates to chemical and biological warfare.

Tilford, Earl H., Jr. *Crosswinds: The Air Force's Setup in Vietnam.* College Station, Texas: Texas A&M Press, 1993.
Comments on the employment of incendiary munitions by the USAF during the early phases of the air war in Vietnam.

Articles

"Assault on Hill 875." *Time* 90 (1 Dec. 1967): 27.
Reporting on the assault of U.S. paratroopers against North Vietnamese; this article comments upon the use of flame throwers in an unsuccessful attempt to burn out Communist positions.

Bers, Julian E. "How to Fight with Flame-throwers." *Chemical Warfare Bulletin* 29 (January 1943): 62–67.
An article which appeared early in WWII, it was filled with generalities, but correctly criticized the inadequate training given to flame thrower operators.

Bostick, Orbie. "21 Months in the South Pacific." *Chemical Warfare Bulletin* 30 (Dec. 1943–Jan. 1944): 5.
This first-hand account of a CWS officer just returned from the combat zone made a strong plea for the organization of special flame thrower assault teams.

"Chemical Warfare Service Opposed to Frightfulness." *Chemical Warfare* 8 (15 January 1922): 19.
This short article chides the *Literary Digest* of 24 Dec. 1921 for implying that the CWS advocated "frightfulness" in war.

Gahan, Theodore P. "The Status of Incendiaries in the Army Air Forces." Unpublished thesis, Air University, Maxwell Field, Ala., 1947.
Author strongly critical of peacetime neglect of incendiary bombs in the years following World War II.

Gilman, Edgar D. "Chemical Warfare—A Lecture Delivered to the ROTC, University of Cincinnati." *Chemical Warfare* 8 (July 15, 1922): 13–15.

Reprinted remarks of an Engineer Reserve officer highly critical of flame throwers used in World War I. Conformed to the opinion held by BG Fries, Chief of CWS.

Greene, L. Wilson. "Prewar Incendiary Bomb Development." *CCJ* 2 (October 1947): 25–30.

Most helpful. One of the few sources that sheds any light on the amateurish and insufficiently funded attempts made by CWS personnel at Edgewood Arsenal to develop prototype incendiary bombs during the late 1930s.

"Japan: The Recent Big Strikes." *Impact* 3 (April 1945): 14–24.

This article covers, with excellent photos, the incendiary raids on Tokyo, Nagoya, and several small cities.

Laughlin, Joseph C. "The Application and Effects of Napalm." Unpublished thesis, Air University, Maxwell Air Force Base, Ala., 1948.

The continued development of incendiaries (or lack of it) is the central topic of this research paper. Significant because it shows how severely Air Force funds had been cut since the end of WWII.

Morschauser, John III. "Blowtorch Battalion." *Armor* (March–April 1960): 30–33.

Interesting account of the training and combat employment of the 713th Armored Flame Thrower Bn. The author was a member of the unit during all phases of its operations in the Pacific.

"Napalm: Fire Bombs Turn Trick Against Holed-Up Nips in Luzon." *Impact* 3 (August 1945): 49–53.

Excellent account of tactical fire bombs used against Japanese defense in the Ipo Dam area of Luzon, Philippines.

Olds, James F. "Early Bougainville Experiments." *Chemical Warfare Bulletin* 30 (Aug.–Sept.–Oct. 1944): 7–9.

What the author lacked as a stylist, he made up for in pertinent information as a CWS officer in the Southwest Pacific.

———. "Flame Throwers Front and Center." *Chemical Warfare Bulletin* [*CWB*] 30 (June–July 1944): 5–8.

Olds wrote this article just after he returned to the United States from a two-year stint in the Pacific. He explains the organization and tactics of the flame thrower platoons that had been employed on New Georgia in 1943.

Twohey, James S., ed. "Pacific Battlefronts: Accounts to December 4th." *Twohey Analysis of Newspaper Opinion* (December 9, 1943): 17–22.

This weekly newsletter, published in Washington, D.C., digested the news services' reporting of major issues. Twohey analyzes the reaction of several major newspapers to the published casualty figures of the Tarawa operation.

Zanetti, J. Enrique. "Strategy of Incendiaries." *CWB* 27 (April 1941): 41–44.
Zanetti's article was the first on incendiaries to appear since 1937 in this CWS service organ. In the article, Zanetti calls for a realistic appraisal of incendiary bombs and their role in modern warfare.

Interviews Conducted by the Author

Barnard, Howard D., COL., USAF. Carlisle Barracks, Pa. October 1, 1993.
An experienced fighter pilot and commander, Colonel Barnard was serving as Senior Air Force Representative at the Army War College at the time of the interview. Most helpful in gathering data on aerial incendiaries.

Campbell, William A., MSGT., USMC. Quantico, Va. June 11, 1975.
Sergeant Campbell participated in several major amphibious assaults in the Pacific while armed with an M1A1 flame thrower. During the period April 1944–February 1945 he saw the number of portable flame throwers allocated to infantry regiments increase three times.

Cohen, Leonard, USA, Ret. Edgewood Arsenal, Md. May 10, 1975.
Mr. Cohen served as an enlisted man in the CWS and Chemical Corps until his retirement in 1958. After retirement, he continued to work at Edgewood Arsenal as a civilian employee.

Colver, Robert M. Duke University, Durham, N.C. November 5, 1975.
Dr. Colver served as a CWS officer prior to and during World War II. While completing training at Edgewood Arsenal during the late 1930s, he did not see any work being done on incendiaries of any kind.

Compton, J. R., MAJ., USAF. Ft. Leavenworth, Kans. January 25, 1977.
This officer discussed USAF doctrine governing the employment, storage, and stockage levels of incendiary bombs in the post–Vietnam era.

Cushing, John, LT. COL., USMC. El Toro, Calif. November 9, 1993.
Lieutenant Colonel Cushing was assigned to Marine Air Group 11 during Operation DESERT STORM. He is currently the Operations Officer of MAG 11.

Hallman, Jerry A., MAJ., USAF. Ft. Leavenworth, Kans. January 26, 1977.
This officer commented upon the varying degrees of effectiveness of incendiary bombs utilized in Southeast Asia.

Jones, Richard H., COL., USAR. Ft. Myer, Va. May 20, 1975.
Colonel Jones was a platoon leader in Co. C, 713th AFT Bn before and during the invasion of Okinawa.

Kaszer, Robert A., MAJ., USA. Ft. Leavenworth, Kans. January 25, 1977.
Recounting the employment of napalm in support of his unit in 1966, the officer interviewed commented in detail upon the limitations of napalm (incendigel) when used in close support of infantry troops.

Turnage, Wilson C., COL., USMC (Ret). Kansas City, Mo. December 6, 1976.

A former Marine Corps fighter pilot, Colonel Turnage commented upon the use of napalm fire bombs by USMC air units during the battles for Iwo Jima and Okinawa. Commented upon the initial shortage of napalm gel during the early stages of the Korean conflict.

Letters to the Author

Kleber, Brooks E. Historian, U.S. Army Training and Doctrine Command. Ft. Monroe, Va. September 27, 1977.

This letter, by a co-author of *Chemicals in Combat*, contains a number of insights regarding the development of flame weapons of World War II.

Ropp, Theodore. Duke University, Durham, N.C. October 6, 1978.

Historian Ropp comments upon the problem of devising controls over weapons before the weapon has been fully exploited during wartime.

SECONDARY SOURCES

Books

Ambrose, Stephen E. *Citizen Soldiers*. New York: Simon and Schuster, 1997.

Provides the American soldier's view of combat in the ETO from D-Day until V-E Day.

Appleman, Roy E., and others. *Okinawa: The Last Battle*. Washington, D.C.: Government Printing Office, 1948.

Official Army history dealing with the campaign conducted by the Tenth Army in 1945. Offers many accounts of flame thrower employment.

Arthur, Robert A., and Kenneth Cohlmia. *The Third Marine Division*. Washington, D.C.: Infantry Journal Press, 1948.

A wartime history of the Marine division. Contains many photos as well as textual material describing flame thrower tactics utilized on Iwo Jima.

Atkinson, Rick. *Crusade: The Untold Story of the Persian Gulf War*. New York: Houghton, Mifflin, 1993.

Popular account of Operations DESERT SHIELD and DESERT STORM.

Auld, S. J. M. *Gas and Flame*. New York: George H. Doran, 1918.

Opinionated account of chemical weapons written by a British officer assigned as an instructor in the United States. Primarily wartime propaganda. No notes, bibliography, or index.

Bailey, Sydney D. *Prohibitions and Restraints in War*. London: Royal Institute of International Affairs, 1972.

Short paperback containing some information on napalm.

Baxter, James P., III. *Scientists Against Time.* Boston: Little, Brown, 1952.
Brief official history of the Office of Scientific Research and Development from 1940 to 1945.

Beaumont, Roger A., and Martin Edmond, eds. *War in the Next Decade.* London: Macmillan, Ltd., 1975.
A collection of essays. Especially interesting is "Science, Technology, and the Future of Warfare" by Roger Williams. See pp. 157–79.

Belote, James, and William Belote. *Typhoon of Steel: The Battle for Okinawa.* New York: Harper & Row, 1970.
Well-written account of Okinawa campaign with a good bit of information from Japanese sources.

Bindinian, Larry J. *The Combined Allied Bombing Offensive Against the German Civilian: 1942–1945.* Lawrence, Kans.: Coronado Press, 1976.
A critique of the Allied bombing campaign that relies heavily on the U.S. Strategic Bombing Surveys for information. Not well written, but a useful document for researchers.

Bond, Horatio, ed. *Fire and the Air War.* Boston: National Fire Protection Association, 1946.
Excellent collection of articles by experts on flame warfare and flame damage. Covers fire raid results in Germany and Japan.

Brodie, Bernard, and Fawn M. Brodie. *From Crossbow to H-Bomb.* Bloomington, Ind.: Indiana University Press, 1973.
Presents a readable account of weaponry in ancient times, including early forms of flame weapons.

Brown, Frederic J. *Chemical Warfare: A Study in Restraints.* Princeton: Princeton University Press, 1968.
Does not provide much information on incendiary munitions or napalm, but does treat the general questions facing nations with regard to chemical and biological warfare. Excellent discussion of CWS problems in the 1920s.

Bruce, Robert V. *Lincoln and the Tools of War.* New York: Bobbs-Merrill, 1956.
Examines Abraham Lincoln's personal fascination with weapons of all kinds and records his exposure to various types of flame weapons during the Civil War.

Caidin, Martin. *The Night Hamburg Died.* London: New English Library, 1966.
Covers the conduct of Operation GOMORRAH, the fire bombing of Hamburg by the RAF and USAAF in July and August 1943.

Cannon, M. Hamlin. *Leyte: The Return to the Philippines.* Washington, D.C.: Government Printing Office, 1954.
Official Army history. Contains information regarding the use of American flame throwers in the Philippines in 1944.

Chamberlain, Peter, and Chris Ellis. *British and American Tanks of World War II.* New York: Arco Publishing, 1969.
    Complete photographic history of U.S., British, and Commonwealth tanks. Has photos of most of the flame-throwing tanks of World War II.

Chemical Corps Association. *The Chemical Warfare Service in World War II.* New York: Reinhold Publishing Co., 1948.
    Short history of the CWS designed as a stop-gap until official history was published.

Cole, H. M. *The Lorraine Campaign.* Washington, D.C.: Government Printing Office, 1950.
    Both American and German use of flame throwers are recorded in this official history of the U.S. Third Army's campaign in the fall of 1944.

Coll, Blanche D., Jean E. Keith, and Herbert D. Rosenthal. *The Corps of Engineers: Troops and Equipment.* Washington, D.C.: Government Printing Office, 1958.
    This official history volume explains how the peacetime role of the Engineers was transformed by the American entry into WWII.

Cookson, John, and Judith Nottingham. *A Survey of Chemical and Biological Warfare.* London: Sheed and Ward, 1969.
    For the educated layman. Exhibits no political allegiance. Authors provide information about various aspects of current chemical and biological warfare weapons and practices.

Craven, W. Frank, and James L. Cate, eds. *Europe: ARGUMENT to V-E Day. January 1944 to May 1945. The Army Air Forces in World War II.* Chicago: University of Chicago Press, 1951.
    This official history contains information on the USAAF incendiary bomb attacks on Dresden and Cologne, Germany.

————. *Europe: TORCH to POINTBLANK. August 1942 to December 1943. The Army Air Forces in World War II.* Chicago: University of Chicago Press, 1949.
    Volume 2 of the USAAF history. Covers in some detail the early stages of the bombing campaign carried out by U.S. bombers and contrasts the American daylight bombing of industrial and military targets with the RAF's night bombing of population centers.

————. *The Pacific: Guadalcanal to Saipan. August 1942 to July 1944. The Army Air Forces in World War II.* Chicago: University of Chicago Press, 1950.
    Volume 4 of the AAF history, this contains a great deal of information about the employment of tactical and long-range aircraft in the South and Southwest Pacific areas. Excellent index.

————. *The Pacific: MATTERHORN to Nagasaki. June 1944 to August 1945. The Army Air Forces in World War II.* Chicago: University of Chicago Press, 1953.

Deals with the last decisive phases of the air war in the Pacific and provides information about the incendiary bombing of Japanese cities by the XXI Bombardment Group.

Crowell, Benedict. *America's Munitions.* Washington, D.C.: Government Printing Office, 1919.
   Hastily prepared and not annotated, this slim history is valuable for what it does not say about flame throwers.

Crowl, Philip A. *Seizure of the Gilberts and Marshalls.* Washington, D.C.: Government Printing Office, 1955.
   Includes numerous accounts of flame thrower action on Tarawa, Makin, and Eniwetok.

Dickey, James. *Buckdancer's Choice.* Middleton, Conn.: Wesleyan University Press, 1964.
   This book of poems contains his poem entitled, "The Firebombing." Ex-bomber pilot Dickey reflects on the excitement he felt and the death below him.

Dod, Karl C. *The Corps of Engineers: The War Against Japan.* Washington, D.C.: Government Printing Office, 1966.
   Provides information on the types of flame throwers used by engineer troops in the Pacific and discusses assault tactics.

Douhet, Giulio. *The Command of the Air.* Translated by Dino Ferrari. New York: Coward-McCann, 1942.
   The writings of the great Italian proponent of bombers. Douhet urged that the Italian government look to the future in the development of a separate and powerful air force.

Dupuy, Trevor N., ed. *Military, Political, and Psychological Implications of Massive Population Casualties in History.* 4 vols. Washington, D.C.: Historical Evaluation and Research Organization (HERO), 1965.
   A contract report, prepared for the U.S. Army Combat Development Command, contains numerous scholarly essays dealing with various aspects of mass casualties as a result of warfare.

Ewing, Joseph H. *29, Let's Go!* Washington, D.C.: Infantry Journal Press, 1948.
   The wartime history of the 29th Infantry Division. Contains a good account of the actions at Fort Montbarey, near Brest, France, in which the Americans were assisted by British flame thrower tanks.

Falk, Richard A., ed. *The Vietnam War and International Law.* 3 vols. Princeton: Princeton University Press, 1972.
   Sponsored by the American Society of International Law, these essays attack the American presence in Vietnam. The U.S. employment of napalm is attacked successfully on moral grounds. Attacks on legal grounds are unsuccessful.

Fredette, Raymond H. *The Sky on Fire: The First Battle of Britain 1917–1918, and the Birth of the Royal Air Force.* New York: Holt, Rinehart and Winston, 1966.

Very well-organized and carefully researched history of the initial use of aerial incendiaries by the German air service in World War I and the reprisals carried out by the British.

Fries, Amos A. *Communism Unmasked.* New York: By the author, 1937.

A polemic tract urging vigilance against the spread of Communism. No notes or bibliography. Fries points to the Fascist governments of Germany and Italy as the primary bulwarks of the non-Communist world.

Garand, George W., and Truman R. Strobridge. *Western Pacific Operations: History of U.S. Marine Corps Operations in World War II.* Washington, D.C.: Government Printing Office, 1971.

The official USMC history dealing with the invasions of Peleliu and Iwo Jima, this volume, number 4 in the WWII series, gives a great deal of information regarding the use of portable, tank-mounted, and LVT-mounted flame throwers by the Marines.

Garrett, Stephen A. *Ethics and Airpower in World War II: The British Bombing of German Cities.* New York: St. Martin's Press, 1993.

Examines the British air bombardment in terms of target selection, ordnance effectiveness, employment techniques, and the moral and ethical questions surrounding the large-scale bombing of population centers.

Green, Constance M., Harry C. Thomson, and Peter C. Roots. *The Ordnance Department: Planning Munitions for War.* Washington, D.C.: Government Printing Office, 1955.

This official history discusses many of the problems encountered by "service" branches prior to WWII in developing weapons for future employment. Especially troublesome was the chronic lack of information about European weapons development.

Greenspan, Morris. *The Modern Law of Land Warfare.* Berkeley: University of California Press, 1959.

Unsuccessful attempt to prove illegality of flame weapons. Author treats flame weapons in the same way he deals with biological weapons.

Harrison, Gordon A. *Cross-Channel Attack.* Washington, D.C.: Government Printing Office, 1951.

Official history of the Normandy invasion by the U.S. Army. Mentions flame thrower training in England only briefly, but gives accounts of flame thrower action soon after the invasion of France.

Havens, Thomas R. H. *Valley of Darkness: The Japanese People and World War II.* New York: Norton, 1978.

Discusses the response of the Japanese population to the bombing of the Japanese home islands in 1944–45.

Hermes, Walter G. *Truce Tent and Fighting Front: The United States Army in the Korean War.* Washington, D.C.: Government Printing Office, 1966.
Useful in its discussion of North Korean and Russian charges that the U.S. was engaged in biological warfare during the Korean War.

Hersh, Seymour M. *Chemical and Biological Warfare: America's Hidden Arsenal.* New York: Bobbs-Merrill, 1968.
An attack on the American possession and use of defoliants and herbicides in Vietnam, this book also calls for an end to all chemical weapons. Discusses the evils of napalm and its discoverer, Dr. Louis F. Fieser.

Holley, Irving B. *Ideas and Weapons.* New Haven: Yale University Press, 1953.
A study in the relationship of technological advance, military doctrine, and the development of weapons, with particular emphasis on the problems Americans had in utilizing air power in World War I.

Horne, Alistair. *The Fall of Paris.* New York: St. Martin's Press, 1965.
Well-written history of the struggle for control of Paris incident to the defeat of France in the Franco-Prussian War. In his discussion of the Paris Commune, Horne addresses the reports of female members of the Communard who threw incendiary devices at regular troops sent to restore order.

Hough, Frank O. *The Assault on Peleliu.* Washington, D.C.: United States Marine Corps, 1950.
This published monograph benefits from the use of still-fresh primary source material and many interviews with veterans of the fighting on Peleliu, to include veterans of the 1st Amphibian Tractor Bn., who had utilized the Canadian Ronson flame projector on LVTA1s.

Hough, Frank O., Verle E. Ludwig, and Henry I. Shaw, Jr. *Pearl Harbor to Guadalcanal.* Vol. 1 of *History of U.S. Marine Corps Operations in World War II.* Washington, D.C.: Government Printing Office, 1958.
Discusses the use of flame throwers by the Japanese invaders of Wake Island in 1941.

Irving, David J. C. *The Destruction of Dresden.* New York: Holt, Rinehart & Winston, 1964.
The author indicts the RAF and USAAF for fire bombing refugee-packed Dresden at the request of the Russians in 1945. Contains an introduction by General Ira C. Eaker and a foreword by Air Marshal Sir Richard Saundby, both of whom were instrumental in the attacks on Dresden.

Israel, Fred L., ed. *Major Peace Treaties of Modern History.* New York: Chelsea House, 1967.
This is truly an excellent compilation of international peace treaties. Divided into four volumes, each with its own index, and also served by an overall index, this collection aids a great deal in quick reference to treaties.

Johnson, Thomas M., and Fletcher Pratt. *The Lost Battalion*. Washington, D.C.:
   Infantry Journal Press, 1943.
   Light reading. History of elements of the U.S. 77th Inf. Div. cut off in the
Argonne Forest in October 1918, when they were attacked by Germans with flame
throwers.

Judges 13:20.
   Illustrates the wonder in which ancient peoples beheld fire when it seemed to
serve as a holy sign.

Judges 15:4–5.
   This passage gives an account of Samson destroying the corn crop of the
Philistines with flaming brands tied to foxes.

Kerr, E. Bartlett. *Flames Over Tokyo: The U.S. Army Air Forces' Incendiary Campaign
   Against Japan, 1944–1945*. New York: Donald I. Fine, 1991.
   Popular account of Twentieth AF bombing of Japan. Describes development of
B-29 bomber and M69 incendiary bomb. Excellent maps, photos, charts.

Kerry, A. J., and W. A. McDill. *The History of the Corps of Royal Canadian Engineers*. Vol.
   2. Ottawa: Military Engineers Association of Canada, 1966.
   Contains quite a bit of information regarding the employment of mechanized
flame throwers by Canadian units during World War II in Europe.

Langer, William L. *Gas and Flame in World War I*. New York: Knopf, 1965.
   A short history of Co. E, 30th Engineer Reg. (Gas and Flame). Account of combat
experience of this unit, which was later redesignated as the 1st Gas Regiment, AEF.
Does not mention use of flame throwers. "Flame" in title comes from designation of
the unit.

Lefebure, Victor. *The Riddle of the Rhine*. New York: The Chemical Foundation, 1923.
   Combines a review of chemical warfare as practiced during World War I with
warnings about the potential hazard of allowing Germany to retain control of large
chemical concerns like the Interessen Gemeinschaft. Not annotated. Appears to
reflect fears of a resurgent Germany as felt by those who were dissatisfied with the
Versailles Treaty.

Liddell Hart, Basil H. *The Tanks: The History of The Royal Tank Regiment*. Vol. 2. New
   York: Praeger, 1959.
   Some chapters written by generals. Those dealing with tank warfare in 1944–45
have a good deal to say about the effectiveness of British "Crocodile" tank flame
throwers.

London Times. *History of the War*. Vol. 10. London: 1917.
   This is less history than histrionics. Still, it does provide an interesting case of
wartime propagandizing in an effort to maintain wavering morale. Made up of news
accounts from the *Times*, it was published each year.

MacDonald, Charles B. *The Siegfried Line Campaign.* Washington, D.C.: Government Printing Office, 1963.
Well-written account of the U.S. First Army's campaign during the fall of 1944. Provides accounts of U.S., British, and German flame attacks.

McKee, Alexander. *Dresden, 1945: The Devil's Tinderbox.* New York: E. P. Dutton, 1982.
British writer provides overview of Dresden attacks. Uses secondary sources from USA, UK, FRG, DDR, and Russia.

McMillan, George. *The Old Breed.* Washington, D.C.: Infantry Journal Press, 1959.
Unit history of the 1st Marine Division, Guadalcanal, Peleliu, and Okinawa. Many accounts of flame actions by the Marines.

Meid, Pat, and James M. Yingling. *Operations in West Korea.* In *U.S. Marine Operations in Korea: 1950–1953.* Washington, D.C.: Government Printing Office, 1972.
This is volume 5 of the official Marine history for the Korean conflict. It provides very good accounts of flame attacks carried out by the Marines using flame throwers, both tank-mounted and portable, of World War II vintage.

Middlebrook, Martin. *The Battle of Hamburg: Allied Bomber Forces Against a German City in 1943.* New York: Scribner's, 1980.
Meticulously researched, based on the author's personal contact with over 500 participants in the bombing or defense of Hamburg. This book contains excellent diagrams explaining attacks upon targets in the Hamburg area. Two of the book's appendices contain specific data on the RAF and USAAF organizations that took part in the bombing campaign.

Miller, John, Jr. *CARTWHEEL: The Reduction of Rabaul.* Washington, D.C.: Government Printing Office, 1959.
Records flame thrower actions by Army and Marines on Bougainville in 1943.

Miller, John, Jr. *Guadalcanal: The First Offensive.* Washington, D.C.: Government Printing Office, 1957.
Official Army history. Mentions some of the first uses of American flame throwers in the South Pacific that met with success.

Milner, Samuel. *Victory in Papua.* Washington, D.C.: Government Printing Office, 1957.
This official history of combat on New Guinea contains an account of the abortive flame thrower actions carried out in December 1942 by the 114th Combat Engineer Bn.

Montross, Lynn, and Nicholas A. Conzona. *The Inchon–Seoul Operation: USMC Operations in Korea, 1950–1953.* Washington, D.C.: Government Printing Office, 1955.
Mentions the extensive use of portable and tank-mounted flame throwers by the Marines in Korea. Also describes attacks by U.S. aircraft delivering napalm bombs.

Montross, Lynn. *War Through the Ages.* New York: Harper and Brothers, 1946.
This very well-written book provides scanty, but interesting information on early flame devices, particularly fire ships.

Moran, Lord [Charles M. Wilson]. *The Anatomy of Courage*. London: Constable and
     Co., Ltd., 1966.
     Interesting study of the effects of stress in battle. Fear and man's reaction to fear
are examined.

Mrazek, James E. *The Fall of Eben Emael: Prelude to Dunkerque*. Washington, D.C.: Luce,
     1970.
     Mentions the utilization of flame throwers by German combat engineers in their
assault upon the Belgian fortress.

Murray, Williamson. *Strategy for Defeat: The Luftwaffe, 1933–1945*. Maxwell Air Force
     Base: Air University Press, 1983.
     Valuable source for its information on the impact of Allied bombing upon the
German industrial base and the response of the German air force to Allied bombing.

Newcomb, Richard F. *Iwo Jima*. New York: Holt, Rinehart & Winston, 1965.
     Contains many accounts of flame thrower use during the conquest of the
Japanese stronghold between 19 February and 14 March 1945.

Nichols, Charles S., Jr., and Henry I. Shaw, Jr. *Okinawa: Victory in the Pacific*. Washing-
     ton, D.C.: Government Printing Office, 1955.
     Official Marine history volume. Many accounts of flame thrower actions, particu-
larly by the tanks of the Army's 713th Armored Flame Thrower Bn.

Noyes, William A., ed. *Chemistry*. Boston: Little, Brown, 1948.
     This collection of articles and monographic studies provides a general history of
the NDRC during World War II.

Numbers 11:1, 16:35.
     God burns wicked people who disobey his commandments.

O'Neill, James E., and Robert W. Krauskopf, eds. *World War II: An Account of Its Docu-
     ments*. Washington, D.C.: Howard University Press, 1976.
     Printed papers and proceedings of the Conference on Research on the Second
World War held on June 14–15, 1971, at the National Archives, Washington, D.C.
Essays by noted historians deal with research procedures used at the National
Archives when working with records in their field.

Palmer, Robert R., Bell I. Wiley, and William R. Keast. *The Procurement and Training of
     Army Ground Troops*. Washington, D.C.: Government Printing Office, 1948.
     Army history of the Army Ground Forces. Indicates how training programs were
expanded with regard to flame thrower training after 1943 due to the increased frequency of flame attacks being conducted in the Pacific.

Partington, J. R. *A History of Greek Fire and Gunpowder*. Cambridge, England: W.
     Heffer, 1960.
     A scholarly treatment of ancient and medieval flame weapons. Hard to read, but
full of information.

Prentiss, Augustin M. *Chemicals in War.* New York: McGraw-Hill, 1937.
  No footnotes, but a full bibliography. Combines a short history of chemical weapons with projected use of chemicals in war. The author, a CWS lieutenant colonel, includes a short chapter on incendiary bombs on pp. 248–61. Foresees the increased use of incendiary bombs.

Rogers, Bernard W. *CEDAR FALLS–JUNCTION CITY: A Turning Point.* Washington, D.C.: Government Printing Office, 1974.
  General Rogers' monograph discusses the use of mechanized flame throwers in the jungles of Vietnam in 1967.

Roland, Alex. *Underwater Warfare in the Age of Sail.* Bloomington, Ind: Indiana University Press, 1978.
  Examines underwater weapons; chronicles the development of mines and submarines, often regarded as dishonorable weapons by nineteenth-century naval officers. Very interesting, especially its treatment of resistance to change among military organizations.

Ropp, Theodore. *War in the Modern World.* Durham, N.C.: Duke University Press, 1959; reprint edition, New York: Collier Books, 1973.
  Standard work on strategy and weapons that stresses the wars of the twentieth century without neglecting what has gone before.

Rose, Steven, ed. *CBW: Chemical and Biological Warfare.* Boston: Beacon Press, 1969.
  Papers presented to the conference on chemical and biological warfare, London, 1968. See chap. 3, "Napalm." Polemic.

Rumpf, Hans. *The Bombing of Germany.* Translated by Edward Fitzgerald. New York: Holt, Rinehart, and Winston, 1962.
  Originally published as *Das War der Bombenkrieg* in Germany. Largely an attack on allied area bombing, with a strong denunciation of fire bombing.

Schaffer, Ronald. *Wings of Judgment: American Bombing in World War II.* New York: Oxford University Press, 1985.
  Provides fresh insights into the decisions that shaped the American bombing campaigns of World War II. Best single volume dealing with the moral aspects of area bombing during the war. Excellent essay on sources should be read by anyone working on this topic.

Shaw, Henry I., Jr., Bernard C. Nalty, and Edwin T. Turnbladh. *Central Pacific Drive.* Washington, D.C.: Government Printing Office, 1966.
  Volume 3 of the official Marine history for WWII, this book covers the fighting on Tarawa, Saipan, Tinian, and Guam, all of which saw extensive use of the flame thrower by Marines.

Shaw, Henry I., Jr., and Douglas T. Kane. *Isolation of Rabaul.* Washington, D.C.: Government Printing Office, 1963.

Volume 4 of the Marine history. This volume, though with a higher number, covers actions that occurred somewhat earlier than those in vol. 3. This book deals with the American drive toward Rabaul and recounts Marine fights on New Britain and Bougainville.

Sherrod, Robert. *Tarawa—The Story of Battle.* Fredericksburg, Tex.: Nimitz Foundation, 1973.
Eyewitness account of flame weapon employment on Tarawa, 1943. Interesting attack upon U.S. civilians who criticized Marines as being too brutal.

Sherry, Michael S. *The Rise of American Airpower.* New Haven: Yale University Press, 1987.
Mandatory reading for anyone hoping to understand the development of the world's strongest air force during World War II. Fully annotated, with a great deal of discussion on the conceptual basis for strategic bombing.

Shore, Moyers S., II. *The Battle for Khe Sanh.* Washington, D.C.: Government Printing Office, 1969.
Vietnam monograph. Tells of North Vietnamese and USMC use of flame throwers during the Battle of Khe Sanh in 1968.

Smith, Robert R. *Triumph in the Philippines.* Washington, D.C.: Government Printing Office, 1963.
An Army history, it recounts in detail the return of MacArthur's forces to the Philippine Islands. Mentions, but does not elaborate on, the use of flame throwers on Luzon and during the recapture of Corregidor.

Spaight, James M. *Air Power and the Cities.* London: Longmans, Green, 1930.
Raises the question of legal/moral restraints upon chemical weapons when such weapons are intended for use against civilian population centers. Contains a useful review of attacks upon civilians. Well indexed, and annotated.

————. *Air Power and War Rights.* London: Longmans, Green, 1924.
Addresses the present and future problems of international law in dealing with the new aerial weapons employed during World War I. The author urges an expansion of the laws of land warfare to encompass air warfare, especially air attacks against civilians.

————. *Bombing Vindicated.* London: Geoffrey Bles, 1944.
Primarily an Allied propaganda tract, this book seeks to apply rulings of international law to the Allied bomber offensive. Interesting because it highlights some of the conflicts that arose in the Grand Alliance during World War II.

Stockholm International Peace Research Institute. *Napalm and Incendiary Weapons.* Stockholm: 1972.
Lengthy attack on the U.S. military. Includes findings of a symposium of European and American doctors and educators opposed to U.S. involvement in South Vietnam. Includes a survey of nineteenth- and twentieth-century international conventions in which the prohibition of incendiaries was urged.

Stouffer, Samuel A., ed. *The American Soldier: Combat and Its Aftermath.* Volume 2 of the four-volume *Studies in Social Psychology in World War II.* Princeton: Princeton University Press, 1949.
This volume contains one chapter, no. 4, which deals strictly with fear in combat. Most interesting conclusions regarding the effect of the anticipation of injury or death.

Thiesmeyer, Lincoln R., and John E. Burchard. *Combat Scientists.* Boston: Little, Brown, 1947.
Provides background of NDRC mission and organization. Good account of NDRC activities overseas. Title is unfortunate. Most of the scientists were located in London, Brisbane, or Honolulu.

Thucydides. *The History of the Peloponnesian War.* Translated by Rex Warner. Middlesex, England: Penguin Books, 1972.
Landmark study of the Greek war during the fourth century, B.C.

Trooboff, Peter D. *Law and Responsibility in War: The Vietnam Experience.* Chapel Hill, N.C.: University of North Carolina Press, 1975.
A collection of essays, the book provides various (and divergent) opinions on the legality of flame weapons—specifically in Vietnam, but in past wars as well.

Verrier, Anthony. *The Bomber Offensive.* New York: Macmillan, 1968.
The best feature of this history is its very complete bibliography. Although the USAAF in Europe during World War II is dealt with, the book is concerned primarily with the RAF.

Waitt, Alden H. *Gas Warfare.* New York: Duell, Sloane, and Pierce, 1942.
General treatment on chemical weapons. The very general discussion of flame weapons indicated the limited development of incendiaries by the CWS prior to 1942.

Walker, Robert M., and Dennis J. Reimer. *One Team, One Fight, One Future.* Washington, D.C.: 1998.
This is the U.S. Army's Posture Statement for Fiscal Year 1999 as presented to the Senate and the House of Representatives.

Wartime Fire Defense in London: The Organization, General Plan and Methods Used by the London Fire Brigade to Control Fires Resulting from Incendiary Bombing as Observed by Members of the New York Fire Department Assigned to London from October 22, 1940 to January 14, 1941. Honorable F. H. LaGuardia, mayor of New York, and John J. McElligott, fire commissioner of New York City. Washington, D.C.: The United States Conference of Mayors, 1941.
Printed on the eve of U.S. entrance into WWII, this text detailed the ways in which Londoners had dealt with German fire bombs.

Werrell, Kenneth P. *Blankets of Fire.* Washington, D.C.: Smithsonian University Press, 1996.
Excellent modern account of the U.S. strategic bombing of Japan in 1945, with specific emphasis on incendiary bombing.

Wilson, Andrew. *Flame Thrower.* London: Wm. Kimber Co., 1956. London: Bantam Books, 1984.

Author served in 141st Regiment RAC in Crocodile flame tanks, 1944–45. Illustrated. First-hand account of British use of flame.

Articles

"A Jap Burns," *Life* 19 (August 1945): 34.

Photographic account of the destruction of a Japanese pillbox in the Southwest Pacific by Australian troops.

Allison, Graham T. "Conceptual Models and the Cuban Missile Crisis," *American Political Science Review* 63 (September 1969): 699–718.

Allison provides a three-part model for examining the decision-making processes in government.

Army Initiatives Group, HQDA. "State of America's Army on Its 218th Birthday," Washington, D.C., 1993.

This short pamphlet describes the Army's role as an integral part of the joint military establishment and serves to reinforce points in FM 3-0.

Atkinson, Rick. "Dresden Remembers Its Destruction," *The Washington Post* (February 14, 1995): A18.

Account of activities involving British and German political leaders and the current citizenry of Dresden on the 50th anniversary of the fire bombing of Dresden.

"Attack By Fire," *Time* 45 (June 4, 1945): 35.

The U.S. M2-2 flame thrower is extolled in this article praising the Marines fighting in the Pacific.

"B-29 Strikes," *Impact* 3 (June 1945): 24–39.

Excellent photo coverage of fire bomb strikes on Kobe, Nagoya, and Mushashiro, Japan, during May 1945.

Bers, Julian E. "Army's Newest Flame Gun," *Chemical Warfare Bulletin* [*CWB*] 30 (June–July 1944): 39–41.

Short presentation of the major components of the new M2-2 portable flame thrower.

"Bomb-Bats," *Time* 67 (January 7, 1946): 46.

Nothing new here, but interesting in that it was one of the earlier public announcements of the aborted bat-bomb project.

Bostick, Orbie. "Mercy Killers," *CWB* 30 (February–March 1944): 16–17.

In spite of the title, this article, written by a CWS officer in the Pacific, presents a thoughtful study of the toxicological effects of flame. This article was one of several printed in *CWS Bulletin* at this period of the war which attempted to portray the flame thrower as a merciful weapon.

Bratt, L. Eric. "All Finalists for Napalm Job Drop Out," *San Diego Union-Tribune* (April 29, 1998): A2
  Article concerning the Navy's failure to find a contractor firm willing to properly dispose of 23 million lbs. of napalm stored in Fallbrook, Calif.

Brophy, Leo P. "Origins of the Chemical Corps," *Military Affairs* 20 (Winter 1956): 217–26.
  Well-written history of the founding of the Chemical Warfare branch of the AEF in 1917 and the Army CWS from 1920 to 1930.

Brower, Kenneth S. "Fuel-Air Explosives: A Blow to Dismounted Infantry," *International Defense Review.* Vol. 10 (1987): 1405–7.
  Article describes the FAE potential for use against infantry strongpoints or unprotected troops.

Bullene, Egbert F. "Chemicals in Combat," *Armed Forces Chemical Journal [AFCJ]* 5 (April 1952): 4–5.
  Lightweight review of chemical weapons used during World War II.

"Bunker Busting," *War Monthly* 25 (April 1976): 42–48.
  Good overview of techniques employed by British and U.S. forces for the reduction of fortifications during World War II.

"Chemical Procurement in the New States," *Chemical Corps Journal [CCJ]* 2 (October 1947): 48–50.
  Very helpful article explaining how the CWS and civilian industry worked together during World War II to develop and manufacture weapons and equipment.

"Chemical Warfare Service Materials Used by the Air Services," *Chemical Warfare* 8 (January 15, 1922): 2–5.
  Surprisingly full discussion of World War I bomb types, fillers, fuses, etc. Also lists desirable characteristics of aerial incendiaries.

"CWS Studies Flame Deaths," *CWB* 30 (April–May 1944): 31–32.
  This staff article discusses the various aspects of the toxicology of flame.

Delo, David M. "Scientists in Uniform," *AFCJ* 3 (April 1949): 20–24.
  This short article comments on the need for technically-oriented officers in the Chemical Corps.

Dolan, Michael J. "Napalm," *Military Review* 33 (September 1953): 9–18.
  Reviews the development of fuel thickeners for use in aerial incendiaries. Helpful because of its clarity and concise nature.

"Finale: With or Without Atom Bomb, Japan War Through," *Impact* (September–October 1945): 103–4.
  Many Japanese are quoted who felt that the combination of U.S. submarine and air attacks had defeated Japan before the atomic bombs were dropped.

"Firebirds' Flight," *Time* 45 (19 March 1945): 3.
Interesting mainly for its pugnacious tone. The news editor obviously felt that the Japanese being fire bombed were getting their just desserts.

Graebner, Norman A., and Martha J. Roby. "Allied Assault on Germany." Pages 51–81 in vol. 3 of HERO study on mass casualties, 1965.
An analysis of the effects of the Allied bombing offensive against Germany during World War II.

Gurney, Gene. "The Giant Pays Its Way," *World War II in the Air: The Pacific.* New York: Franklin Watts, 1962, pp. 247–65.
Chronicles the employment of the B-29 bomber in the Pacific during 1944–45.

Hollingsworth, E. W. "The Use of Thickened Gasoline in Warfare," *AFCJ* 4 (April 1951): 26–32.
This article reviews the attempts (mostly twentieth century) to thicken gasoline in order to provide a viscous flame munition.

Hopkins, George E. "Bombing and the American Conscience during World War II." *Historian* 28 (May 1966): 464–69.
Discussion of criticism of U.S. bombing attacks against German and Japanese population centers.

"Hotter Than Napalm," *Army Times* (26 February 1975): 43.
The newly developed 27-lb flame projectile launcher is pictured in this article. Designed to replace the standard flame thrower, this weapon was issued to selected troop units in the late 1970s.

Howard, Michael. "Military Science in an Age of Peace," *RUSI Journal* 119 (March 1974): 3–9.
Thought-provoking essay on the impact of technology.

Josephy, Alven M. "Jungle of Stone," *Infantry Journal* (September 1945): 12–13.
This article provides an eyewitness account of the use of flame throwers by the Marines on Okinawa.

Kleber, Brooks E. "The Incendiary Bomb," *AFCJ* 7 (October 1953): 24–27, 58–59.
A review of various types of incendiary bombs used during World War II.

Kononenko, Alexei. "Attack on a Fortified Inhabited Point," *Infantry Journal* 51 (May–June 1944): 62–63.
Soviet flame thrower techniques are explained here. Soviets used portable and tank-mounted flame throwers.

"M-69 ... The Fire Bomb that Falls on Japan." Standard Oil Co. of New Jersey. April 1945.
An industrial public relations pamphlet, this demonstrates the employment of gelled gasoline bombs against Japan.

Martin, Harold H. "Black Snow and Leaping Tigers," *Harpers Magazine* 192 (February 1946): 151–55.
A contemporary report of the survivors of the B-29 fire raids on Tokyo in March and April 1945.

Meyers, Lewis. "Tactical Use of Flame," *Marine Corps Gazette* (November 1945): 19–22.
Unofficial statement of what had become official tactical doctrine regarding the employment of flame weapons by the USMC.

Miller, Walter L. "Flame Helps the Infantry," *U.S. Army Combat Forces Journal* 2 (December 1951): 16–19.
Well-written article which somewhat overstates the capabilities of flame throwers.

Montgomery, Edward. "The Role of the Chemical Corps in Air Power," *CCJ* 1 (April 1947): 19–21.
The author was attached to air staffs in Europe during World War II and comments upon the difficulties experienced by CWS officers serving two masters—the field commander and the chief, CWS.

Morton, Louis. "The Decision to Use the Atomic Bomb," *Foreign Affairs* 35 (January 1957): 334–53.
Morton examines the condition of Japan prior to and after the dropping of the atomic bomb.

Munhall, John H. "Were the Japs Defeated by CWS Incendiaries?" *CCJ* 1 (October 1946): 41–42.
Biased account of the incendiary bombing of Japan in 1945. Author implies that atomic bombs were not essential for the defeat of Japan.

"Navy Set to Move Napalm Stockpile," *Boston Globe* (22 March 1996): 8.
U.S. Navy attempts to dispose of 23 million lbs. of napalm that had been stored in Navy depot of Fallbrook, Calif., since 1973.

Otto, Carl E. "Fires from Incendiary Bombs," *CWB* 27 (July 1941): 94–98.
Demonstrates renewed U.S. interest in aerial incendiaries spurred by German use of flame against British cities.

Perry, Tony. "Waging a Low-Key War on Napalm," *Los Angeles Times* (5 December 1994): 4–5.
Discusses the Navy's plans for disposing of napalm stocks held in California.

Prentiss, A. M. "Incendiaries," *Combat Forces Journal* 2 (October 1951): 22–25.
Nicely done review article which explains, in simple terms, the importance of incendiary bombs during WWII. Prentiss also wrote *Chemicals in War* (1937).

Ropp, Theodore. "Political and Economic Considerations." Pages 25–28 in vol. 4 of HERO study on mass casualties, 1965.

Ropp explains the short-term and long-range effects of massive casualties and great destruction on the social, political, and economic fabric of society.

St. John, Adrian. "Chemical Warfare in the European Theater of Operations," *Military Review* 29 (December 1944): 57–66.
Colonel St. John was the chemical advisor to the SHAEF CG at the time this article was written. It correctly reflects the official policies of the CWS regarding flame in the ETO.

Shaw, Fred B., Jr. "Packing Incendiary Bomb Clusters: A Container Problem," *AFCJ* 3 (April 1950): 20–21, 40.
Sheds light on the problems of packaging and shipping incendiary bombs from the United States to Europe.

Shaw, Samuel R. "Non-nuclear Attacks" [on Japan]. Pages 83–102 in vol. 3 of HERO study on mass casualties, 1965.
Casualty effects of the fire bombing of Japan.

Sorensen, Henry. "History of Flame Warfare," *Canadian Arms Journal* 2 (July, August–September 1948): 31–32.
This article, which appeared in two installments, provides a good review of flame warfare in modern times. In the July installment, he cites at length vol. 4 of *History of the Great War, Military Operations, France and Belgium.* James E. Edmond (London: Macmillan & Co., 1928).

Struve, Kenneth D. "Yokohama M69 Day," *CCJ* 2 (January 1948): 29–30.
Short treatment of the incendiary bombing of Yokohama, Japan, on 29 May 1945, in which napalm-filled M69 bombs were extensively utilized.

Sullivan, Gordon R. "America's Army: Into the Twenty-first Century." Published by the Institute for Foreign Policy Analysis as National Security Paper Number 14 (1993).
Explains the Army leader's view of the future force.

Terry, William K. "24 Japs in a Hole," *CWB* (April–May 1944): 19.
Battlefield reporting by a USMC combat correspondent. Excessively gory, but tends to follow facts while providing a bit of propaganda for the CWS.

"The Fires of War: Napalm and Other Incendiary Weapons," *UN Monthly Chronicle* 10 (February 1973): 48–54.
A group of experts on incendiaries, mostly from Third World nations, collaborated on the production of this article hailing the UN General Assembly's call for steps leading to the outlawing of napalm and other incendiaries.

"The Massacre at Dak Son," *Time* 90 (15 December 1967): 32–34.
Pictures and text report the use of flame throwers by North Vietnamese troops in an attack upon a South Vietnamese village.

Thompson, Paul W. "Engineers in the Blitzkrieg," *Infantry Journal* 47 (September–October 1940): 429–30.
In this article, Army Captain Thompson presents a glowing report of the technical and tactical expertise of German engineers.

———. "How the Germans Took Fort Eben Emael," *Infantry Journal* 51 (August 1942): 22–29.
One of several articles by this author, who was a U.S. military attaché in France during the German blitz. Very pro-engineer without being pro-German.

Townsend, Earle J. "Hell Bombs Away!" *AFCJ* 4 (January 1951): 8–11.
Explains the use of napalm bombs during the Korean War. Light reading.

Unmacht, George F. "Flame Throwing Seabees," U.S. Naval Institute *Proceedings* 74 (April 1948): 425–27.
The contribution of Navy engineers to the flame tank construction project in Hawaii forms the focus for this article.

———. "Flamethrower Tanks in the Pacific Ocean Areas," *Military Review* 25 (March 1946): 44–51.
The best single published account of the work done by Colonel Unmacht's group in the last year of the war, with comments about the effectiveness of the flame tanks in combat.

"U.S. Military Making Plans to Dispose of Lost Napalm," *Baltimore Sun* (5 December 1994): 3.
Short article provides an account of Navy plans to contract a firm to extract napalm from obsolete bombs. The extracted napalm would then be used as fuel for high-temperature kilns at cement-making plants.

Waitt, Alden S. "Assault Troops Silence Pillboxes with Fire," *Popular Science* 141 (August 1942): 38–41.
Appearing before American combat troops had used flame in combat, the author, a CWS officer, explains the workings of a flame thrower in simple terms.

West, Togo D., and Dennis J. Reimer. *Meeting the Challenges of Today, Tomorrow and the 21st Century*. Washington, D.C., 1996.
This is the U.S. Army's Posture Statement for Fiscal Year 1997 as presented to the Senate and the House of Representatives.

Wheeler, Richard J. "The 'First' Flag-Raising in Iwo Jima," *American Heritage* 15 (June 1964): 103.
This article, written by a veteran of the Iwo Jima battle, contains many references to flame thrower employment by the USMC.

White, Gilbert. "Armor for the Flamethrower: Staff Gave Us 60 Days," *CWB* 30 (August–September–October 1944): 4–7.
This article describes the activities of the CWS Technical Division in late 1944.

Wing, H. Gilman. "Flame," *AFCJ* 7 (July 1953): 8–15.

A review of the manner in which flame weapons of all types were employed during World War II and the Korean War.

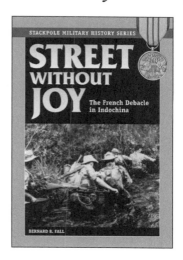

Stackpole Military History Series

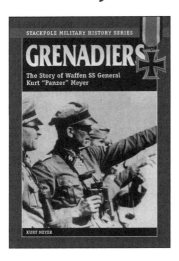

GRENADIERS
THE STORY OF WAFFEN SS GENERAL
KURT "PANZER" MEYER

Kurt Meyer

Known for his bold and aggressive leadership, Kurt
Meyer was one of the most highly decorated German
soldiers of World War II. As commander of various
units, from a motorcycle company to the Hitler Youth
Panzer Division, he saw intense combat across Europe,
from the invasion of Poland in 1939 to the 1944
campaign for Normandy, where he fell into Allied
hands and was charged with war crimes.

Paperback • 6 x 9 • 448 pages • 93 b/w photos

WWW.STACKPOLEBOOKS.COM
1-800-732-3669

Stackpole Military History Series

ARMOR BATTLES
OF THE WAFFEN-SS
1943–45
Will Fey, translated by Henri Henschler

The Waffen-SS were considered the elite of the
German armed forces in the Second World War and
were involved in almost continuous combat. From
the sweeping tank battle of Kursk on the Russian
front to the bitter fighting among the hedgerows
of Normandy and the offensive in the Ardennes,
these men and their tanks made history.

Paperback • 6 x 9 • 384 pages • 32 photos, 15 drawings, 4 maps

WWW.STACKPOLEBOOKS.COM
1-800-732-3669

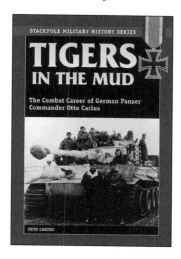

Stackpole Military History Series

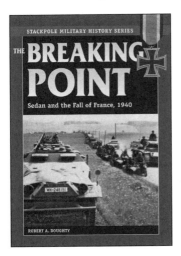

THE BREAKING POINT
SEDAN AND THE FALL OF FRANCE, 1940
Robert A. Doughty

Over the course of a week in May 1940, German general
Heinz Guderian's panzer corps swept through the
Ardennes and across the Meuse River and launched a
swift attack against France, winning a "miraculous"
victory near Sedan and breaking through into the French
interior. With refined tactics and commanders who led
from the front, Guderian's success was less a miracle and
more a triumph of a superior military force over an
inadequate one. Dissecting this World War II battle in
alternating chapters that cover the French and the
Germans, *The Breaking Point* is classic military history.

Paperback • 6 x 9 • 416 pages • 8 maps

WWW.STACKPOLEBOOKS.COM
1-800-732-3669

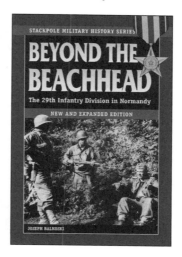

Index

183